Memoirs of a City Radical

Memoirs of a City Radical

Nicholas Davenport

Weidenfeld and Nicolson
London

© 1974 Nicholas Davenport

First published by Weidenfeld and Nicolson
11 St John's Hill, London SW11

ISBN 0 297 76796 8

Printed in Great Britain by Willmer Brothers Limited, Birkenhead

Contents

To my wife Olga with love, who has now inspired me to write two books and a play when my natural inclination was to cultivate the garden.

Foreword

A very long time ago – and quite by chance – I embarked on a career in the City which led on to financial journalism and involved me in the public debate about the future of the capitalist system. I had inherited from my father a gnawing social conscience, a deep-rooted feeling that the workers, particularly in the coal mines near our home town, were not getting a fair deal. I was confirmed in my opinion by what I discovered about the City under Montagu Norman and later on about the 'old boys' brigade' which I joined as a City director. Being privileged, however, to be guided in my weekly column by two eminent economists – Maynard Keynes and Hubert Henderson – I came to share their conviction that the capitalist system could be reformed, could be made more humane, more respectable and more efficient, and could really become an instrument of great economic good by applying Keynesian economics in a mixed economy

The *New Statesman* socialists, of course, thought otherwise. They believed that the capitalist system would have to be destroyed, and in the public wrangle which went on between the Fabians, who said that it could be done by degrees and by persuasion, and the Marxists who believed that it could only be done by force and revolution, I was brought into personal contact with three great Labour leaders – Hugh Dalton, Stafford Cripps and Herbert Morrison – and with two Marxist intellectuals – Harold Laski and Kingsley Martin, not to mention Richard Crossman who kept clear – and perhaps clear left – of both Marxists and Fabians. In the case of Hugh Dalton my journalistic contact ripened into a close friendship and through him I came to know the younger generation of Fabians to whom he had given a helping hand – Hugh Gaitskell, John Wilmot, Anthony Crosland, Douglas Jay, Roy Jenkins and James Callaghan – and

A*

finally Harold Wilson. Politicians are not easy friends but I have attempted to give pen portraits of those who came to visit or stay with us at our house near Oxford.

This house happened to be an historic place which had been involved with the socialists or Levellers of the Puritan revolution in the seventeenth century. I had the feeling in the Dalton era that the Labour leaders were re-enacting the part played by the Levellers – their 1945 manifesto had proclaimed the new Socialist 'Commonwealth' – and that they were riding for a fall, similar to that which befell the Commonwealth of 1650, because, like Cromwell, they had lost touch with public opinion. In the Tory restoration which followed – so reminiscent of the Restoration of 1660–89 – I became alarmed by the growing alienation of the working-class from the moneyed ruling clique. I then wrote a book – *The Split Society* – to warn the politicians against the coming confrontation between us workers and them rulers. I had hopes that Harold Wilson would heal the split but to my astonishment he adopted the monetary techniques of his predecessors and made the split society more divided than ever. As a result we now have a threat to our two-party Parliamentary democracy. When one party is financed by big business and the other party is financed by the trade unions, now increasingly dominated by militant Marxists, we have set ourselves on a collision course. It is the more regrettable seeing that the silent majority now has the means and desire to pursue a more comfortable and interesting life.

Philip Guedalla said that history does not repeat itself : historians repeat one another. This was a typical Oxford Union epigram of his time and it hid the truth that English history does have a habit of repeating itself when the lessons of the past are not learned. This particularly applies to the pound sterling and to our socialism. Crises of the pound have followed one another almost every other year since 1945 because politicians never understand the monetary system and are advised by a closed monastic order – the Treasury – which has no experience of business life outside. It saddened me to see Dalton and Cripps, who meant so well and tried so hard, physically destroyed by the rigours of this monetary-monastic flagellation. As for our socialism, the Puritan social conscience kept pressing the Fabians to take over in the 'public interest' more and more enterprises, which they could not run properly, which could only be run efficiently, if at all, on communist lines, this is, by the denial of the freedom to strike and the fixation of wages and prices. Blind to these facts and obsessed by that doctrinaire abstraction, egalitarianism, these Fabian social reformers never knew when to stop. The communists are, of course, waiting to pick up the pieces when the whole pretentious edifice of the 'Socialist Commonwealth' collapses.

In the economic debate I was conducting in my weekly column, first in the *New Statesman* and then, after the war, in the *Spectator*, I was never diverted from my main purpose, which was to show how a dangerously split society could be unified in a mixed economy if the workers were brought into the game of capital growth on the lines I put to Harold Wilson in 1964 (see Chapter 12). I cannot see why free enterprise and public enterprise cannot combine and flourish if the rival politicians would only learn from the past mistakes of capitalism and socialism and exercise some creative imagination. But Lord, O Lord, how long?

Acknowledgements

I am grateful to Lord Kahn for permission to quote from Lydia and Maynard Keynes's letters, and to Mrs Paul Einzig for permission to quote from her husband's letters to me. My thanks are also due to the following for allowing me to quote from their publications or letters: Lord Boothby, Sir Roy Harrod, Harold Wilson, George Brown, Jim Callaghan, Douglas Jay, Mrs Richard Crossman, Douglas Houghton, Sir Vaughan Berry, Sir Derick Hoare, Lady Gaitskell and Harry Oram.

I wish to thank the *New Statesman* for their permission to reproduce parts of an article by Maynard Keynes which appeared in the issue of 24 September 1956, Harold Laski's review of my book *The Vested Interests or Common Pool* (15 August 1942), the article by Wilfred Beckerman and the letters by Brian Walden which are quoted in the epilogue; the *Economist* for permission to reproduce their review of my book *The Split Society*, the *Spectator* for allowing me to to quote from some of my articles, and Victor Gollancz Ltd for permission to quote from my earlier works.

I am indebted to the following authors and publishers for allowing me to quote from their works: Lady Faith Henderson, *Oxford Economic Papers 1953* (OUP); Francis Williams, *Nothing So Strange* (Cassell & Co. Ltd); H. N. Brailsford, *The Levellers and the English Revolution* (Cresset Press, Barrie & Jenkins); Christopher Hill, *God's Englishman* (Weidenfeld & Nicolson); Denis Robertson, *The Marshall Lectures 1960* (Cambridge University Press). I am also grateful to Frederick Muller Ltd and David Higham Associates Ltd for permission to quote from *High Tide and After* and *The Fateful Years* by Hugh Dalton.

The cartoon of Maynard Keynes by David Low appears by arrangement with the Trustees and the London *Evening*

Standard. The photograph of the north-east view of *Hinton Manor* was taken by Tania Midgeley. I am indebted to my wife Olga for giving me most of the others. The letter of Bernard Shaw to me on how to write a play is copyright © 1974 the Trustees of the British Museum, the Governors and Guardians of the National Gallery of Ireland, and Royal Academy of Dramatic Art.

NICHOLAS DAVENPORT

I
Quite by Chance

I had never intended to go into the City. If anyone had suggested it in my young radical days in the twenties, I would have laughed at the idea as a bad joke. I regarded City people as incredibly stupid and reactionary. A stockbroker was then a music-hall figure of fun. A banker was a wicked capitalist sitting on a pile of money which grew larger and larger as the funds entrusted to his care grew smaller and smaller. I would not have dreamed of being caught in such a thieves' kitchen. But dire circumstances subdue arrogant thoughts and a domestic tragedy brought me into the City quite by chance.

It was having deeply religious parents which started me off with the idea that the working-class would eventually inherit the earth, like the meek, but I was never sure whether this would occur after or before the Second Coming of Christ. My mother brought me up on the huge illustrated Bible, given to her by her aunt Bullivant. There was everything in it – poetry, passion, sexuality, spirituality, bestiality, humanity, materialism and metaphysics. The metaphysical communism of Jesus made a deep impression upon me.

My parents were High Anglicans. They loved the ritual of the High Church, the smell of incense, the gorgeous vestments, the crossings and genuflexions before the altar. I was always being dragged to church. The choral Communion was their heaven. My father, who died when I was a very small boy, was a saint as well as a business man and ran a mission as a lay preacher for the hard-working and hard-drinking coal miners of Ashby-de-la-Zouche. He probably had a guilt complex, having inherited a number of public houses and a thriving business in beer, brewing, bottling and marketing. Every Sunday night I was taken to the mission hall to join in the service and listen to his sermon, which I found very tedious, but I was carried away by the rumbustious singing of the hymns which the miners shouted at the top of their voices. From that time I have always had a warm respect for coal miners, whose fine earthy qualities derive from the bowels of the earth where they work in danger of their lives. They were then miserably paid and exploited and if they are now paid well enough to be able to choose just when they want to work it bears witness to our improved sense of social justice.

After my father's untimely death, my mother devoted herself to good works among the poor. She would always give a loaf or a pudding to any hungry woman who came to her back door. These were the days before Social Security, when you could honestly play the part of a Good Samaritan. Her work among the poor taught me to respect and understand the feelings of the under-paid and under-privileged. This understanding was a great help when I took up Keynesian economics later on.

Fifty years later, when I was appointed by a Labour government to serve on a commission of enquiry into football, under Sir Norman Chester, Warden of Nuffield College, I found the working man had not changed since these Leicestershire years. He still lived for the three F's – fun, football, and fucking. Fun in the working men's clubs, where the beer and entertainment are superb; football in the gladiatorial stadia where the cup finals send him wild with excitement and sex on a Sunday afternoon after a booze-up. Sex came last in order of importance. Whether the liberated working girl of today will cause the order to be changed remains to be seen. I recall this experience because it influenced my attitude to economics and politics. I knew that the British worker, like any other, could become bloody-minded and revolutionary when conditions went against him, as they did in the twenties and thirties, but fundamentally he was a hedonist, with his eye on a good time without too much hard work. He had and still has a philosophy of life surely superior to that of the neurotically hard-working nations like the Germans and Japanese.

So simple was the faith of my father that he once told me that the undulations on the surface of a field were the mark of Noah's flood. I did not become free from this Biblical make-believe until I went to school at Cheltenham and was introduced by the underhousemaster 'Dolly' Drew – so called because he had the sweet regular features of a Victorian doll – to the great Victorian scientists – Spencer, Darwin and Huxley. I read the lot and was particularly fascinated by T. H. Huxley, who engaged in ferocious controversy with Gladstone and the bishops over monkeys and man. Could any Prime Minister but Gladstone have found time to write a pamphlet in defence of the historicity of the Garden of Eden? The fact that there are two contradictory accounts of creation in *Genesis* did not worry him : he swallowed them both.

The Victorian scientists shattered my early faith, and at Oxford I became a worried agnostic. I read everything I could about the origin of the earth and the evolution of man. The idea of vast clouds of hydrogen gas condensing into stars and the stars blowing up or spitting out planets like the earth filled me with amazement. Was there a first 'big bang'? A period of racking doubt overcame me. The precarious nature of man's evolution over millions of years was so astonishing. Was human life really the product of chance, the unpredictable result of a pure accident? It was fortunate at that time that molecular biology was not advanced. If I had been confronted with Professor Monod's *Chance and Necessity* I would have been in despair, for not only, according to this eminent biologist, is man an accident based on *chance* but the accident is perpetuated by the blind *necessity* of chemical reactions which produce the succeeding genetic mutations. All I knew in the 1920s was that an errant gamma ray, shooting out from our local sun, fell by chance on some peculiar amino-acid compound and started up the living cells which eventually became a fish and then a mammal and finally a man with a mind. How could we be certain that there had not been a ghastly mistake, that God had really intended to create a vegetable universe of beautiful flowers and trees but that an errant gamma ray had fallen on the wrong amino-acid compound, producing a fish instead of a rose?

If you could swallow, I thought, the incredible piece of luck which led from the ape-man *Australopithecus* to Plato, Jesus, Mozart and Einstein you would swallow anything. You would be caught up in the animism which began with the dark myths of the primitive savage and ended up in the dialectical materialism of Marx. I just could not take it.

This period of shocked agnosticism lasted while I was up at Oxford and debated with philosophers and theologians. I grappled with Bradley's metaphysical essay *Appearance and Reality* and I think this steadied me down. After all, Bradley had said : 'Space and time are appearance. Reality is not in the appearance'. So I came to the conclusion that there must be some reality or principle behind the chance material appearance. I felt that if there was a principle behind Life there might be a principle behind mine, though I realised that that was a *non sequitur*.

At Oxford I formed a debating club which I called the 'X Club' because it was primarily to discuss the subject which obsessed me – the Unknown God. Once, on the occasion of a club dinner, I pitted the famous theologian Canon Streeter, the Dean of my college, Queen's, and a reverend man called Talbot, the nephew of the Bishop of Winchester, against a well-known Victorian atheist, Joseph McCabe, whom I had invited down from London. It was great fun. Talbot became very angry with McCabe in the course of the discussion and accused him of never having met a real gentleman. I felt like Shaw's *Black Girl in Search of God*. Clearly one did not get nearer to Principle through this sort of childish acrimonious debate. Nor did Canon Streeter, the most eminent divine of his day, resolve my doubts. We used to go for long walks together on Headington Hill but his answers were always equivocal. He was a dear man but he was torn by grave metaphysical anxieties. We called him 'Christ' because of his large feet : they were the size of those of the ascending Christ in the stained glass window of the chapel. A Dutch artist had painted footprints on the Mount of Olives of gargantuan size.

I mention these early philosophical trials because, being a serious and introverted youth, they made a deep and lasting impression on my inner self, the Freudian Super Ego. In fact they changed my whole attitude to life. I could no longer regard sensual consciousness as the whole of reality. I could no longer regard the face I saw in the mirror as the real me, which was a great comfort seeing that I had nothing to boast about. Matter and mind, it seemed, could not be separated. The later scientists gave the reason why when they broke finite matter into infinitesimal particles of energy. If matter-mind was a state of consciousness it could be uplifted by improving the matter (curing disease and abolishing poverty) and improving the mind (through the study of the ethic of scientific knowledge). The purpose of life, if it had any, must therefore be the uplifting of man into a higher form of consciousness. This became my philosophy and shaped my subsequent attitude to politics and economics. From that date I have never been able to take seriously the conventional politician. Nor the conventional economist. It was only Keynes, I felt, who saw the economic emancipation of man as a way to the higher purpose of living more intelligently and more enjoyably.

I was confirmed in my beliefs by a curious incident which happened during the serious illness of my first wife when I was living temporarily at 25 Cheyne Walk in Chelsea. A friend had sent a Christian Science lecturer to talk to me about healing and he called at a most inopportune moment – when I was about to go upstairs to bed with an acute attack of influenza – aching limbs and high temperature. With reluctance I invited him to the drawing-room and let him talk. While I listened as intently as I could I was conscious of a peculiar sensation – as if a tight stocking garment was being pulled off my body. Then I felt relaxed. When he had gone I turned to go upstairs to the bedroom where the maid had put the hot water bottles and as I mounted the steps I suddenly realised that I was entirely cured of the influenza. I was feeling free and normal. Not a weight in my legs. Not an ache. Not a pain. I took my temperature : it was normal. Yet the man had not known that I was ill. There could have been no faith cure or hypnotic suggestion. It was an instantaneous healing, the science of which I am still trying to discover.

But to go back to Oxford. I do not believe that I have ever again laughed so much as we all did in the summer term of 1914. Not a week passed without some exquisitely funny moment, for my friends were dedicated wits and intellectual show-offs, and would take any preposterous stand to produce a laugh. The environment in 1914 was ideal for such gay irresponsibility and intellectual snobbery. The world had not assumed the grim visage which dries up laughter today. No world war had occurred, no Russian Revolution, no mass slaughter, no gas chambers, no genocide. We could discuss Marx without associating him with the savage tyranny and purges of Stalin. We could discuss women

without mixing them up with a sex war or permissive, porno-
graphic societies. We could organise a rag without being
reminded by the media of the starving millions in the rags of
poverty and oppression. Even Aldous Huxley was 'blissfully un-
troubled'. Perhaps there will never be another Elysium like
Oxford in the Summer Term of 1914.

The debates at the Oxford Union were often hilarious. I
rejected the conventional label of Tory or Liberal and called
myself a Guild Socialist, a label I took from the Magdalen
economist, G. D. H. Cole, the author of *Guild Socialism*. Having
been moved by the miserable lot of the Leicestershire coal miners
in my youth, I felt bound to be against the Establishment, but I
must confess that in these frivolous Oxford years one never took
politics very seriously. Nor was my pose taken seriously at the
Union. Once, when I was making an impassioned speech in
favour of 'votes for flappers', C. E. M. Joad, the popular philosopher to be, held up a pair of female knickers and made some
lewd remark as he often did. I forget my epigrammatic reply, but
the house was convulsed and thereafter I was taken to be a wit
and was never after allowed to make a dull, serious speech.
Having a strong sense of humour I enjoyed the new pose. Douglas
Jerrold and I used to meet in my rooms in Queen's before a
Union debate and manufacture epigrams which we would supply
to anyone who would stand us a drink. Victor Gollancz told me
later that the epigrams were not particularly funny, but as I used
to get passionately wound up in my argument and wave my arms
about in the perorations I became a popular speaker. I cannot
remember now a single word I said.

The First World War broke out before I had taken my final
schools. I had organised an August reading party with some
undergraduate friends who were as deeply serious about getting a
'first' as I was, and we were staying at the remote Fosse Bridge
Hotel in Gloucestershire, close to the Roman Villa at Chedworth
which we had planned to explore. We cut ourselves off from life
and refused to have newspapers or take telephone calls. One
morning our landlord broke into our studies to say that war had
been declared. We stared at him in amazement : 'What war?' we
asked. 'Is it Ireland?' I asked. I had recently been taken by my
godfather, who was a director of Worthington, the brewers, to
Belfast where, having been given the secret pass-word by a Tory

MP we had watched the Ulster rebels being drilled with their rifles in a brewery yard behind locked gates. 'No, no,' said the landlord, 'world war'. We were vaguely conscious of some international tension, but had not heard of the assassination of the Archduke. We rushed into Cirencester to buy the papers. Not a word was spoken while we read the horror story. Immersed in our reading of ancient and medieval history, we were aghast at the thought that civilised European statesmen could plunge the world into war over such trivialities.

At the beginning of next term we joined up for medical examination. Having overstrained my heart on the cinder track – some foolish friend had said that, as I had won the hundred yards in record time at Cheltenham, I should go all out for a running 'blue' – I was not passed by the doctors and was told to finish my schools and report again. I then threw myself into serious work, day and night, and within one year managed to get a 'first' in the history school and at the same time win the Lothian historical prize with a thesis on the obscure subject of *The Pseudo-Isidorian Decretals*. It pretty well wrecked my health again. I was put into a B medical class but was applied for by a friend in the War Office and posted to the War Office staff as a civil servant.

I was not sorry to leave Oxford. It had become desolate. Gone were the outrageous rags and the hilarious scenes at the Union. I had been elected 'acting-president' and had presided over the closing-down of the debates. There was silence in the quads. No longer came the sound of laughter and talk from the open windows. The flower of a brilliant generation of undergraduates had gone to die on the bloody fields of Flanders for a cause which we now see as utterly unworthy of their sacrifice.

It was strange to find myself a civilian in the seat of the military. As a resident clerk on night duty at the War Office, I was opening secret telegrams, taking telephone calls from ladies for the Quartermaster General and handing on reports of the latest Zeppelin raid. I shall never forget the night when the Zeppelin was destroyed over north London in 1916. I had asked Harry Strauss (now Lord Conesford) and his fiancée to dine in my flat in King's Bench Walk and after dinner we went out into the garden to watch the searchlights, having had warning of a raid. Suddenly the huge airship was caught in the beam of a searchlight and in a few seconds we saw a faint flash and then a tongue of flame enveloped the whole ship and it was ablaze. A red glow spread over the Temple garden. As we stood silent with amazement, a distant roar of cheering from the crowds which had been watching came flowing down from the northern heights of London to the river. Then it was taken up and answered from the southern bank. It was like the chorus in a Greek drama. We went silently indoors feeling that we had witnessed a sacrifice to some evil god.

After a time I was transferred to army finance and became private secretary to Sir Charles Harris, the Financial Secretary. Sir Charles was one of the most brilliant civil servants of his time. He was almost as deaf as a post and wore a hearing aid which enabled him to hear what he wanted and miss what he thought was worthless. Believe it or not we were trying to cut down useless war expenditures. Sir Charles introduced cost accounts into the army to help the more intelligent generals to run their establishments with greater economy and efficiency. He devised a cost unit for hospital beds and persuaded medical officers to compete with one another in a race for the lowest weekly return. Medical attention, I hasten to add, was excluded from the cost unit. We had less success with the cost unit per horse per week in the remount depots. Cavalry officers seemed to consider it unsporting.

Sir Charles persuaded Kitchener, the Secretary of State, to sanction the establishment of a Corps of Cost Accountants. Many rude jokes were made about them, but the House of Commons took it seriously and a Select Committee to enquire into the national expenditure was set up. I was appointed Secretary of the War Office Sub-Committee, whose chairman was Herbert Samuel. Our committee became convinced that a lot of avoidable waste went on in the artillery engagements. The effectiveness of shelling, they said, declined after a period, but the shelling went on and millions of pounds were wasted. So with the approval of the High Command our committee went over to France to interrogate the gunner generals. We were a party of five – three backbench Members of Parliament, our distinguished chairman and myself. I was asked to draw up charts showing the curve of shelling – with cost figures of millions of pounds on the bottom line – and the point in the decline curve after which it would become ineffective. We were generally regarded by the gunner generals as raving lunatics.

We were invited to visit the Commander-in-Chief at his head-quarters. Outside a beautiful old château in faded red brick, with a formal hard-edged garden in front, was posted a squadron of lancers, their pennants flapping in the breeze. Their horses were finely groomed as for a Horse Guards' Parade. Captain Sir Philip Sassoon, clad in beautiful suede top boots, came to meet us and conducted us to the presence of General Sir Douglas Haig. The Commander-in-Chief was also clad in beautiful suede top boots. He discoursed to us on the trench warfare, pointing to the various fronts on a huge map on an easel, and as he reeled off the targets I felt inwardly sick. My brother Tom, a gunner officer, had just been blown up in his billet by a German shell which might have been regarded as a useless waste in the eyes of my committee. As we left the exquisite *parterre* of the château, I heard the distant thunder of the guns. I thought of my elder brother Arthur, who was then in action as a major in the Royal Engineers. I was glad not to meet him, for he might have been contemptuous of me and my committee. Happily he survived and took up a Fellowship at Sidney Sussex College, Cambridge, was made University Lecturer in Engineering and became the best, being the most practical, college bursar of his time.

When we had returned home from France I was engaged on our committee's report which was presented to the House of Commons. I cannot remember whether it was even debated, but the work had so aroused my interest in the Parliamentary control of expenditure that I wrote a book on the subject called *Parliament and Tax Payer*, with a foreword by Herbert Samuel. It was published by Skeffington in 1918. The last sentence is perhaps worth quoting : 'The fate of the British taxpayer lies in the hand of his Member of Parliament. The way of controlling public expenditure is plain : the will of the politician is uncertain. Nothing will be achieved until the House of Commons acquires a financial conscience.' It is still trying to do so.

I shall always be grateful to Sir Charles Harris who set me on a financial path from which – to my astonishment – I was never to be diverted. He gave an intellectual distinction to the control of money. I shall always remember his flashing replies to the Public Accounts Committee in the House. He was the Keynes of the Civil Service. He was married to the sister of the German philosopher Schiller and had two sons – Reggie who became a Fellow of All Souls and three times a doctor, and Allan who followed his footsteps and entered the Civil Service of the War Office. They remain my friends and remind me of this incongruous period of my early life.

The war ended and I was transferred as a civil servant to the private office of the Minister of Supply, Lord Inverforth, a shipping magnate, head of the firm Andrew Weir. I remember representing him at a House of Lords enquiry into some peculiar, if not shady, transactions of his office when I was suddenly struck down with typhoid fever. I had been eating contaminated water cress at a house in the Chilterns. I very nearly died in the fever hospital in Grays Inn Road. After a long convalescence spent mainly in reading the works of Walter Pater, I wondered what to do next. Stay in the Civil Service? It was too dull and I was exhausted and tired of files and minute writing. Become an academic? Having got a good degree I was offered a history fellowship at Keble. But I was not attracted by the miniscule salary offered – it started at around three hundred pounds and went up to five hundred after five years – and I could not stand the architecture of Keble with its sham Gothic and hideous red brick. I was also nauseated by the sickliness of Holman Hunt's painting the *Light of the World*, which hung, life-size, in the chapel. I realised that I could not live in surroundings which were aesthetically abhorrent. This feeling has lasted down the years. Aesthetic starvation was only overcome when later on I acquired a beautiful Elizabethan manor house, and later still a beautiful second wife, who was an artist with similar intellectual tastes and sense of humour, and a delightful girl to talk to.

At Oxford I had eaten dinners in the Inner Temple, and after the war I took the examinations and was called to the Bar. Should I embark on the conventional career in law and politics? I had been attracted by the career of the brilliant lawyer-politician F. E. Smith, the first Lord Birkenhead. He had been at the height of his fame when he came to speak at the Oxford Union. As junior librarian I had been one of the welcoming committee. He was already 'under the influence' when he arrived but we gave him brandy to steady him down and were amazed to hear a faultless speech, each sentence perfectly constructed, each word carefully chosen. He merely swayed a little on his long legs.

I was actually tempted for a time to plunge into Conservative politics not by F. E. Smith, but by a wonderful old gentleman, Sir Henry Birchenough, a baronet, who was chairman of the British South Africa Company (Chartered). His delightful daughter Elizabeth had become a close friend of mine. Sir Henry was so honest that he died with a comparatively modest fortune. He looked, and was my idea of an aristocrat, because he would never enter a barber's shop. He had a man to shave him and brush his hair every morning in his house in Eccleston Square. He introduced me to Lord Milner, talked to me about Cecil Rhodes and saw in me a young Joseph Chamberlain if only I would join the Tory Party. I found him and his daughter fascinating. Under his encouragement I went around the public houses in Leicestershire mining villages talking to the coal miners about the new Tory democracy. These were the men for whom my father had conducted his mission and I thought the name of Davenport would be remembered with affection. It was, but they went on drinking bottles of port, singing bawdy songs and voting Labour. Not being convinced that they were wrong I gave up the idea of Tory democracy and party politics.

What made me decide finally to leave the Civil Service was the offer of a lucrative commercial job. It came from Lord Inverforth. He was still Minister of Supply but his firm, Andrew Weir, and Lord Pirrie of Harland and Wolff had formed a new oil company – the British-American – to supply oil for the Cunard and White Star fleets which had been converted from coal to fuel oil burning. The fact that I had been called to the Bar and knew something of company law made them think that I should be a suitable secretary to the new company. It was an exciting new experience. The two lords had contracted for their oil supply with Doheny of the Huasteca Petroleum Company of Mexico. We all went – Inverforth as well as Pirrie – to New York to negotiate a new contract. This Doheny was a talkative Irishman who was later to be accused of bribing Secretary Fall of the Interior Department over what was known as the Tea Pot Dome concession. At our conferences in the Plaza Hotel, New York, I used to see a seedy-looking gentleman with a wet moustache sipping endless scotch in an ante-room. He was Secretary Fall and he did, in fact, eventually go to gaol for twelve months. Doheny was a great actor, being an Irishman, and he told the two lords that their ships would sail into New York harbour and never get out because an oil famine was coming and they would never be able to buy enough fuel oil to raise steam. 'We must pay that man the price he wants,' they whispered to me as they left the conference room. They did and within three months the company was 'bust'. A glut of oil, not a famine, broke the market. Doheny's price had been outrageous and the company became insolvent. Of course the contract had to be revised. The Lord Pirrie was very angry. There was an unfortunate incident on the White Star liner which carried us home. Lord Pirrie accused me of leaving some confidential papers in the squash racket court of the liner. So we parted company. Lord Inverforth offered me another job but I declined.

The loss of the oil job could not have happened at a worse time. I was in financial trouble. My young wife whom I had met at Oxford – she was the cousin of a Cheltenham school friend, Harry Hinchcliffe (now Sir Harry) – had had a serious breakdown in health, and the specialist and nursing home fees had been shattering. She had been a beautiful girl with flaming auburn hair – I saw her as a Burne-Jones painting – but she was far from robust. I was anathema to her mother who was a Boote of Staffordshire, a family of potters contemporary with Wedgwood. This lady was the typical old fashioned Victorian moralist who regarded Bernard Shaw as an evil atheist and anarchist. When I announced that I was an ardent Shavian she felt that her daughter had married a dangerous social revolutionary. The climax came when I presented her at Christmas with an abbreviated edition of Nietzsche which convinced her that I was a devil. This was too much for her, and I was made to feel a social outcast. The tension of this family conflict caused my poor wife 'Freddy' (short for Winifred) to have a nervous breakdown. She overcame this illness splendidly and had a child – my son Antony – but later on her health collapsed again. Every doctor was tried, and Christian Science too, but she never recovered, and died.

At the height of this crisis I had taken a house in the country and had installed an expensive nurse. I was too distracted to think of another commercial job and took to writing on oil, capitalising my experience with the British-American company. My first two articles on oil and politics appeared in the centre pages of *The Times*. Then I became the oil correspondent of the *Manchester*

Guardian under the direction of Oscar Hobson who guided me into financial journalism. Suddenly as a reward from heaven, in which I had then ceased to believe, I received a summons from Maynard Keynes to write two articles on international oil for the famous supplements of the *Manchester Guardian* on *Reconstruction in Europe* which he was editing. This was in 1920.

I had been introduced to Keynes some years before by my Cheltenham school-friend Sidney Russell Cooke who was an undergraduate at King's College. I had gone to spend the weekend with him. Sidney's rooms in college were always alive with good talk and the most fascinating argument used to come from a long-legged man lounging deep in his chair whom they called 'Maynard'. I was struck by his odd appearance. His lower lip was thick and sensual but the sensuality was disguised by a short military moustache which seemed incongruous for an intellectual. I thought he should either have been clean-shaven or bearded. Although Sidney was an extremely good-looking young man it never occurred to me that this was of any special interest to Maynard. It was many years later that I met him by chance on a Paddington station platform and said: 'Hello Maynard'. 'My name is Keynes' he said with the frostiest of smiles. But he mellowed as we talked in the train going down to Oxford about the politics and economics of oil. From then on Keynes became the great influence on my intellectual life. I had taken economics as part of the history school at Oxford and now I studied all his writings. In this I was greatly helped by Hubert Henderson, another distinguished Cambridge economist. Hubert's wife Faith had a younger sister Georgina, who had been a close friend of my wife. I owe to Hubert my first lessons in applied economics. He had a fine analytical mind and was to become Keynes' fiercest critic of *The General Theory*. Hubert never liked any 'general' theory on economics.

Writing about oil for the *Manchester Guardian* gave me the idea that I should write a full-length book about the international oil war. Until very recently, it seemed hard to believe that the American Government could be worried about the exhaustion of its domestic oil supplies. It was then suspicious that Great Britain was trying to achieve an oil hegemony and exclude foreigners from her lion's share of the huge Middle East oil fields. There was, in fact, an 'oil war' between the two great powers and I took the line in my articles that a lot of bad blood was caused by the fact that the British Government was actually owning fifty-one per cent of the equity shares of the Anglo-Persian Oil Company. There would be less dangerous politics in oil, I argued, if governments kept out and left it to the commercial interests.

Keynes approved of my idea and the book was financed by my friend Sidney Russell Cooke on condition that his name appeared as co-author. I readily agreed and he was extremely helpful as a literary critic. The book was published by Macmillan in both England and America under the title of *The Oil Trusts and Anglo-American Relations*. It created quite a stir in 'left' circles because I condemned the oil 'imperialism' of the British Government which derived from Winston Churchill, when he was First Lord of the Admiralty in the First World War. I took the view that there was no half way position between an international control of oil production – the ideal, but then unattainable – and complete freedom of competition between the privately owned oil companies. I proposed that the Government should sell all or part of its Anglo-Persian oil shares to Shell and divest itself of control. The Soviet Government was particularly interested and had the book translated into Russian and sold as a paperback by the War Ministry in Moscow. I suppose they thought it was good anti-Imperialist stuff. They had no permission to do so and no royalty was ever paid, but as there were still intellectual links between London and Moscow at that time, Sidney Russell Cooke took up the question with Kamenev to whom he had been introduced. Incredible as it may seem, Kamenev and a friend spent the weekend at Sidney's house in the Isle of Wight. He brought no bodyguard or security men, but had a pistol in his suitcase. Nothing came of this curious encounter.

My suggestion that the Government should sell its Anglo-Persian oil shares to Shell brought me a summons to call on Sir Robert Waley Cohen, a managing director of the Royal Dutch Shell group. He said he disapproved of my book, but as he had been trying to buy the Government holding of Anglo-Persian, he thought it ought to be read widely. Later on I was to write some pamphlets on oil economics for this remarkable man. I had regarded him as a tough business tycoon – he was certainly tough with his Dutch partners – but he was an intellectual manqué and was devoted to charitable works and the Jewish cause. When I dined with him in his immense house in Highgate, called Caen Wood Towers, his wife, who was charmingly fat, would go fast asleep at the table by the time the cheese had arrived. Our fascinating conversation used to act on her like a sleeping pill.

My book also attracted the attention of an oil jobber on the Stock Exchange who showed it to the great Lancelot Hugh Smith, the almost royal head of a leading firm of stockbrokers called Rowe and Pitman. He graciously declared that he would like to meet the authors. Sidney, already a partner of a firm of stockbrokers, Capel Cure and Terry, was produced on the floor of the House, and as he was a good-looking young man with dark brown hair and brown eyes, an aristocratic nose and the somewhat arrogant manner of the upper-class, he made a favourable impression on the rich bachelor Lancelot Hugh Smith. In a few days he was offered a partnership in Rowe and Pitman and had the magnaminity to tell the great man that although he was greatly flattered, he could not accept the offer unless he could bring with him a young friend called Davenport who wrote 'all his economic stuff'. So Davenport found himself writing 'economic stuff' for a leading firm of stockbrokers in the City. I had arrived at the gates of Mammon. In the nick of time, I thought, for the huge doctors' bills were pressing hard.

2

The City under Montagu Norman

Arriving in the City for the first time I had the feeling that I had travelled to a foreign country, although it was only half an hour by tube. The inhabitants were wearing such curious clothes. Messengers in the uniform of the Corps of Commissionaires were marching about in military gait carrying millions of pounds worth of cheques and company scripts as though they were parcels from the local store. Fresh-looking stockbrokers, absurdly dressed in top hats, were darting into dark alleys to call on merchant bankers who were never seen, I was told, in the light of day because of their foreign appearance. In the centre of the 'square mile', which is the confine of the old Roman fort, rose the hideous mix-up of a building, towering over the fine classical wall of architect Sloane, whose statue, expressing, I thought, extreme disgruntlement, was placed facing the back street. This was the Bank of England – a pseudo-Classical building, decorated with neo-Georgian sculptures, rising up to an incongruous Mansard roof. In the entrance hall stood tall dignitaries in scarlet robes and coachmen's hats, embroidered with tassels and gold braid, proclaiming their late seventeenth-century origin and uselessness. They were forbidding access to vulgar sightseers, for this was the holy of holies – the seat of the City Pope – the Vicar-on-Earth of the Great Gold Mystery.

When the Bank of England was responsible for operating the international gold standard a terrible economic power lay in the hands of the Governor of the Bank of England. He could put prices down and throw men out of work or put prices up and start a boom, simply by manipulating Bank rate and through Bank rate the general rates of interest. He did not do this arbitrarily, of course, but if our export prices were relatively high in world trade, and if, as a result, the Bank's gold was being shipped out to pay for a deficit on the balance of trade – or if the maximum of paper notes allowed to be issued without gold bars had been reached or exceeded – the Governor of the Bank was obliged by the rules of the gold standard game to put up Bank rate and contract credit, so that businessmen should slow down their trading, reduce employment and force labour to accept lower wages through the fear of the sack. The underlying idea was to reduce our costs of production, stimulate our exports and so restore our balance of payments. That, by the way, is still the policy of the 'hard money' school.

The Governor of the Bank of England at this time was the fabulous Montagu Norman, who was to preside over the City of London for twenty-four years – up to 1944 – as absolutely as the Prince Archbishop used to rule over the city of Salzburg. I was told that the dictate of the Pope-Governor was never questioned. He had only to summon the bill brokers or the merchant bankers or the chairman of the Stock Exchange or the chairman of Lloyds to his sanctum, for his word to become law. Even the private lives of City financiers were subject to his nod of approval or disapproval. If any misbehaved, his colleagues would have a word with the Governor and the sinner would quietly vanish into oblivion.

The Governor chose his own staff meticulously as if he was running a security department of State, which, in his opinion, he was. The members of the Court of the Bank, whom he selected personally, mostly from the Old Etonians, were all paragons of virtue, wealth and breeding. I remember seeing one of these deities drive up in his Rolls Royce to a Saturday point-to-point meeting and win a race on one of his own fine horses. That was the type Montagu Norman loved – gentlemen with good horse sense.

It was said that the Governor himself had been sent down from Cambridge for bringing his hunter up to his rooms in a protest against the rustication of a fox-hunting friend. He was always eccentric in his ways. I would often see him travelling to the City in the rear coach of a Central London tube train with his ticket tucked into the band of his black Homburg hat which he wore at a rakish angle. Sometimes he would be talking to himself. The only deference shown to him was to be allowed to leave the train through the guard's door. With his pointed beard he looked Mephistophelean but not evil – a charade version of Mephisto. A poseur, I thought, and perhaps a little dotty as, indeed, he turned out to be.

I was brought one day by Sidney Russell Cooke to meet the City Pope in the Governor's parlour at the Bank of England. Montagu Norman was worried at that time by the inflationary nature of Australian Government finance. Could I write a critical pamphlet, he asked, to expose it without leaving any trace of his having inspired the attack? I said I could, and I did, and the secret was well kept. The Governor was delighted. Much of his work was always done secretly behind the scenes. He loathed publicity and would always travel *incognito*, which, of course, directed more attention to himself.

It was a sobering experience to find myself in the sacred Courts of the Establishment which I had hitherto been holding up to ridicule. What struck me at first sight was the jolly vitality of stockbrokers. They were like healthy schoolboys, telling each other dirty stories, ragging around when the markets were dull, and occasionally de-bagging an outsider who intruded into the 'House' in Throgmorton Street. They were exceptionally quick-witted; their reactions to the ticker-tape were like lightning; they saw the future just a day ahead. Their intellectual level was about form four in the schools they had never really left. But they were doing their job efficiently – they were activating the capital market which is the key-stone of the whole capitalist system. To call their attention to the need for social change at that time would have been an unpardonable *faux pas*. They had tacitly sworn an oath of allegiance to the Establishment and the pound sterling. But what distinguished them from some of those who scoffed at and derided them – they were really prepared to fight and die for their Establishment. They were always among the first to join up to defend the *status quo* whenever a national war broke out.

I found myself in a snobbish upper-class firm. Lancelot Hugh Smith, the head of Rowe and Pitman, had royalty among his friends, his clients and even his relations. He was the father figure of the great Hugh Smith clan which had brothers, nephews and cousins entrenched in the merchant banks, investment trusts and other financial institutions throughout the City. For me Lancey stood for the Establishment as I had imagined it to be – pompous, powerful, upright, unbending, alert to defend the pound sterling to the last million of the reserves and to the last million of the wretched unemployed. All the immense Stock Exchange business of the Hugh Smith clan poured through Rowe and Pitman. In addition to this bread and butter the firm floated many company issues and handed out underwriting to the life insurance companies and banks whose Stock Exchange business it handled. The profits of the firm were therefore enormous. The partners enjoyed fabulous incomes. Naturally they lived in great style with town and country houses and many of them hunted in the 'shires'. Sidney Russell Cooke and his wife Melville hunted with the Pytchley and looked magnificent on their splendid mounts.

Encouraged by their shining example I even took up hunting myself but not too seriously. I found myself one day in a top hat hunting with the Old Berkeley, which was nearer to London and less upper-class. I excused myself indulging in a cruel blood sport by saying that the fox had a much better chance of surviving the hunt than I had. I could not afford then to keep a hunter, so I depended on hire-lings which were not always reliable. On one hunt with the Old Berkeley I was about to take a fence when a lady, swearing loudly, rode her horse in front of mine. I pulled up, cursing also – one quickly imitated class habits – and gave the horse a kick. Before I was ready, it cleared the fence and sent me sailing over its head in a fine parabola. I heard a crunching sound and thought my neck was broken. I had landed on my top hat which was crushed flat. I was covered in mud and blood – the bridle bit had actually gone through my cheek – and was semi-conscious when I heard the loud voice of a City gentleman calling : 'Take hold of your bloody horse; I can't hold it all day.' I grabbed the horse, still dazed, and as the whole field cantered past me, swearing and yoicking, I had a vision of the Norman Knights charging at the battle of Hastings.

The rise in my income was a great relief – I was able to pay off all the heavy doctors' bills – and I found the management of a portfolio of securities a fascinating sort of game. You were always expected to do better than the *Financial Times* index of ordinary shares or gilt-edged, which was never easy. These were the days before the investment analyst had appeared on the scene with their tables of price-earning ratios and cash flows. There were no

B

research departments with earnest university graduates looking into company accounts and plotting the growth of future earnings. I remembered Hugo Pitman, one of Lancey's partners, calling me into his room one day to ask me to explain a balance sheet. There was really no reason why Hugo should have bothered to understand a balance sheet. His family's immense clientele was not built up on his understanding of company accounts, but on his integrity and charm. He had rowed for Oxford and was a friend of Augustus John, whose paintings he had collected. He was given the first issue of the Ford Motor Company to handle, because a Ford family connection had been up at Oxford with him and had rowed in his college boat.

Lancey's clientele was even more impressive than Hugo's for it included royalty and most of the dukes and earls. I was called to his office one day to hear him on the telephone saying 'Yes, Your Majesty; no, Your Majesty', but it was merely, he smilingly explained, the King of Greece. The Yorks used to come occasionally to lunch in the office – the late King George VI and our present Queen Mother – because one of Lancey's partners was Jock Bowes-Lyon, Elizabeth's brother, who was adored by the staff because of his perfect manners. Jock was never rude to clerks.

It was obvious that Rowe and Pitman were playing an important part on the national investment scene. I began to realise how immensely rich were the old aristocratic families with their great landed estates. I had never before seen such evidence of vast private wealth. The inequalities of wealth which so distress the left today are little ridges on the surface of the economic globe compared with the mountains of private real estate of the 1920s.

I soon began to wonder how long I could go on writing 'economic stuff' for a firm of stockbrokers who were not really interested in what I wrote. Certainly it was right and proper to pay off debts and make some money, but I was also acquiring knowledge and expertise; I had powerful friends and I felt that a chance would come to make use of the reforming urge which I had inherited from my parents and had merely talked away at Oxford. There were many City people – merchant bankers and stockbrokers – who were quite alive to the needs of reform. The Stock Exchange Council itself was a democratically elected body, fully aware of its national importance. The City was, in fact, the power house of the capitalist system. It provided the capital market where the savings of the people – collected by life insurance companies, pension funds and the like – were channelled into investment. As we all know, the economic progress of a nation depends on saving a proportion of current income and converting it into factories and plant for the creation of more wealth. If you are running an advanced capitalist system you are bound to have a Stock Exchange to effect the conversion of savings into investment – to bring the savers into touch with the capital spenders. The savers would not be willing to accept the securities of the capital spenders unless they knew that they could convert those securities back into cash at any moment on the Stock Exchange in Throgmorton Street. The only trouble is that there is no guarantee that the savings handed over to the financial machine in the City will emerge as the right sort of investment which the national economy needs. They might from time to time turn up in the pockets of unscrupulous company promoters. As Keynes once said : 'When the capital development of a country becomes a by-product of the activities of a casino, the job is likely to be ill-done.'

What amazed me to find was that it was left to the whim of simple life assurance directors, advised by merchant bankers who had no responsibility to the public, and by stockbrokers who had no economic training to do what they liked with their invest-ments. However well-meaning they were, they might invest in South African gold shares or in Australian pastoral companies or put the whole lot into American utilities, ignoring the claims of the home economy. They had no investment directive from the Government and there was no reason why their bankers or their stockbrokers should ever consider investment from the national economic point of view. They may have been aware that the capitalist system would not work unless the savings of the people were directed into the productive sort of investment, that is, the sort which made for the growth of the economy and employment of the workers, but growth at that time was not a word one heard – it was not even in the index of Keynes' *General Theory* – and there was nothing to compel them to take that point into consideration in their investment policy.

What concerned the Council of the Stock Exchange, which was a private club and not constrained by any Act of Parliament,

was to see that the capital market was working efficiently and
freely and that the process of turning savings into investment was
conducted with absolute honesty and fair dealing. This, on the
whole, it achieved, although there were lapses from time to time.
Clarence Hatry was not the only company promoter who went to
gaol. John Howeson, the tin king, and his co-director Bishirgian,
went in for twelve months for issuing what was judged to be a
fraudulent prospectus (though it misled no one but City under-
writers who ought to have known better) and even Lord Kylsant,
the chairman of the Royal Mail, followed suit for publishing a
misleading balance sheet, although it was passed by the
accountants. Much sympathy was extended to Lord Kylsant and
on his release from prison the villagers gave him a royal reception,
pulling his beflagged Rolls Royce with ropes up to the porch of
his mansion. These were considered misdemeanours compared
with Hatry's outrageous forgeries of municipal script – Hatry was
not out of the top drawer – but they showed how strictly the good
name of the City was guarded.

Investment practice in the City in those days was not the
sophisticated affair it has become today. The usual portfolio was
conventionally   distributed   between   gilt-edged,   debentures,
preference shares, equities and property. Had they never heard, I
thought, of the trade cycle which gave rise to regular fluctuations
in interest rates and security prices? Here was a chance to make
money out of trading in securities which they never seemed
adequately to exploit. Personally I had no capital at the time to
exploit but I managed to make an extra thousand or two a year
by trading in the stock markets without taking undue risks or
gambling on borrowed money.

I had a friend, Major L. L. B. Angas, who was the first to
publicise a system for trading in stocks and shares by exploiting
monetary cycles. He was attached to the stockbroking firm of
Myers and had written two books – *Investment* and *Investment
for Appreciation*. He had made an analysis of the trade and
monetary cycles over the years from 1800 and had found that the
average trade cycle before the First World War was eight years –
four years up and four years down. (When 'stop-go-stop' was
introduced by the Tories after 1951 the average cycle became a
four-year one – two years up and two years down). The Major's
rules were simple. When a boom was coming to an end you sold

every equity share you had – near the top if you were lucky – and went into cash. Then after a while you used the cash to buy gilt-edged stocks because the rate of interest would fall as the recession deepened and bonds would begin to rise. Long before bond prices had reached their top you came out and switched into equity shares just as they were rising in anticipation of the next boom. But you had to be careful to choose the right groups. Major Angas would, of course, advise you for a fee.

The Major, who was short of stature and rather plump, looking like a well fed bull-finch, had a flair for the publicity. He would produce a pamphlet called *The Coming Collapse in Rubber* or *The Coming Rise in Gold* which made everyone rush to buy the pamphlet and telephone their brokers. Naturally there was a form inside the pamphlet on which you could subscribe for the Angas Investment Service. He did very well for himself and after exhausting the London market he went to New York to set up a hotter service where the clientele would be more active and extensive. He wanted me to join him. 'You can write,' he said, 'I can't. But I've got the right ideas and together we could make a fortune.' I did not fancy it. He went away to New York and, as far as I know, flourished. There are always new mugs to entice on to the investment merry-go-round to replace those who have fallen off.

Many investment systems have been devised since Angas's. Nicky Kaldor invented for Vickers da Costa an 'investing in success' formula based on very stringent rules, and they applied it with much success for a time. But companies which have had a brilliant record over the past ten years sooner or later run into management or technological trouble. My own trading system was a compound of three formulas :

(a) Investing in failure.
(b) Investing in aggressive acquisitiveness.
(c) Investing in technological innovation.

For (a) you pick a company which has got into a mess and is being put right under new management. For (b) you pick a company managed by a business genius whose Freudian aggression complex compels him to take over fresh companies every year. For (c) you pick technological innovations such as Xerox or IBM computers.

The capital appreciation which results from (a) or (b) or (c) will generally be much greater than the capital appreciation from normal growth. The steepest rise in market values always occurs when the investment status of an equity is changing from a high yield basis to a low yield basis, especially when an acquisitive business genius is acquiring companies on a twenty per cent earnings yield basis and paying for them with his own shares valued on a five per cent earnings basis.

In recent years investment trading has been madly exploited by mutual funds (unit trusts) and their satellite 'off-shore' funds and a huge amount of good money has been lost by the frantic gambling of their young 'go-go' managers. Why inexperienced young graduates from the American economic and technical schools were ever allowed to play around in Wall Street with the savings of the people invested in the mutual funds, I have never understood. The 1969 slump in Wall Street after the outrageous build-up of these mutual funds in the 1968 boom probably caused more damage to small investors than did the 1929 panic forty years earlier. The collapse of Bernie Cornfeld's IOS (the 'Fund of Funds') after his super-salesmen had collected over $2000 million from innocent savers spread disaster round the world markets. In the late twenties, when I made my humble debut in the City, investment trading in the market was not looked upon with favour by the City élite. Keynes was the first to give it the seal of respectability and apply it to a life assurance fund when he became chairman of the National Mutual Life Assurance Society in 1921. Keynes was to develop in his *General Theory* the idea that the trade cycle was really a cyclical change in the marginal efficiency of capital, although complicated by changes in the propensity to consume and the preference for liquidity. He once said : 'The right remedy for the trade cycle is not to be found in abolishing booms and thus keeping us permanently in a semi-slump but in abolishing slumps and thus keeping us permanently in a quasi-boom.'

Later on Roy Harrod was to advance the theory that booms and slumps were not deviations from a static equilibrium but oscillations round a line of steady growth. Growth, he said, depended on the rate of saving for investment, on the increase in technical developments and on the rate of increase in the population subject always to the ceiling of full employment. This was undoubtedly correct in theory but Nicky Kaldor, with perhaps a keener perception of human nature, remarked that an economy was likely to grow at the rate its business men expected it to grow, because that would govern their rate of investment. It was only, he said, when the optimism of business men kept straining at the leash of full-employment that the economy would attain its full potential growth. Inflation at that time was not a problem he had to consider.

I had my own ideas about the trade cycle. It seemed to me that all these economists were not taking enough account of the psychology of ordinary business people. When profits were excessive the entrepreneur, being greedy as a rule, would tend to over-invest in plant in pursuit of this bonanza. He thereby sowed the seeds of the next slump by creating an over-supply of the means of production. When the first signs of over-production appeared, his greed would then be replaced by fear. He would begin to de-stock and new industrial investment would come to a standstill. Thus the psychological feature of trade cycles in these unenlightened days seemed to me to be the alternation of excessive greed and excessive fear. I have never been able to understand how economics could ever be divorced from psychology. The most successful operators in the stock market trading have always been those who knew little about economics but a lot about human behaviour.

Just when I was tempted to say 'enough is enough' for me in this City firm of stockbrokers my horizon suddenly broadened out. I was invited by Keynes to write a weekly City column for *The Nation*. In 1923 Keynes and a group of other Liberals – Walter Layton, the Cadburys and the Rowntree Trust – had bought control of *The Nation and Athenaeum*. Hubert Henderson, the Cambridge economist, became the editor, and he and Keynes asked me to write the City page in co-operation with Sidney Russell Cooke. This made my life in the City seem much more worthwhile. My experience of investment and the capital market would henceforth, I hoped, contribute something to the efforts which Keynes, Henderson and other socially-minded economists were making to reform and civilise the capitalist system and make it more respectable and efficient. I was particularly concerned to expose the inefficiencies of the financial machinery of the capital market as it then worked. It was clearly being exploited far too often by the less scrupulous financiers who were not interested in turning the savings of the people into productive investment but in lining their own pockets out of the promoters' fees and share dealing profits. They are, of course, still doing it today but much more discreetly.

The City Establishment, in 1924, was preparing for the return to the gold standard. When the dollar exchange had been un-pegged after the war an Act of Parliament had been passed in 1920 prohibiting the export of gold except on licence. So the pound was left floating and it seemed obvious to Montagu Norman and the City Establishment that at all costs it should be put back on to gold at its old parity. I do not suppose he even appreciated the risks involved. For him gold stood for stability, respectability and sound money. But it was in fact extremely risky to go back to a gold exchange standard when America had acquired during the war, and was firmly sitting on, an immense pile of gold – actually three times larger than the stocks held in 1914. The Federal Reserve had sterilised most of its huge war-time acquisition of gold and so had left the world's stocks of gold maldistributed, in fact, inadequate to support a revival in world trade on the gold-exchange standard.

I was of course familiar with Keynes' monetary theories and shared his hatred of the old gold standard which required a deflation of the economy – the creation of idle plant and surplus labour – whenever there had been a sizeable loss of gold from the reserves. A monetary system which required the imposition of human idleness and misery as a means of checking a business inflation was, he felt, senseless and inhuman. So it appeared to me who had been brought up in the parental mission for the Leicestershire miners – generally the first to be thrown out of work. When Keynes discovered that the Establishment intended to return to gold at the pre-war rate of $4.84 he was furious. In their articles in *The Nation* he and Henderson warned the Government that to do so would be to over-value the Pound by ten per cent and that this would depress the export trades, create worse unemployment and force down wages. Their warnings were disregarded. Keynes prophesied industrial unrest. The working class, he said, would be subjected to a cut in money wages without any guarantee that there would be a fall in their cost of living. 'They are bound to resist so long as they can,' he said 'and it must be war until those who are economically weaker are beaten to the ground.' This was as far as Keynes ever got to a belief in the Marxist class war.

At that time we were never really far from a class war. It was obvious to all of us Keynesians that the workers were being shamefully exploited and that an explosion could occur if wages were forced down too cruelly. The Russian Revolution had undoubtedly inflamed class hatreds, particularly on the Clyde, and had put the fear of God into the ruling Establishment. In October 1920 the Government had passed the Emergency Powers Act which enabled it to make emergency regulations by Orders in Council and set up courts of summary jurisdiction in the event of a general strike. The Triple Alliance of miners, railwaymen and dockers, formed in 1914, was still a menace and a general strike was only just averted in 1920 and 1921. The mood of the workers was distinctly revolutionary and in May 1921 the Communist Party Secretary was jailed for six months for publishing a British translation of Comintern propaganda.

In spite of Keynes' denunciations the pound was put back on to gold at its old parity in Chancellor Churchill's budget speech of 28 April 1925. It is said that Churchill never forgave Montagu Norman for the wrong and inhumane advice he had tendered. But he knew so little about economics that he told the House of Commons that the return to gold was no more responsible for the distress in the coal industry than the Gulf Stream. Keynes contemptuously referred to ministerial statements of this kind as 'feather brained' in his devastating pamphlet called *The Economic Consequences of Mr Churchill.* He excused Churchill personally only because he had 'no instinctive judgement to prevent him from making mistakes' and because 'he was gravely misled by his experts'.

The Nation brought me into the fierce Keynesian war on the narrow minded financial Establishment of the City personified by Montagu Norman. That the moneyed ruling clique in the City could cheerfully subject the working population to the scourge of unemployment for the sake of the gold exchange rate of sterling and the well-being of the merchant banks seemed to all of us wicked and immoral. I wrote in my column that the preservation of a particular exchange rate in terms of gold was not an end in itself. The exchange rate for the pound sterling was only a means

B*

to an end – the end being a healthy and expanding economy and a sufficient surplus on the balance of payments to finance overseas investment. If the particular rate of exchange was not bringing about that desirable result, then sooner or later it would have to be changed, as indeed it has been – not infrequently. No one can say today that there is anything sacrosanct about the sterling exchange when the pound has been devalued in 1914, upvalued in 1925, devalued in 1931, allowed to float from 1931 to 1939, devalued again in 1939, pegged at $4.03 for the duration of the war, devalued by thirty per cent in 1949 by a Labour Government, devalued again by sixteen per cent in 1967 by another Labour Government and left to float downwards by a Conservative Government in 1972–4. At the time of writing it is still floating against the dollar.

To go back deliberately to a higher rate of exchange in 1925, which was bound to damage the export trade and bring on a slump, was, as Keynes said, a *folie de grandeur*. But the Establishment in 1925 had a concept of Britain entirely divorced from the interests of the working population. It wanted a gold-fixed pound because it desired to see the overseas investments of the nation built up and the international banking and brokerage business of the City flourish. It was not concerned about the degree of unemployment at home, which it believed to be due to British workers working less hard and being more highly paid than foreign workers. The finance houses in the City were not even interested in domestic industry : they knew far more about the capital requirements of South Africa with its gold and diamond mines than about Lancashire, Yorkshire, Tyneside or the Clyde. Week after week Keynes, Henderson and I in my City column would expose the inefficiencies, the wastefulness, the immoralities of the prevailing system, but the Government went on allowing money to be pumped into the financial machine without seeing that it came out in the form of useful productive industrial investment which could put the unemployed millions into work. The finance-capitalism of the twenties and thirties may have provided thick bread and butter for the merchant banks and stockbrokers of the City but it dropped precious few crumbs for the working-class.

In my writings for *The Nation* I was afraid I might be catching some of the intellectual arrogance from which Keynes at that time suffered, but Hubert Henderson, who had a gentle and kind nature, convinced me that Keynes' ferocious criticism of official stupidity was correct and just. The fact that Sidney Russell Cooke shared my feelings, being a disciple of Keynes, eased the spasms of conscientious objection I felt to working for a firm of stockbrokers whose senior partner embodied what I most disapproved of in the hard-faced monetary Establishment. I looked on my column in *The Nation* as my weekly penance and good work.

Hubert's wife, Lady Faith Henderson, has left a fascinating account of 'Editing *The Nation*' in the *Oxford Economic Papers* of 1953. I must quote the following which seems to reproduce so vividly the atmosphere of the late twenties:

> We remember one or two great events – the General Strike, the Locarno Treaty – but the general impression that remains is vague, a sense of frustration and frivolity, Mr. Baldwin conserving his energies at No. 10 while the bright young people held midnight treasure hunts in Trafalgar Square. [I confess to having joined them once.] In reality the twenties when Hubert was Editor of the *Nation* (1927–30) were a bitter prelude to the full tide of disaster which followed in the thirties. They may well go down to history as the Wasted Years, wasted in political disputes at home which played into the hands of reaction and inertia, and in industrial conflicts more bitter than had been seen in this country before or since.

I was to write later:

> Exactly as Keynes and Henderson had warned, unemployment grew worse after the return to gold. By December 1926 it had risen by nearly 25% to 1,432,000. The 'distressed areas' were emerging. What the country was needing was not a severe deflation forcing wages to be cut, but the rationalisation of industry and the modernisation of industrial plants. There were far too many small uneconomic units in all the staple industries but the employers simply preferred wage cuts to modernisation. The coal-owners persisted in their demand for a substantial reduction in miners' wages. The Samuel Commission, reporting in March 1926, recommended that a cut should be made – not by as much as the owners had demanded but by enough to bring wages down to below the pre-1914 level![1]

[1] Extract from my book *The Split Society*, (Gollancz 1964).

Driven to desperation the miners struck and with left-wing leaders then in temporary control of the trade unions the general strike followed on 3 May 1926, when the Government broke off negotiations on the refusal of the machine men at the *Daily Mail* to print an anti-strike editorial. Fortunately for the City, the workers had no revolutionary leaders to guide them. The General Strike met with the well organised opposition of the entire middle-class. Stockbrokers joined up to a man to unload at the docks, to run the buses, to help the railways and maintain essential public services. Montagu of Beaulieu, the father of the present Lord, drove a passenger express train and was so adept that he was made an honorary member of the firemen's union when the strike ended.

On the whole ugly incidents were just avoided in spite of the provocations of the *British Gazette*, edited by Winston Churchill, and the calling out of troops for the docks and other vital places. My personal sympathies were with the miners who were having a raw deal, but as a responsible Keynesian and financial writer I could not support revolutionary action such as a general strike which might upset the economy and throw up a huge deficit on the balance of payments. On the first day of the strike I was motoring to the City from Gerrards Cross, where I then lived, and my car was held up by an angry crowd of strikers in Acton Vale. I managed to get through without being overturned but it was a near thing. A barrister school-friend Geoffrey Hutchinson (now Lord Hutchinson), whose actress wife Janet had become a close friend, offered to put me up for the duration of the strike at his house in Hampstead. This offer I gladly accepted and in conscientious support of the forces of law and order I joined up at the Hampstead police station and was assigned to night transport duty with my car.

The trouble area was Camden Town. With wire fixed over the windscreen as a protection against stone-throwing I motored policemen to Regents Park, where the London buses were stored and petrol dumps maintained. But there were few unpleasant incidents and no violence. There was no one prepared even to throw a petrol bomb. This seems the more strange today when violence has come to erupt on any demonstration of dissent in the streets.

The senior trade union leaders were terrified of revolution.

They had realised that to call a general strike in a modern industrial state was a revolutionary action which was bound to invoke all the forces of the State against it. They had no heart for such a confrontation and in nine days the General Strike had collapsed. The aggrieved miners feeling that they had been let down, as indeed they had, went on striking for another six months and finally had to forfeit everything they had fought for. A chastened Labour Party gave up further industrial action and went back to a Parliamentary line. J. H. Thomas said in his illiterate way in the House of Commons : 'I have never disguised the fact that in a challenge to the constitution, God help us unless the constitution won.' George Brown remarked in his memoirs that the General Strike was one of the great formative influences on the life of Ernest Bevin. 'Until then,' he said 'he had been very much a left-wing trade union leader but his experiences in the conduct of the strike, during which he became contemptuous of many of the colleagues he was dealing with, had a marked impact on him.' In fact Bevin was thereafter to become the dominating anti-communist force in the trade union movement, an event which turned out to be of great importance in the political history of the thirties.

It was significant that in the 1929 election, when Labour won 287 seats, the Conservatives 261 and the Liberals 59, the Communists lost every one of the twenty-five seats they had contested. The hot-heads were in full retreat. This marked the turning-away of the Labour movement from direct industrial action to Parliamentary democracy.

The Stock Exchange naturally cheered up after the humiliating defeat of the activist trade unions and the cut in wages which was enforced. By 1928 there had been a rise of thirty per cent in industrial shares. This is the beastly side of the City which always upsets me. It was not that the merchant bankers and stockbrokers were hard, selfish people. They were honourable and intelligent men, but they were hidebound by their class traditions and drew their monetary ideas from Montagu Norman who really believed that it was necessary to throw men out of work and cut their wages so that exports could revive and the pound sterling remain safe. The fact that this also meant that the City would be more prosperous and that government bonds and equity shares would rise in value was the pleasant sequence of events but they would not regard this as the motive for a monetary policy which we would now regard as inhumane.

The recovery on the Stock Exchange after the General Strike was marked by a new issue boom. It was largely a company promoters' boom which dished out huge capital profits to the vendors of some speculative business – often a new gadget for the affluent consumer – and their merchant bankers and brokers. It was exposed in my weekly column as evidence that the financial machine in the City was again not working for the investment good of the economy – that money pumped into the machine was not coming out in useful productive industrial investment which would help to put the wretched unemployed to work.

Throgmorton Street in the late twenties began to be caught up in the great stock market boom which was gathering pace and fury in the USA. The Wall Street boom and crash of 1928–9 was the most shattering blow the capitalist system has ever suffered. As it came soon after my entry into City life and brought tragedy and change with it I must devote a page or two to relating its fascinating and terrible story. The boom was said to have been officially ushered in in 1927 when the Federal Reserve cut its discount rate from four to three and a half per cent in response to pleas from Montagu Norman and other European bankers. But it had begun long before that. There had been two 'bull' markets under President Coolidge followed by a real estate boom in Florida. People began to think, as Professor Galbraith put it in *The Great Crash*, that 'God had intended the American middle-class to be rich', that is, if they played the market correctly. After Hoover had been elected President in a landslide of votes at the end of 1928 a great 'victory boom' broke out on Wall Street. Company profits rose conveniently to back it up but equity share prices soon began to outpace the rise in equity earnings which 'the bulls' projected. A speculative fever took hold of everyone, rich and poor, manager and office boy, husband and wife, son and daughter. In those days you did not have to pay for your stock; you bought 'on margin'. The rise in brokers' loans were $3,500 million. By the end of 1928 they were over $6,000 million and in the first nine months of 1929 they rose to $7,700 million. Call money rates soared – to 12 per cent and over – drawing in millions of loan money from Europe.

What makes the Wall Street boom and crash such an Old

Testament sort of story is the decline in financial morals which went on with the rise in stock prices. To get rich overnight was too tempting for slick company promoters to resist. They were soon forming holding companies to hold the stock of operating companies in the electric, gas and utility fields, so that they could float new shares on the market at ever rising prices. Then they formed conglomerate companies to hold the holding companies and finally investment trusts to hold the conglomerate-holding-operating company shares. In 1928 no less than 186 new investment trust companies were formed and in 1929, before the crash came, they had marketed no less than $3000 million of securities – a third of all the new capital floatations. The share prices of these new issues used to double in a few weeks after their introduction to the market. Unscrupulous financiers could make a fortune overnight.

It seems incredible, but even reputedly sane and conservative bankers joined in this mad market gamble. They conceived it to be their duty to invest their depositors' money in the craziest speculation the world has ever seen since the South Sea Bubble. The President of the Boston Five Cent Savings Bank said, a week or so before the crash : 'We must serve our depositors by investing in the type of securities that they desire. It is their money that we are handling. If we do not invest it according to their wishes, then they will withdraw it from our institution.' Charles Mitchell, chairman of the National City Bank and a member of the Federal Reserve Bank of New York, was typical of his breed. He could see no end to American prosperity or to the Wall Street boom. He was blind to the danger of erecting paper pyramids upside down with the tips resting on a few conglomerate equity shares. It only needed a slight turn-down in the growth of the underlying operating companies to bring the whole paper edifice crashing down.

The peak of the monstrous boom was reached on 1 September 1929. There had been warning signals of the sellers' wrath to come – like the rumblings of an approaching volcano – but they had been ignored. Major Angas had surpassed himself with a new pamphlet *The Coming Crisis of 1929* and had cried : 'Get out! Stay out! Wait for the Panic!' On 30 August 1929 London had sent out a red warning flash when the forger-financier Clarence Hatry crashed and plunged the London Stock Market into a dangerous slump. Liquidation from those caught in the Hatry débâcle started the wave of selling which began to engulf Wall Street. London operators, being five hours ahead of Wall Street time, were the first to jump off the market toboggan. There was another spasm of selling on 21 September and then, after a brief recovery, panic caught hold of the market on 29 October. Stocks were thrown overboard regardless of price and $16,000 million was wiped off the value of equity shares in a single day. From the peak on 1 September, when the market was valued at $90,000 million, the fall by the end of the month was over $26,000 million on the 'big board' alone. If we take account of the 'curb' and 'over-the-counter' markets the total drop in paper values was $40,000 million! It was enough to plunge the whole of America into a catastrophic business slump. Every business firm, every trust, every family, had been investing its savings and surpluses in the paper of Wall Street, which vanished almost overnight. Yet this fantastic stock market boom was generated in a period of stable money. Americans had enjoyed seven years of stable commodity prices. It goes to show that the human race – or that part of it running an acquisitive society – gets bored from time to time with respectability and sober growth, and likes to go on a mad, get-rich-quick rampage. It is an expression, I suppose, of the subconscious destructive drives of the human psyche.

One good result for America of the Wall Street crash was to discredit the bankers and drive them out of the political ruling clique where they had been entrenched for generations. The votes of the middle- and working-classes were solicited by Roosevelt to carry through his radical reforms of the financial system, which included the setting up of the Securities and Exchange Commission. American trade unionists, instead of being alienated, as the British were, by harsh deflationary policies imposed by a moneyed ruling clique, became supporters of the renascent capitalism which Roosevelt was sternly reforming. This explains why American labour has been so much more productive and so much less obstructive in the working of the capitalist system.

I do not believe that there can be another Wall Street slump or depression of the 1929–32 dimension. The American banking structure at that time was thoroughly unsound. The financial management of companies was often both unsound and corrupt. The stock market facilities for gambling were outrageously extended. After the sizeable recovery in the market from the autumn of 1929 to May 1930 there came the prolonged and deadly decline in stock market values for another two years which brought the prices of the mushroom-growth utility companies down to ten per cent or less of their former heights. It was this protracted fall which knocked every investor out. In the winter of 1932–3 the banks everywhere were closing their doors and going bust, wiping out the savings of countless families. I remember a Canadian bank manager, who had an office facing the American frontier, telling me that he could see from his window a long traffic-jam of motor cars waiting to cross the border. It was the panic-stricken American fathers trying to get into Canada to deposit what was left of their family savings in a sound Canadian bank.

I have vivid memories of this earth-shattering stock market slump because I had been privileged, as a young man in the City without capital, to participate in a syndicate formed by the partners of Rowe and Pitman and Shroeders merchant bank to take up a block of Chase National Bank common stock – one of the high-flyers of Wall Street. For some weeks the shares sky-rocketed and we were counting our wonderful profits and then came the crash. The stock fell by twenty or thirty or forty points a day. I saw the partners of Rowe and Pitman hanging on to the ticker-tape, their faces white and drawn, watching their money vanish into thin air. My participation was only the dollar equivalent of £500 : the average partner lost over £5,000 in this little flutter. In the general panic, many worthy investors lost their entire savings and some committed suicide. The story is told of two young men who threw themselves out of the top window of a skyscraper, hand in hand, because they had been running a joint account – on borrowed money – in General Motors.

A tragedy also came to me and Rowe and Pitman. Sidney Russell Cooke was a highly sensitive young man beneath his acquired panache – he was in fact, an intellectual *manqué* – and I could see that partnership worries were breaking his nerves. One day during the nerve-wracking bear market he said to his senior partner : 'Lancey, the time is coming when you will go into the market and not find a bid in a hundred War Loan' (meaning £100,000) The great man replied : 'Sidney, I think you are losing your judgement.' Turning his back on Sidney he walked out of the room. The young man, who had been the 'blue-eyed' boy of the firm, now found himself cold-shouldered by his senior partner. It was more than he could bear. A nervous breakdown followed soon after. After nursing-home treatment Sidney went off on a voyage. He came back apparently restored to health. I went to dine with him alone in my flat in the Inner Temple which he then rented from me. He seemed calm, but a little distrait. We played *bézique* in silence. The next morning, 3 July 1930, he was discovered dead with his sporting gun beside him. I had lost my best friend, and Rowe and Pitman their most intelligent partner.

3
Working with Keynes in the City

The shock of Sidney's death turned me sharply against the hard upper crust of City life. I wanted to get out as quickly as possible. I was horrified by their harsh treatment of a highly intelligent and over-wrought young man. As I was thinking of their insensitivity, I remembered the vision I had on the hunting field when I was thrown dazed in the path of their hunters – the vision of the Norman knights charging on the field of Hastings. Here was the clue, I thought, to their callous behaviour. They were carrying on the traditions of their ancestors.

We always seem to have enjoyed or suffered in England an extremely tough ruling-class. For example, our Norman overlords conquered and held not only England but southern Italy and Sicily, and built great castles – some of them still standing – in the Peloponnese, Cyprus, Rhodes and the Holy Land in their incredible drive to oust the infidel from Jerusalem. The Tudors ushered in a brilliant new aristocracy fattened on the plunder of the monasteries. Then we had the fighting landed gentry of the Cromwellian revolution who fattened themselves in turn on the confiscated estates of the Royalists. In every age we seem to have had a vigorous and resourceful class of *nouveaux riches*. Indeed, the Whigs and Tories of the eighteenth century founded a new ruling clique which possessed the same powerful and acquisitive qualities of the Normans. It is this same ruling clique which dominated our politics and society right up to the First World War and beyond. They were not, in fact, dispossessed until the General Election of 1945 which brought into power for the first time the lower-class of villeins and labourers with the help of a few landless and rootless intellectuals from the universities.

Happily our upper-class has never slipped into the decadence which fell upon so many European aristocracies. Today they are displaying the adaptability and resilience of their ancestors when they convert their stately homes into show-grounds complete with lions and giraffes or motor car museums in order to pay their taxes and death duties. Only a few of them now believe that social importance depends upon the length of their family pedigree : the majority will cash in upon it by inviting the public inside to see how the last of the pedigree live. The great merit of their class lay in their feudal sense of discipline and duty. Just as the Norman baron had his feudal code of honour and would put on his armour to fight for his king and overlord, at home or overseas in France, so the landed upper-class of England would be prominent in the field abroad whenever a national war had been declared. Their sons who joined up in 1914 and were virtually wiped out on the field of Flanders were acting in the tradition of the Norman knights who fought at Hastings. Their grandsons were probably among the first to volunteer in 1939. 'Thank God for Colonel Blimp', wrote Keynes at the beginning of the Second World War when he was having trouble with the pacifists and fellow-travellers at *The New Statesman and Nation*. Incidentally, it was the Norman system of primogeniture which kept the family estates of the upper-class intact, for the eldest sons, and sent the adventurous and buccaneering younger ones into the army or the City. The City certainly seemed full of them in the late 1920s when I arrived.

While I was feeling depressed over the tragedy of Sidney Russell Cooke, I happened to meet a friend in one of the alley-ways of the City who seemed to be exuding bonhomie and confidence. He was Robert Boothby, now Lord Boothby. Besides being a Member of Parliament he was then a partner of a Stock Exchange firm called Chase Henderson and Tennant to whom his father, Sir Robert Boothby, head of a Scottish life assurance society, had transferred his Stock Exchange business. With his usual gaiety, wit and cock-sureness Bob suggested that I ought to leave Rowe and Pitman immediately and join Chase Henderson and Tennant as a partner. This was against my inclination but I was at a loss to know what to do. If I had stayed with Rowe and Pitman I would have been offered a partnership eventually, I was told, but Sidney's death had made their office feel like a morgue.

I accepted Bob Boothby's offer and have regretted it ever since. I did not know at the time that the offer was made on the suggestion of Brendan Bracken who, aware of my distress, had telephoned Bob and put the idea in his head. This was the first of many kindnesses I received at Brendan's hand.

A Stock Exchange partnership was not my line. It was worse than marriage. You can always walk out on your wife if you have such an inclination but you cannot walk out on your partners. There are too many legal documents in the way. Indeed, my first experience of the legal nature of a City partnership was having to pay my share of Robert Boothby's debts when he over-speculated, as he loved to do, and lost his shirt. That was not too upsetting, because my share was small and it was worth paying something to have the constant pleasure of Bob's witty and exhilarating conversation. Like me, he felt like a fish out of water in the City, and really had nothing in common with his partners. They particularly seemed to resent my arrival and to harbour a suspicion of intellectuals and especially writers of the radical type like myself. Certainly they resented my writing a column for a liberal paper like *The Nation*. They said I must not criticise bankers, however stupid and deflationist they might be, because they might be clients of the firm. They warned me that I must never attack the Bank of England. On one occasion when I had done so in my weekly column, the senior partner called me in and said menacingly : 'You have been attacking the Bank of England again. Well, I've just had lunch with one of the managing directors (Humphrey Mynors it was) and he told me to tell you : "LAY OFF!"' Of course, I did not. My criticism of the Governor of the Bank as the arch-priest of deflation and unemployment was, as a Keynesian, my constant theme. Besides, Keynes' speeches to the policy-holders of the National Mutual Life Assurance Society were replete with scorn of bankers and their deflationary policies.

The ignorant and prejudiced young fanatics of the left seem to imagine that the City stockbroker is always a conservative and dull-witted dog. I met many who were extremely intelligent and some who were highly emotional. Such a one was H. P. Chase, the head of Chase, Henderson and Tennant. He was fascinated by Bob Boothby's political career and, having been introduced to Churchill, became obsessed with the menace of Nazi Germany and furious with the appeasers whom Churchill and Bob were denouncing. He also became addicted to scotch. He had great strength of body as well as of mind and once threw the heavy volume of the *Stock Exchange Official Intelligence* at my head when enraged by some trivial political argument. John Tennant had a gentler nature. He was the eldest son of H. J. Tennant, the ex-Liberal minister, and was the nephew of Margot Asquith. He married Antonia Benson who is now the wife of Lord Radcliffe. Bob once confided to me that he had only performed one noble act in his life, which was to introduce Antonia to Cyril Radcliffe who took her away from John.

John Tennant was immensely rich. He had the air of the *grand seigneur* but intellectually was a non-starter. He told me that at the Dartmouth Naval College there were only two officers below his intellectual level – the Prince of Wales and the future George VI. He was also very snobbish. When accused of this on one occasion in the presence of his clerk he denied it hotly, saying that if he were to meet his clerk in the street when he was going into his great house in Gloucester Square in company with a Lord or a Duke he would certainly stop and acknowledge the clerk's greeting.

As for Henderson, he was a dour Scot who made me feel that all Scots were distant foreigners suspicious and distrustful of the native English. If people so dissimilar and so distrustful of one another as the English, the Scots and the Welsh can more or less live peacefully together there is surely hope for racial integration almost anywhere.

I was fascinated by Bob Boothby's extraordinary character. His gaiety and wit reminded me of happy Oxford days. He had adored Oxford where he had been immensely popular and in some ways he remained an undergraduate. His charm and good looks certainly allowed him to get away with some outrageous undergraduate behaviour. He was a born gambler in both love and money, and it clearly gave him a kick to live dangerously. He would sooner gamble than do the hard work necessary for making money in the City. In fact the City bored him stiff. His real passion was politics. While the devil might be driving him on in his personal affairs he was invariably on the side of the angels in his politics. He opposed Snowden's deflationary budgets and the mean economies of the May report. He opposed appeasement in the thirties and was one of the very few Members of Parliament who stood by Churchill in his rearmament campaign. He attacked the terms of the American loan of 1946 and especially the clause for the convertibility of sterling. As he said in a passionate speech in the House of Lords in 1968 : 'Those who have most consistently opposed the Treasury policies during the past forty-five years have been the most consistently right and I am nearly at the top of the list.' It was no idle boast. Of course it is not always right to be opposed to an occasional deflation but Bob was a perpetual expansionist. Expansion suited his temperament and particularly his portfolio of equity and gold shares which he was always buying for a rise.

It was, I think, his desire to make money quickly to secure independence for his political career that made Bob such a compulsive gambler. How often I heard him say, when I went to have breakfast with him in his flat in Pall Mall, when I was living at the Athenaeum : 'Tell me, Nicholas, just how to make five thousand pounds in the next account. Don't give me lock-ups, I'm not interested in long-term investments. I want short-term gains. I want big short-term gains. I want five thousand pounds in the next account.' It was said with his usual joking manner. He was an exceedingly bad gambler. Later on in life he gave up gambling on his own account, and asked his friend Beddington Behrens to manage his portfolio for him, which he did with great success.

The offices of Chase Henderson and Tennant were in a gloomy street – New Broad Street – where the sun never penetrated. It was a hideous provincial-style building with the arms of some northern cities worked in stained glass. As I entered it a depression would fall over me with the half light. I was very miserable there and soon began to feel that my change of venue in the City had been a ghastly mistake. But fortunately my financial journalism became more exciting when *The Nation* was taken over by the *New Statesman* in 1930. And to my great delight I was suddenly thrown into closer working contact with Keynes.

Sidney Russell Cooke had been a director of the century-old National Mutual Life Assurance Society of which Keynes was chairman. On Sidney's death I was invited to fill his place on the board. The then actuary and general manager, Geoffrey Marks, explained that they wanted someone on the board who could answer Keynes back. That was impossible. Keynes could get the better of any argument and was impish enough to enjoy tying up an opponent in dialectical knots. So I took my seat on the board in 1931 with some trepidation.

It was a great lift for a young man without personal backing to be elected to the board of one of the City's oldest financial institutions. The fact that my public school was Cheltenham and not Eton made a lot of difference to my prospects. To the old Etonian, every financial door in the City was open. He had as a rule inherited great wealth and his mind was trained to think in terms of money and its management. He would not know how to make money out of manufacture or bourgeois retail trade. Eton would have destroyed that capacity although his father might have made his fortune out of such vulgar enterprise. The moneyed and Eton-educated son would turn his nose up at factories and shops and would drift naturally into the merchant banks, the discount houses, Lloyd's, the Stock Exchange and the investment trusts of the City. With the exception of Catto and Leslie O'Brien, all the Governors of the Bank of England within my working lifetime have been old Etonians. When the Labour Party made an enquiry some twelve years ago, it found that 44 out of 148 directors of the joint stock banks, 46 out of 149 directors of the insurance companies and 35 out of 107 directors of big City firms were all old Etonians.

It was therefore a rare piece of luck to be invited on to the board of an old financial institution in the great life assurance business. It meant a foot on the City ladder of promotion and gain, for you could count on being re-elected to the same institution for the rest of your working life if you observed the rules. City boards of directors are self-perpetuating oligarchies. When the annual meetings of shareholders come round, the managements pack the meeting with their paid staff, who are ordered to vote for the re-election of the retiring directors. How many times have I heard the secretary at general meetings read out: 'Mr Bonehead and Mr Setface retire from the board and being eligible, offer themselves for re-election.' The chairman grunts: 'Those in favour' – the signal for a forest of hands springing up from the paid staff – 'Those against' – not a sign! 'Carried unanimously.' Of course, on the rare occasion when a disgruntled or crackpot shareholder gets up to object to the gross mismanagement of the board and opposes the re-election of the retiring directors, the resolution is still carried by a huge majority of proxy votes which have been fixed by the management beforehand. Once elected, a director could look forward to, say, forty years of boardroom life – a deadening prospect, it is true, and one likely to shorten the span of life – but he could rely on receiving from each board at least £100,000 subject to tax, over the span.

The City's Establishment at that time was, in effect, an old boys' racket. It was immensely respectable and enjoyable enough if you like to indulge at lunch in smoked salmon and white wine and trivial conversation. The millions spent each year on guzzling in the City board-rooms and guilds, and in the Lord Mayor's junketing, would amaze the under-privileged and enrage the poor. It was a sort of Mafia in reverse – a gang based on honest dealing instead of blackmail, on good 'hard' money (lots of it) instead of easy loot and on simplicity instead of cunning. The only rules were playing safe, resisting change, opposing new ideas, upholding the Establishment and being willing to dress up and go on the pompous dinner parade in the City halls.

The 'old boys' network' then extended beyond the City to the boards of industrial and trading companies throughout the country, in which the City institutions had family or vested interests. The network is no longer what it was, for many old families have died out, but in those days boards used to interlock and cover 'the commanding heights' of the economy which the Labour Party has never yet been able to capture. By means of the 'old boys' network' of directorships the money power of the old ruling-class before the Second World War pervaded the whole of British industry. That is why British industry lagged behind its foreign rivals in the quality and expertise of its management. On the Continent, and in the USA, a man with brains and technical expertise acquired from some Institute of Technology would quickly go to the top, regardless of his social background and old school tie. But not in England, especially if he had a foreign name. However, do not imagine that British management would be any better off if it were replaced by another 'old boys' network' of trade unionists and Labour Party hacks. The second would probably be much more conservative and bone-headed than the first.

When Keynes took on the chairmanship of the National

Mutual Life Assurance, this old mutual society, dating back to the 1830s, became in some ways an exception to the 'old boys' network'. Thanks to its forward-looking actuary and manager, Geoffrey Marks, it had an unusual board which contained some outstanding and unconventional intellectuals. There was the eccentric Oswald ('Foxy') Falk, Keynes' stockbroker and collaborator in financial speculation. There was Walter Layton (later Lord Layton), then editor of *The Economist*. The heated arguments we had when there was the inevitable dispute about economics and investment policy were enlivened by Falk's sharpness of tongue. There could not have been two more dissimilar minds. Falk was quick, rude and decisive. Layton was slow, academic and indecisive. Indeed, Layton saw so many sides to every question that he could never make up his mind. There was an amusing incident years later at Strasbourg where I had gone to meet Dalton, who was then Britain's delegate at the Council of Europe. Layton had arrived as leader of the Liberals and his hotel put to him this fearful question : would he prefer an ante-room to his bedroom where he could hold meetings or would he prefer his own bathroom and lavatory: he could not have both. Walter simply could not decide. He saw good reason for either but no overwhelming reason for one as against the other. I made him in the end plump for the lavatory and bathroom on the grounds that the local sea-food could bring on diarrhoea.

'Foxy' had a brilliant mind and an explosive personality. He once threatened to throw a member of the board out of the window after an angry dispute and whether or not he intended it he had such a strong physique and such powerful shoulders – he was a champion golfer – that one always felt that his intellectual violence might end in physical violence. He was head of the stockbroking firm of Buckmaster and Moore but would not look after any private client unless he was given *carte blanche* to do what he liked. The poor victim either made a killing in the market or was wiped out completely. Foxy was always ruthless in investment matters. Having passed the stiff actuarial examinations he was regarded as an authority on life assurance investment. He and Keynes were the first to put equity shares into a life fund as a permanent or trading section of the investment portfolio.

Foxy had worked at the Treasury during the First World War and had joined Keynes as a Treasury delegate at the Paris peace conference. He told me that Keynes had written *The Economic Consequences of the Peace* in a white heat of fury because he had heard, before he left Paris in a huff, that Lloyd George was going to sack him. This may explain the wicked picture Keynes drew of Lloyd George's character, which was so fiendish that it had to be left out of the first public printing of the book. 'How can I convey to the reader,' he had written 'any impression of this extraordinary figure of our time, this syren, this goat-footed bard, this half-human visitor to our age from the hag-ridden magic and enchanted woods of Celtic antiquity? Lloyd George is rooted in nothing ... he lives and feeds on his immediate surroundings ... a vampire and a medium in one.' The venomous tone of this writing lends credence to Foxy's story that Maynard knew he was to have been dismissed from the Versailles conference. If vindictiveness had not motivated him he might have written a better balanced book; he might never in fact, have conjured up the national guilt complex about the Versailles treaty which led on to our appeasement of the Nazis.

Foxy was always sharp in his personal relations. He had been a close friend and adviser to Montagu Norman until they quarrelled over the return to gold in 1925. Foxy had been in favour of devaluation of the pound. The Governor sent for him and said : 'I don't know what you mean by devaluation. I have heard of default.' Foxy never spoke to him again. Like Montagu Norman, he was an authoritarian by nature and favoured the rule of the élite. He hated socialism. He once called me 'a bloody socialist', and in spite of my conventional reply of 'you bloody fascist' we remained firm friends. I enjoyed talking to him about art. He was a discerning collector. His early Picasso's, which he had sent to America for safe keeping when the First World War broke out, were badly sold on Government account for the dollars they needed. I remember seeing on his walls after he had retired several Cézanne water-colours. He knew far more about art than Maynard Keynes. Today the City leaves art to Kenneth Clark.

In spite of his contempt for party politics Foxy was a close friend of the Asquiths. He was playing bridge with the Prime Minister at Sutton Courtenay on the famous occasion when Lloyd George called and is said to have been kept waiting until the rubber was finished. This story, he told me, was a gross exaggeration. He became a bosom friend of the brilliant Violet

Asquith who married Maurice Bonham Carter ('Bongie'). Their conversation must have been scintillating. I used to meet her younger sister Elizabeth Bibesco at the *New Statesman* lunches and there was nothing to match a female Asquith in full conversational flood. It was said that Foxy always refused to answer the telephone at home because it ruined the art of conversation. When he gave up stockbroking and formed a finance house – O. T. Falk and Partners – Bongie became Foxy's joint managing-director. In the wider field of a financial house, Foxy's genius was more usefully employed. He acquired a brilliant staff which included Thomas Balogh, the economist, and Lancelot Law Whyte, the physicist. It was Lance Whyte[1] who was sent to investigate the jet engine invention of Whittle, and persuaded Falk to finance him. Foxy's hatred of socialism turned into explosive fury when Stafford Cripps in the last world war used his powers as Minister of Aircraft Production to take over Power Jets at the ridiculously low price of 63s 6d per share.

Foxy's abruptness seemed to have worsened when the Second World War broke out. Violet and Bongie had been accustomed to stay the weekends with Falk at his country house in Wiltshire. This marriage *à trois* suddenly broke up when Falk sold the house and retired to the exclusion of a flat in the High at Oxford. He was never seen except at our board meetings of the National Mutual. Of all his violent decisions this was the most dramatic. He subsequently retired to live on Boar's Hill, and until he died in 1972, he was looked after devotedly by the Bonham Carter nursery governess with whom he had, in fact, secretly 'eloped' to the flat in Oxford.

Incidentally, Foxy was responsible for Keynes' marriage to Lydia Lopokova. He had chided Maynard, who had then no great passion for the ballet, for his lack of interest in Russian music. In the 1920s Diaghilev was the dominant force in the art world, but Maynard had never been to a Russian ballet until Falk booked the seats when they had a season at the Coliseum. Lydia was the doll in *La Boutique Fantasque* and was introduced to

[1] I believe Lance Whyte helped Whittle to steer the jet engine through its initial difficulties. Later on he left Falk to work out his own philosophy of life. His books *The Unitary Principle in Physics and Biology* and *The Next Development in Man* were fascinating in their penetration. He became a popular lecturer in America but was hardly known in this country although Rebecca West once described him as the 'cleverest man in England'. He died in September 1972.

Maynard at a party afterwards. Her conversation was so amusing and quaint that Maynard fell a helpless victim to it. She specialised in choosing the wrong words which would sound funny and bizarre, but whether she did this deliberately or by misadventure I was never able to discover. Once when she was staying the weekend at the country house of a grand lady, who was very proud of her large aviary of exotic birds, she called out to a new guest arriving : 'You must come and see Lady B's ovary; she says it's the largest in England.' The atmosphere at the supper parties at 46 Gordon Square – Keynes' town house – when the Russian artistes were entertained, must have been fantastic. At one of them, Foxy told me, Pavlova asked : 'Do you like my dress?' 'But I adore your dress,' he replied. 'Then you can have it.' And she rose, tore the dress into two pieces, handed it to him while she sank back into her chair in the few underclothes she wore and continued their eternal conversation about life. According to Caroline Blackwood, in a recent talk on the BBC, Foxy had been for a time Pavlova's devoted lover. Lydia and Maynard must have been naturally joined together in this exotic atmosphere.

I can still see Keynes sitting in the centre of the board room table at the National Mutual. His constant shafts of scorn aimed at stupid City bankers were always entertaining because we had a banker on the board, Francis Curzon, the brother of the great marquess, who never failed to be provoked. One day Keynes turned on him and said : 'Really, Curzon, you have all the pomposity of your brother and none of his intelligence.' Keynes' smile was always friendly and his great charm took the sting out of his rude ripostes. Once when a member of the board asked him to explain an economic point he said : 'No, really I can't, for if I did, you would never understand it.' It was said with an engaging smile.

Maynard's stoop, and his sallow complexion suggested that he had never taken exercise in his life and apart from a stroll I never saw him physically in motion. He could not be called good looking; in fact, he was what the French call '*joli laid*'. Yet he was extremely sensitive to the looks of others. In *Two Memoirs* he described how repulsive were the first Germans he met at the peace conference – 'Erzberger fat and disgusting in a fur coat' – but when he encountered Dr Melchior – 'His eyes gleaming straight at us with extraordinary sorrow in them, yet like an honest animal at bay' – he fell almost in love. 'In a sort of way I was in love with him', he wrote, after the meetings had showed up the harsh meanness of the French. There were deep emotional forces about Maynard which one could always feel under the flow of his intellectual argument. One could sense his humanity. There was nothing of the cold intellectual about him.

I have never met anyone so gay, so brilliant and so witty in conversation as Maynard Keynes. He carried you away on his flights of fancy or argument; it was as exhilarating as listening to a Mozart symphony. My friend Paul Einzig described in an article in *Twentieth Century* of 1968 how his first meeting with Keynes inspired him to write his best book:

In January 1963 he [Keynes] invited me to lunch to 46 Gordon Square in order to discuss a controversial topic on which we could not come to terms by correspondence. I can well recollect every detail of that occasion even to the extent of remembering my amused surprise when I beheld my hero in the essentially human role of carving roast chicken – presumably because my hostess, Lydia Lopokova, being a great artist, had been even less domesticated than the great economist. I also remember that we were drinking champagne, because before the War it was quite unusual in my experience to drink champagne at such an informal lunch at which there was only one other guest – his old friend Nicholas Davenport.

What provided a turning point in my life was his remark that he was in the habit of reading most of what I had written. I very much doubt if he realised what an immense source of inspiration that remark would become for me. Since that moment, for over thirty years, whenever I was writing something that I considered important, I tried to write as if I were addressing it to Keynes.

In much the same way, Maynard had had a like influence on my own writing, particularly as I knew he had to read my weekly column as a director of the *New Statesman*.

Roy Harrod, in his immaculate life of Keynes, devoted a lengthy passage to Keynes' practice of speculation. Maynard began in 1920 by speculating in currencies and lost his entire fortune, which at that time was very modest. He borrowed

£10,000 each from his father, from Falk, and from another friend, and his father said : 'I do hope, Maynard, this will be a lesson and you will be more cautious in future.' Instead he plunged more deeply than ever into another gamble in currencies and commodities which came off splendidly. By the end of 1924, says Harrod, his net assets were worth £60,000 and by the beginning of 1937 a little over £500,000. I believe that at one time he was worth £1 million. When markets were active there was not a bond or an equity share or a commodity or a currency which he and Falk did not gamble in, sometimes on the 'bull' tack, sometimes on the 'bear' tack. I believe he made his biggest 'killing' by taking a 'bull' position in lead. But as his wealth grew by what we should regard as imprudent speculation he never altered his sober academic way of life. He remained a don, living comfortably in a town and country house, but not extravagantly.

The reason why Maynard was successful as a speculator was partly because he never stopped, partly because his forecasting of money and commodity prices was generally accurate, partly because he obtained a lot of inside information. He never used direct inside information in an improper way but he was often asked for advice by company chairmen and given an insight into their company affairs. One of his ex-pupils married a whaler's daughter. When Maynard was convinced on economic grounds that the price of whale oil must go up he bought heavily into Hector Whaling shares when the ships sailed for the Antarctic. There was a heavy catch and the price of whale oil began to rocket. He made a small fortune out of Hector Whaling. But I always felt that he was more interested in his theory of probability than in the winning of hard cash. He never allowed speculation to upset the quiet rhythm of his intellectual life.

Maynard constantly used his expert knowledge of the money system to speculate in the gilt-edged market. It was easier then than it is now because the Bank of England under Montagu Norman was hide-bound in its conventional reactions. I remember an occasion in 1934 when Maynard made his annual speech to the policy-holders of the National Mutual. He strongly advocated a cut in Bank rate and stressed the crying need for cheaper money. The next day the papers were full of his cogent arguments. Such was his influence in the City and his reputation abroad that the gilt-edged market immediately rose several points. No doubt he had heavily backed his judgement in the market on his own personal account, as he was fully entitled to do.

Harrod says that he only spent half an hour in bed each morning telephoning to his broker. But I happen to know that he spent a lot of time with Falk and that, however quickly his mind worked, the gestation of his complicated currency and commodity deals would occupy far more than half an hour each day. At first I was puzzled by the dichotomy between the economist searching for the economic good and the speculator gambling for his own financial profit. But he gambled for his college as well as for himself and he was, in fact, merely trying out his economic and commercial views. Speculation improved his economics and economics improved his speculation.

It was his understanding of the speculative business instinct which made Keynes such a great economist. The academic economist never really knows what makes a business man tick, why he wants sometimes to gamble on an investment project and why sometimes he prefers liquidity and cash. Maynard understood because he was a gambler himself and felt the gambling or liquidity instincts of the business man. He once said to me: 'Remember, Nicholas, that business is always a bet.' He also understood the techniques which made for success in speculating on the Stock Exchange. It was, he said, 'by beating the other fellow to the gun'. I have never known a man so quick off the mark in the Stock Exchange race.

But quickness did not always pay in the long-term investment which the City institutions have to make on behalf of life-policy-holders. In 1924 Keynes and Falk and a Scottish accountant, Gifford, formed the Independent Investment Trust and appealed for institutional money in a somewhat arrogant prospectus which said, in effect: 'We will not bother to estimate our future profits. You can leave it to us because we understand the money system and will exploit the moves in the rates of interest.' In six years the Independent Investment Trust had lost its entire capital (around £1 million) which had been heavily invested in Wall Street in a mixture of preferred and equity shares of investment trusts and utilities. Gifford, the accountant, retired, and Keynes and Falk had to hand over the trust management to Helbert Wagg, a City firm of merchant bankers. There was a flaming quarrel between

Keynes and Falk : not the 'some disagreement' which Harrod records. They may have remained friends but they never again worked together in investment affairs.

These were very difficult times in the security markets. After the first Wall Street crash of September 1929, which brought the market down by about forty per cent there was a sizeable recovery in the early part of 1930. It was the subsequent fall from May 1930 to December 1932 bringing the investment trusts and utilities of Wall Street down to ten per cent or less of their 1929 values, which caused the great distress in the investment world. While the clever intellectuals were being wiped out of the market, shrewd operators like Barney Baruch and old Joe Kennedy were making fortunes by going 'short'.

What was so endearing about Maynard was his obvious humanitarianism. He had a genuine feeling for the sufferings of the unemployed man who had been thrown out of work by the deflationary policies of the hard-faced bankers. Keynes had loved fun in his early life and wanted to see the mass of people having fun in their lives. When I first met him, and later when I worked with him on *The Nation* and the *New Statesman* and on the National Mutual board, it never occurred to me that he was or had been a homosexual. He had none of the usual mannerisms. Although my first meeting with him was in the undergraduate rooms of a very attractive looking young man, my school friend, Sidney Russell Cooke, it would never have occurred to me that there was any homosexual affair between them. Sidney was too interested in women. If he was a potential catamite to Keynes, it was merely a fanciful make-believe affair. Michael Holroyd, in his *Life of Lytton Strachey* describes Strachey's mortification when he discovered that Keynes had taken away from him the much beloved Duncan Grant, the painter, but he also mentions Strachey once complaining to Grant about Keynes' 'irremediable lack of passion'. Duncan Grant and Keynes were sharing the same house when Keynes was writing his *Theory of Probability*. I feel that affection, and not very active sex, was much more of a probability. Indeed, Michael Holroyd tells us not to take the obscenities in the correspondence between Strachey and Keynes too literally ' "To propose" [he writes] would seem to indicate little more than the slightly ambiguous pressure of one hand on another : "to rape" or even "to bugger" usually means a peck on

C

the cheek or a dubious embrace.' I once asked Roy Harrod why, in his biography of Keynes, he failed to mention or even to hint at the homosexual background of his early Cambridge days. He told me that he thought it might lessen Keynes' influence upon economic thought if he had done so. Besides, at that time, the law regarding homosexual practice among consenting adults in private had not been changed.

I was glad to receive a letter from Paul Einzig after the publication of Holroyd's *Life of Lytton Strachey* which revealed that he was sharing my view of Keynes' over-publicised sexuality. With his permission I reproduce it:

DEAR NICHOLAS,

I am enclosing the current issue of *Twentieth Century* which is devoted to turning points in various people's lives. In my essay I give my first meeting with Keynes as my turning point, and since it is you who had arranged that meeting it seems to me fair to send you a copy of the issue which you might overlook otherwise.

I stressed the importance of that meeting on my subsequent career and the immense help and inspiration I derived from Keynes. My object in writing it this way is to repay a fraction of the debt I owe to his memory by striking a blow for him in the middle of the smear campaign to which he has been subjected in recent months. I neither know nor care whether the "disclosures" about his private life have any foundations. Someone who knew him well wrote to me saying that all these relationships were just talk and talk and more talk and no action. Anyhow, it was an outrageous thing for Max Beloff to attack him the way he did in *Encounter*, and I feel there ought to be a counter-offensive on the part of those who owe him a debt of gratitude.

There is of course nothing to be said or done about the actual subject of the smear campaign. But I feel that everybody should seize any opportunity to emphasise his true greatness and his immense kindness as a man as well as an economist. By such means we could counteract indirectly the harm done to his memory. The smear campaign itself should be ignored, but now is, I feel, the time for coming out with anything we can say in his favour.

I conveyed this suggestion to some of his old friends who had been much closer to him than I had been, but so far I have not met with much of a response. Yours ever,

PAUL

Keynes ruled over the National Mutual Life as chairman for nineteen years. He did not succeed in doubling the funds as he did for King's College. You cannot make a lot of money out of investments if you have to work through a committee. He retired in October 1938 because he was tired of disputing with directors of the board and because he took a personal dislike to the actuary. He was always prone to strong personal likes or dislikes.

When he had gone I was plunged in gloom. There was a tremendous boardroom row over the appointment of his successor. The two intellectuals – Falk and Layton – were not seeing eye to eye and the conservatives were afraid that Falk, the deputy chairman, would dominate and endanger our investment policy if he became chairman. He was always set against British industrial equities; he had never budged from the line of his famous letter to *The Times* after the First World War when he declared that British industry was finished. In his view American industry with its advanced technology and management skill was the only fit medium for equity investment. He therefore specialised in American common stocks and was captivated by IBM (International Business Machines) – the wonder stock of Wall Street which was doubling in market value nearly every other year. He was also fond of quoting the famous statistic that £2,000 invested in General Motors in 1916 would have become £1,428,000 in 1955. In support of his rejection of British industrial equities he would often recount a remark which Sidney Webb made at a Political Economy Club dinner between the wars. He began his speech by saying: 'Gentlemen, the profits game is up.' G. D. H. Cole followed him and argued to the same effect. They were more nearly right, said Falk, than some of the City critics at this dinner like Bob Brand. There is no doubt that Falk saw more clearly than others the fatal tendency of guilt-ridden Liberals to bow down before the anti-profit cries of the Marxists. Perhaps he had a prophetic vision of British capitalism being hamstrung by the militant trade unions of today.

This addiction of Falk to Wall Street was enough to cause the conservative members of the National Mutual Board to feel that he should not succeed Keynes in the chair when he retired in 1938. Perhaps they shared the prejudice of their late colleague Lord Montagu of Beaulieu who had turned down an investment in Wall Street because 'investment in silver currencies was always risky'. (This was the only memorable remark made by his lordship during his tenure of office on the board from 1908 to 1929). In view of their prejudice and the perpetual quarrel between the intellectuals – Falk who would make up his mind too rigidly and Layton who could not make up his mind at all – the Board decided to elect a conventional business man and accountant, Kenneth Moore, to fill the chair. I regarded it as a tragedy for an investment institution to elect a chairman who was not interested in the science or art of investment as we had practised it under Keynes. Kenneth's hobbies were yachting and fishing, in both of which he was an acknowledged expert. He could think unconventionally and brilliantly about yachting and fishing – he devised some marvellous inventions and patented a new compass – but he could not think unconventionally about investment. He would adopt the old boys' approach. 'I say, I was lunching at Brooks the other day and ran into old Lord so-and-so who is chairman of Blanks. He told me that there was no harm in buying his shares just now. I gathered they were going to put up the dividend before long. It wasn't a tip but you know what I mean. I think it's a share we could add to our portfolio and forget all about. You know what I mean. I do like a share we can forget all about.' As if there were any!

After the regime of Keynes, when we did honestly attempt to apply our knowledge of money and the trade cycle to some investment advantage, it was like a return to the dark ages under our new chairmen. I should have resigned there and then but at the time I needed the director's fees which had enabled me to give up lecturing at the City of London College on the boring subject of 'The Principles of Investment' – a burden I had undertaken in order to supplement my income.

Board room rows are as frequent as strikes on the shop floor. Kenneth Moore stood in my eyes for the business 'old boys' brigade' just as Lancelot Hugh Smith had stood for the upper-class capitalist Establishment. Kenneth remained chairman for thirty-two years. The CBI have recently proposed five years as

the maximum tenure of a chairman's seat. Kenneth had, however, a sense of humour which made life on the board just
bearable and one of his funny stories revealed exactly what
enraged me about the 'old boys' brigade'. He had been playing
bridge at Brooks with a Duke who said at the end of the rubber :
'I say, Kenneth, what do you do for a living?' 'Well,' replied
Kenneth, 'I am on various boards and chairman of the National
Mutual Life.' 'Oh,' said the Duke, 'that's interesting, I am on a
life board too!' 'Oh, which one?' The Duke hesitated. ' 'Pon my
soul, Kenneth, I can't remember.' Meeting him in the club the
following week a smiling Duke came up to Kenneth and said 'I've
just remembered that life board I'm on; it's the General Accident.' As we all know, General Accident is one of the best-known
of the great composite-life companies.

The years went by and eventually I became deputy chairman
of the National Mutual life from 1960–9. This involved me more
deeply in the routine problems of portfolio management and the
selling of life assurance. The society had an exemplary staff, loyal,
hard working, self-sacrificing, whose interest I continually fought
for. They had been condemned, however, to a slow business
decline until a new actuary and manager had been appointed in
1956. This was Harry Oram, son of a Speaker of the New
Zealand House of Commons, who restored the morale of the staff
by going all out for expansion, particularly in house-mortgage
loans linked with life cover. He achieved it, and the funds of the
Society are now approaching £90 million. Harry brought in a
sense of military discipline with his efficiency drive and I supported him up to the hilt.

On my retirement from the board I received only two letters.
One was from an ex-lord Mayor of London Sir Derick Hoare :

My Dear Nicholas,
I did not get a chance to have a word after lunch today as I
expect you were telephoning about your *Spectator* article. All I
wanted to say was two things.

First that I shall miss your thought-provoking views on so
many things very greatly, as well as missing the company of
someone who I have always found to have a very warm and
very human outlook.

Secondly I would like to tell you that I have greatly admired your outstanding contribution to the N.M. Both your most valuable financial contacts and your own exceptional gifts of understanding deep problems of our economy have been of the very greatest help to the company. All the very best. Yours,

DERICK

It made me feel not only that I had once belonged to the 'old boys' brigade' but that some members of it were extremely courteous and charming men.

The other letter was from Harry Oram, our excellent general manager, which with his permission I reproduce.

THE NATIONAL MUTUAL LIFE ASSURANCE SOCIETY
5, Bow Churchyard
London E.C.4
20 May 1969

MY DEAR NICHOLAS,

It seems strange to be preparing to-day for a Board meeting knowing that you will not be here. I certainly will miss you very much. So many other things had to be dealt with on the AGM day that I hope you did not in any way feel that insufficient justice had been done to all that you had contributed to the Society over the many years in the Boardroom. I have much enjoyed and looked forward to our Friday sessions.

In many other ways as well you have been a great help to me and one thinks specially of some of the causes which you and I alone have supported and triumphed – 39 King Street and T.U.U.T. It is good to look back on them. Yours ever,

HARRY

The first item in his last paragraph referred to the rebuilding of our old office in King Street on a ninety-nine-year lease from the City Corporation. The conservative members of the board had foolishly thought it was too risky but it has turned out to be a dream of a profit, both in capital and income, especially in our present inflation. The second item referred to the Trade Union Unit Trust, which had been organised by Desmond Hirshfield (now Lord Hirshfield). Harry and I persuaded the board to agree to provide the life cover for the T.U.U.T. savings plan which honest workers will find a great blessing when they retire or find themselves redundant. It was the first time that the National Mutual had looked outside the middle-class.

The experience of a life-time on the board of a mutual life office was invaluable, for it convinced me first, that the collection of the people's savings and the investment thereof should not be left to the whim of individual directors but should be brought under the guidance of the State for the purpose of getting the investment right for economic growth and full employment; secondly, the expertise of life insurance, coupled with savings, should be brought to the service of the working-class as well as to the middle- and upper- and that the working-class should be given the same chance of making a capital profit. This I proposed to Harold Wilson in 1964 when I put before him my scheme for a public unit trust, which will be told in Chapter 12. But now I must resume the story of the growing attack on the City by the Marxist left of the Labour Party.

4
Meeting Dalton and the Fabians

For me 1930 was a climacteric year, for it widened the scope of my financial journalism and brought me into personal contact with three of the Labour leaders – Dalton, Cripps and Morrison. I was drawn more deeply into the fierce controversy then raging over the future of the capitalist system and its power house in the City.

In 1930 *The Nation* was merged with the *New Statesman* and Kingsley Martin, a socialist and embryo Marxist, was appointed editor. I was surprised but delighted when he asked me to write the City column. In his history of the *New Statesman* Edward Hyams wrote : 'Kingsley Martin did not hesitate to put an end to Emil Davies' seventeen-year-old series of City pages in favour of *The Nation's* Nicholas Davenport. Davenport was the younger and better journalist.' I must say, I thought at the time that Kingsley was right.

A year after he had won office in the 1929 General Election, Ramsay MacDonald had set up an Economic Advisory Council and had invited my former editor, Hubert Henderson, to be its joint secretary. MacDonald had been greatly impressed by the Liberal manifesto (the famous 'Yellow Book') entitled *We can Conquer Unemployment* which was written for the 1929 Election by Keynes, Henderson and Seebohm Rowntree. This advocated the new Keynesian economics, that is, deficit spending to generate employment through public investment in roads, housing and the like. If only they had had my experience of public spending in 1947 when Dalton put me on the board of one of the New Towns! Nothing absorbs so much public money so quickly as building an entire new town out of fallow fields complete with land drainage, sewage, roads, houses, flats, shopping centres, car parks, concert halls, pubs and churches of every denomination. Keynes had never thought of building a new town.

I cannot say that Hubert Henderson was overjoyed to get the job which Ramsay MacDonald offered. He hated woolly thinking and theorising. Of all the occupants of number ten, Ramsay MacDonald was perhaps the woolliest, and Hubert scorned Labour's economic theories. One of the last of his erudite and salty articles in *The Nation* had the title : *The Limits of Insular Socialism*. The more he had to deal with Ramsay MacDonald and Philip Snowden, the more he detested their economics. Yet he served them for four years and only departed when he was elected to an All Souls Fellowship in 1934. He gave them many useful ideas which they ignored and one of them on exchange rates I have never ceased to believe in. 'Why', he wrote, 'should there not be several different currency systems in the world independently managed, say, a sterling bloc, a dollar bloc and a gold bloc? I believe it is in this direction that we shall be carried by the drift of events'. How right he was! But at Bretton Woods the powers believed that the trading world is one world. It just isn't. Each nation pursues its own trading policy, striving for a surplus, or sinking into a deficit, making a nonsense of the equilibrium which Bretton Woods pre-supposed.

The army of workless had reached one and a half million by January 1930, two million by April and two and a half million by October. There was great public alarm and despondency. Chancellor Snowden thereupon appointed a distinguished Committee of Enquiry into Finance and Industry. The lawyer, Lord Macmillan, was chairman, and Keynes, McKenna of the Midland Bank, Brand of Lazards, Ernest Bevin and Professor Gregory were members. At the *New Statesman* we all thought that at long last some useful official action would be taken to check the spreading plague of unemployment. In the City the stock markets were terribly depressed. Industrial shares were half way down the slide to the bottom which they reached in July 1931. This was fifty per cent below the summer peak of 1929. All of us in the City who traded in the stock markets had long since turned shares into cash.

At the *New Statesman* we were anxious to see the lords of deflation – the Governor of the Bank and the Chancellor of the

C*

Exchequer – exposed by the Committee as the ignorant creators of misery for the working man. At the famous confrontation with Montagu Norman during the meetings of the Macmillan Committee, Keynes, aided and abetted by Ernest Bevin, actually forced an admission from the Governor of the Bank that the main purpose for raising Bank rate was to create unemployment. I quote from the minutes of evidence at the Macmillan Committee :

> *Keynes:* So it is of the essence of the case that the Bank rate should have an important effect : that when it is raised it should have an effect in the direction of unemployment. That is what you want. Am I right?
> *Norman:* Yes, I should think it was.

We Keynesians hoped that to expose the evil social consequences of the orthodox banking policy would be sufficient to get that policy eliminated or radically changed. But we were far too optimistic. MacDonald and Snowden learned nothing and took nothing from Keynes or Henderson. They pursued the same foolish type of deflationary economics as their predecessors. Their vision was just as limited, their political actions just as restricted by the old financial orthodoxy. The scandal of it all was that the suffering which their deflationary policies inflicted had to be borne by innocent working people.

The only Labour leader at this time who learned from Keynes was Ernest Bevin. George Brown has remarked in his memoirs that work on the Macmillan Committee gave Ernest Bevin 'a new understanding of industry, the City and financial matters'. Certainly, after that debate with Norman, he never lost his hatred of the gold standard. Alas, when he came to power in 1945 he was denied the chance to put his Keynesian economic ideas into practice : he was switched from the Treasury to the Foreign Office by his short-sighted party leader.

At the beginning of 1930, Chancellor Snowden, worrying about the pound, could only think of balancing the budget and cutting incomes – the exact opposite of the policy which Keynes and his City columnist were advocating in the *New Statesman*. Snowden proclaimed in the House of Commons : 'An expenditure which may be easy and tolerable in prosperous times, becomes intolerable in a time of grave industrial depression.' This one sentence revealed how deeply the orthodox banking madness had taken hold of him. The pathetic J. H. Thomas, Lord Privy Seal, had been put in charge of employment and was given three ministerial assistants, one of whom was Oswald Mosley. It was ironic that Mosley was the only minister to resign in protest against Snowden's deflationary policies. Mosley's February manifesto, expounding the action he would take to solve the unemployment problem, drew heavily on the Liberal manifesto *We Can Conquer Unemployment* and won the approval of Keynes and Henderson. In December Mosley published his second manifesto which was signed by seventeen left-wing MPs, including Aneurin Bevan and John Strachey. Early in 1931 Mosley erupted and formed a new party which was joined by John Strachey and Harold Nicolson. Strachey resigned as soon as he saw it was turning towards fascism, but Harold Nicolson, sentimental always, was the very last to leave his old friend.

In February 1931, Snowden, more worried than ever because foreign bankers were beginning to lose confidence in the pound, appointed Sir George May, secretary of the Prudential, to lead a committee to advise on cuts in the pay of government servants (including the Services) and in the dole. Snowden uttered all the well known clichés of the City bankers. 'Drastic and disagreeable measures' he said, 'will have to be taken if the budget equilibrium is to be maintained, and if industrial progress is to be made.' Of course the drastic and disagreeable measures fell most heavily on the workers and the unemployed. By July the unemployed army had risen to 2,800,000. The pound came under heavy selling pressure and the Bank began to lose gold. Montagu Norman, Governor of the Bank, had foolishly allowed the merchant banks of the City to lend short-term money on longer term to Germany. By 31 March Germany had actually received in loan money three times the amount she had paid in reparations. The strain of the financial crisis which broke in May 1931 with the failure of the Credit Anstalt bank was too much for Montagu Norman. At the beginning of August he suffered a nervous breakdown and was shipped off to Canada for a complete rest.

In August the May Report was published. It shocked us all at the *New Statesman* and Keynes called it 'the most foolish document I have ever had the misfortune to read'. It also shocked the public with its drastic slashing of the salaries of the police, teachers and the armed services, a ten per cent cut in the dole and higher contributions to the national insurance scheme. A flight from the pound immediately followed. The foreign bankers – American and French – made it clear that no further loans would be granted to save the pound unless the Government balanced its budget on the lines recommended in the May report. This so-called 'bankers' ramp' caused a terrific Cabinet row. Indeed, the majority of the Cabinet were against cutting the dole. So MacDonald went off to the King – not, as they thought, to tender the Labour Government's resignation, but to rat on his colleagues and accept the King's nomination to form a National Government with Baldwin as Lord President of the Council. Only his 'stooges', Thomas and Snowden, followed (Snowden still as Chancellor of the Exchequer) and poor Lord Sankey as Lord Chancellor.

The new Government immediately complied with the May Report and imposed the hated means test for National Insurance. But the pound was not saved. The cut in the services pay produced a mutiny in the fleet at Invergordon. Sterling was again heavily sold and the Bank began to lose gold at the rate of £2½ million a day. This was not surprising, because France had decided in 1928 to take nothing but gold in settlement of the huge surplus accruing to her on her balance of payments through the under-valuation of the franc. (A steady repatriation of French capital had followed on the strong measures taken to restore stability in 1926.) M. Rueff, the gold fanatic, was actually in London acting for the Bank of France, demanding each day, like a Shylock, his bars of gold and refusing to accept sterling.

On 21 September 1931 sterling was finally divorced from gold. Rolph, in his delightful life of Kingsley Martin, tells Graham Hutton's story of how this occasion broke at one of our *New Statesman* lunches :

Maynard Keynes arrived late from the Treasury rubbing his hands and chuckling like a boy who has just exploded a firework underneath someone he doesn't like. There were a dozen of us there, including Nicholas Davenport who was writing a City page for Kingsley. We all said : 'What's the matter? What's happened?' and Keynes said : 'At one stroke Britain has resumed the financial hegemony of the world.'

But it was not to be for long.

The pound fell sharply from $4.86 to $3.23, to the great relief and stimulus of the export trade. Two days later, Montagu Norman returned to London. His colleagues at the Bank had sent him a wire on 20 September : 'Old Lady goes off tomorrow'. He thought they were referring to his mother who was about to go on holiday.

Angry demonstrations, hunger marches, riots and arrests followed one another in 1932. I shall never forget the sight of a column of out-of-work, half-starved Welsh miners singing as they marched on the long and fruitless road to Downing Street. It would have moved a scrooge to tears. 'For the first time within memory,' wrote G. K. Chesterton, – at that time the essayist I most revered – 'the Government and the nation have set out on a deliberate campaign to make the poor poorer.' He was not exaggerating. When the meagre National Insurance benefit had been exhausted, a man and his family had to prove need before he could obtain National Assistance. I remember that one unemployed worker in Wigan had his benefit cut from 23s 3d to 10s a week because he had two sons earning between them 31s a week!

During this period I was invited by Ramsay MacDonald's doctor to attend a dinner party in honour of the Prime Minister on the eve of his departure to some international conference on world trade. A number of economists and financial writers were present and we were asked over the port and cigars to give the great man our personal views. When my turn came I was as brief and cynical as I could be and then gracefully handed the ball back to the Prime Minister. His reply was pathetic. It was obvious that the poor man was mentally exhausted. He mumbled and bumbled – no sentence was properly finished – and the gist of it all was the terrible burden that fell upon the Head of Government in a time of business collapse. All I can do, he said, was to put one foot forward and consider all the problems at this step and then to put another foot forward and consider all the problems which followed the first step, and then if it was possible to see how another step forward could be made in the light of what you gentlemen had said – for which he was very grateful – the words ended in an inarticulate mumble. Before another meaningless sentence could begin the good physician intervened to thank us all and we hastily departed. The secretary telephoned the next day to ask me to put down in writing my recollections of the memorable evening which the doctor was recording in his diary – no doubt for later publication. I felt that I was reporting the sad occasion of a last supper.

The catastrophe of the pound proved an economic blessing in disguise, as we hastened to point out in the *New Statesman*, for the economy began to expand. Keynes did not miss the opportunity to lay the blame for the 'tragedy' on the French who had pursued the same selfish policies he had exposed in *The Economic Consequences of the Peace*. When the Exchange Equalisation Fund had been set up, the floating exchange took the economic strains and insulated our economy against the deflation which had become rampant abroad. We were therefore able to cheapen money, reduce Bank rate, and set the economy and the Stock Exchange moving up.[1]

What pleased Keynes was the success of this floating experiment. It proved that an exchange rate can be managed if the managers of the Equalisation Fund knew their business, something which ours undoubtedly did. The pound settled down by the end of 1931 at around $3.40. In 1932 it averaged $3.50 and in 1933 $4.22. This was the year when the dollar was driven off gold. In 1934 the price of gold was raised by Act of Congress from $20.67 to $35 per ounce. It was said that President Roosevelt had got bored with having to fix a daily price for gold and asked his secretary one day at breakfast to think of an easy-to-remember number. 'What about thirty-five', the secretary suggested. 'Excellent', said Roosevelt. 'Make it $35 an ounce – once and for all.'

The devaluation of the suspect dollar caused the sterling exchange in 1934 to float up to $5.04 but it did not hold. By the time war broke out it had fallen to $4.46 and it was pegged at $4.03 for the duration of hostilities. Nimble speculators on the Stock Exchange made fortunes out of gold shares in this lively and exciting period.

These formidable events provoked much comment in the *New Statesman* but we were not all agreed upon policy. We Keynesians and the socialists – Martin, Cole and Brailsford – did not see eye to eye. Edward Hyams in his history of the *New*

[1] See Chapter 7.

Statesman remarked : 'He [Kingsley Martin] contrived somehow to reconcile the opinions of J. M. Keynes, G. D. H. Cole and Davenport of the City page, and to present a reasonably coherent policy.' Kingsley put it more simply in *Father Figures* : 'My job was to see that they did not contradict each other.'

But they often did. We were only at one when it came to attacks on the capitalist Establishment for its failure to cope adequately with the spread of massive unemployment. Keynes was pressing the Government to spend its way out of the depression and in my City column under the pseudonym of 'Toreador' I was exposing the shortcomings of the capital market. My constant theme was that money put into the financial machine in the City was not getting out into productive investment. A large part of a new issue went into the pockets of the vendors, the merchant banks, and the brokers. The new issue market was, in fact, being exploited at that time by the less scrupulous financiers of the City who were not interested so much in turning the savings of the people into productive investment as in feathering their own nests as company promoters.

We Keynesians did not want to destroy the capitalist system, but to make it more efficient and more humane and withal a more dynamic instrument for the creation of wealth. We all knew that as it stood it was not an equitable system for the distribution of the wealth it creates – that it tended even to widen the gap between the very rich and the very poor. As Churchill wittily said : 'The inherent vice of capitalism is the unequal sharing of blessings : the inherent virtue of socialism is the equal sharing of miseries.' We realised that serious sociological reforms were overdue but at that moment capitalism was down and out; we wanted to put it on its feet so that it could start employing again the more 'down-and-out' workers. Clearly, a rescue operation was the clamant need of the hour. Roosevelt showed in America how it could be done by his New Deal, setting up a Public Works Administration and a Reconstruction Finance Corporation. Indeed by adopting the Keynesian economics of full employment after the war the USA was the first nation to prove that technologically advanced capitalism is the most effective system for the creation of wealth the world has ever conceived.

Unfortunately Kingsley Martin did not share our views. He never wanted to reform or revitalise the capitalist system; he wanted to see it destroyed and replaced by a native form of communism. But he had never thought out how it could be done and he simply did not understand the economics envolved. He was as ignorant of the monetary system as the simple working man. In *Father Figures* he wrote :

> University students and others, *including* the *New Statesman* [my italics] were converted to a modified form of Marxism by John Strachey and Harold Laski because what they said was substantially true. Strachey's *Coming Struggle for Power* was an analysis in class terms of English social history. Laski's journalistic books were all designed to convince people that unless the social system could be changed peacefully, violence must soon follow. Nothing of the sort happened, not because the arguments were wrong but because rearmament solved the economic problem for the time being and war put an end to the dilemma.

In point of fact the arguments were wrong. John Strachey, Harold Laski and Kingsley Martin were deceiving themselves in their social diagnosis. The Parliamentary process in Britain had always been able to provide for sufficient social change to avoid violence. As the late Geoffrey Hudson, fellow of St Anthony's, Oxford, remarked in his *Fifty Years of Communism* : 'The Labour movement in England has always showed a disposition for pragmatic and non-revolutionary politics. English thinking was predominantly empiricist and allergic to Hegel and therefore also to Marx.' Our Marxists at the *New Statesman* were running counter to the whole trend of our social history since the Peasant Revolt of 1381.

I remember a discussion with Kingsley in 1932 when he had produced a special issue of the *New Statesman* on disarmament and I had turned my City column to an analysis of the economics of rearmament. This proved, he said, the dependence of capitalism on armament expenditure. That, of course, was totally untrue, even at that time. But Kingsley had become convinced that salvation could only come through Marx. There was no changing his faith. As the world depression deepened, he came more and more under the influence of John Strachey who was now proclaiming that a British form of Marxist communism was the only way out for Britain.

The ideological disputes at the *New Statesman* at Great Turnstile were re-enacted in the Labour Party headquarters in Transport House, Smith Square. After the MacDonald betrayal in 1931, the Labour Party rumbled into a terrible soul-searching debate. For the first time I was brought into personal contact with some of their leaders and I found that the split between us intellectuals at Great Turnstile was the same split which divided the politicians in Smith Square. Indeed, their right, centre and left wings, it seemed to me, were irreconcilable. Labour was not a party at all; it was – and still is – an awkward and sometimes ramshackle coalition – 'a coalition of irreconcilables' as Dick Taverne said recently. The right were the social reformers. The centre were professed Fabian socialists but because they believed that the Parliamentary process could produce socialism by persuasion and were not prepared to use force they were, in effect, also social reformers. The left were the Marxist socialist revolutionaries, who really believed in the class war necessitating violence. The right and the left had very little in common to keep them bound together. Unlike the right and the left of the Tory Party, which are tied closely together by the common attachment to private property, private enterprise and private profit, the extreme right and the extreme left of the Labour Party had no common beliefs at all except a hatred of Tories. In fact they had deeply antagonistic beliefs, for the extreme right, led by Morrison and Bevin, were opposed to Marxism and to the revolutionary class war, while the extreme left believed in the class war and were convinced that it must end in violence. Even Cripps for a time came to share the views of the extreme left.

The younger intellectual right wing of the Labour Party had no outstanding political leader until Hugh Gaitskell appeared on the scene, but the centre – the Fabian socialist social reformers – had Lansbury, Attlee, and Dalton, and it was they – together with Morrison – who controlled the party apparatus. These centre leaders were never Marxist revolutionaries; they were evolutionary socialists. They had convinced themselves that they could eventually bring about a Socialist Commonwealth in Britain – without recourse to force – by the gradual persuasion of the professional- and middle-classes. The irony was that when they eventually came into power in 1945 and carried out their first instalment of Fabian socialism, the leaders ran out of socialist breath. Most of them – Attlee certainly – regarded the nationalisation of half a dozen industries as a sufficient measure of social reform. None of them believed that it was possible to go forward to the complete nationalisation of all the means of production, distribution and exchange.

Although the Labour Party was committed to destroying capitalism by its original construction, it did not start as an activist revolutionary party. It was formed in 1900 as a union of various labour and socialist societies for the express purpose of getting working men into Parliament, not of destroying Parliament. The party temporarily acquired a revolutionary ferment after the Russian Revolution in 1917. Led on by the aggressive 'triple alliance' of miners, railwaymen and dockers (which only held firm from 1917 to 1921) it had adopted a 'revolutionary' socialist constitution in 1918 with a full-blooded Marxist clause – the famous Clause 4 – which ran as follows : 'To secure for the workers by hand or by brain the full fruits of their industry and the most equitable distribution thereof that may be possible on the basis of the common ownership of the means of production, and the best obtainable system of popular administration and control of each industry or service'. Later on, at the annual party conference of 1929, this clause was amended to read : 'The common ownership of all the means of production, distribution and exchange'. But none of the leaders dreamed of achieving this by force.

The centre political leaders were, of course, always being egged on by the Marxist intellectuals, but they had really convinced themselves that they could eventually achieve Clause 4 by peaceful persuasion, in spite of Strachey's and Laski's denials. They were particularly influenced by H. N. Brailsford whom I came to know well as a contributor to the *New Statesman*. In 1925, Brailsford had written a book called *Socialism for Today* in which he said :

> We aim at transferring power from the small directing class of to-day to the whole body of workers by hand and brain. Must it be at any point a violent and catastrophic change or can we throughout proceed by way of evolution ? The State through its coercive mechanism and its command of force had been the

indispensable instrument which enabled the capitalist system to establish itself. Must we then think of the State as a capitalist institution which we must contrive to overthrow by revolutionary violence? That was a natural view in the middle years of the nineteenth century. . . . But the outlook for our own generation was radically changed. We realise that the balance of power within the capitalist state is shifting and unstable. It ceases to lour upon us like a Norman keep which we must storm and overthrow. The belief grows that it can be transformed. . . . Visibly it seems already to be in process of transformation.

Here was Shaw's Fabian socialism almost poetically restated. Brailsford realised of course, that while the Labour Party might be ready enough to proceed by democratic means towards its goal, their opponents might not always consent to play the constitutional game. They might try to upset a Labour government by an organised financial panic or they might, he said, as a last resort 'call out their sons in every officers' mess and bring about a revolt within the army'. On the whole, he thought that a Fascist movement on the Italian pattern would not be created easily in this country. He warned, however, that if Labour were to try to nationalise everything at a stroke, and drive the possessing class to desperation by refusing compensation, they would soon provoke a civil war. He counselled a cautious advance until they had won over a large part of the professional and managerial class. He always knew, of course, that behind the Parliamentary party there stood the industrial 'army' organised in trade unions. A general strike would be their last weapon to use – and it would be a revolutionary weapon. But when the General Strike came in 1926 it collapsed within nine days because the union leaders were not prepared for revolution and were unwilling to oppose by force the organised instruments of law and order. Perhaps Brailsford foresaw this happening. At any rate he made it clear in his book that it would be folly to abandon Parliamentary forms. He went on : 'If ever we have to fight to impose our will, our most hopeful course would be to fight with the Parliament behind us as the Puritan middle-class fought against Charles I. In defence of a threatened Parliament, Labour in power would repeat the revolution of the seventeenth century.'

Here Brailsford was creating the great myth of the Labour Party in the thirties – that they were re-enacting the revolutionary part played by the Cromwellian Parliament. They did not appreciate that the Cromwellian Parliament had no middle-class; it was composed of the landed gentry class who were in fact anti-proletariat as well as anti-King Charles. When he became dictator, Cromwell completely destroyed the left-wing Leveller movement.

One could not help liking the honest Brailsford. He had a worried look, a charming personality and was always listened to with respect by the Labour Party leaders. But the Marxist revolutionaries on the extreme left were by no means content to follow his policy of Fabian gradualism. They wanted more aggressive action. They went out and formed the Independent Labour Party under Maxton. John Strachey joined later after he had been converted to Marxism in 1931. So ardent did they become in their Marxist propaganda that the ILP disaffiliated itself from the Labour Party in 1932. And Brailsford eventually joined them.

After the disaffiliation of the ILP rump, another ginger group was formed from the Marxist camp, in 1932, calling itself the Socialist League. This combined those of the ILP who were against disaffiliation and those of Cole's SSIP (Socialist Society for Investigation and Propaganda) to which Stafford Cripps belonged. (Out of Cole's SSIP came the New Fabian Research Bureau.) The Chairman of the Socialist League was Frank Wise and at a Labour Party Conference at Leicester in October 1932 he moved and carried against the platform a resolution to nationalise the joint stock banks.

Frank Wise was a dark political horse, a suspected Marxist revolutionary. It is clear from Dalton's autobiography that during the Labour Government of 1929, Wise was in close contact with the Soviet Government. Dalton relates that when the Labour Government had decided to exchange ambassadors with Russia (King George would not shake hands with one of the gang who had murdered his dear cousin the Tzar, and left it to the Prince of Wales to receive him) he had told Frank Wise that Kamenev would be impossible and suggested Sokolnikof. 'Wise expressed agreement and bustled off and the change was made.' This certainly pointed to a very close intimacy between Wise and the

Soviet leadership. Soviet Russia, said Dalton, was still the subject on which they were under most pressure from the left wing of their own Labour Party:

> There is a swarm of would-be intermediaries, politicians, Labour journalists and business men buzzing round our head. Frank Wise buzzed loudest. He knew all the answers and was always offering himself as a go-between. Sometimes he went with our portion of blessing, sometimes without it. We doubted his discretion and he had, as he freely admitted, a personal axe to grind as an employee of the Centrosoyus.

I gathered from Dalton that he always suspected Frank Wise to be a Russian agent. No doubt Wise was instrumental in making many converts to communism among the Labour left. Perhaps it was a blessing for the country that he died suddenly in 1933. It was significant that Ernest Bevin at this time grew to distrust and hate the Labour Party's intellectuals on the extreme left. He shared Dalton's distrust of Frank Wise. As George Brown expressed it in his memoirs: 'Bevin became violently anti-communist and cracked down on anyone who wanted the TUC to affiliate with the Red Internationals of Labour unions.'

Much to Dalton's annoyance Stafford Cripps joined the Socialist League in 1932. Stafford at this time had moved sharply to the left, having become obsessed with the Fascist peril. He made the jump from Fabian socialism to Marxist activism under the influence of Laski and Strachey. He now wanted a root-and-branch socialist revolution. Indeed, he expected another general strike and warned his followers that they would have to overcome 'opposition from Buckingham Palace and other places as well'. 'This man,' wrote Dalton in his diary in May 1933, 'is really becoming a dangerous political lunatic.' They did not become friends again until the 1945 Government.

As the Socialist League was still affiliated with the Labour Party it was able to assert a strong Marxist influence at the annual party conference. In self-defence against this Marxist barrage the Labour Party Executive appointed a policy committee to work out a practical socialisation programme – a blueprint for the first instalment of Fabian Socialism they would carry out when they achieved power. The first of these policy reports dealt with currency, banking and finance. In this I was concerned because Hugh Dalton and Stafford Cripps consulted me about it.

I first met Hugh Dalton in 1931. This is how he described the meeting in his diary of September 1931 :

> Davenport, Toreador of the *New Statesman,* to lunch with me and Cripps. Intelligent and helpful. We of the Policy Committee are trying to meet as many City blokes as possible these days. (The year we were pushed off gold). This was my first meeting with Nicholas Davenport, with whom and with his charming wife Olga, Ruth and I later became great friends. . . . We have spent many happy days and also many useful hours, with them in London, at their house in Berkshire and at West Leaze. They will recur later in my story.

Dear Hugh, if only you had understood the banking and money system before you set out to replace capitalism with socialism in half the economy! Whenever I tried to explain its financial workings you used to bawl out: 'Stop talking details, Nicholas! Stick to principles.' I do not believe that you could absorb the details of a complicated money system, which was alien to your way of life. But you were one of the big men of the Labour movement – how very few there were! – and your party should remember you, as I do now, with affection and understanding.

Dalton's appearance was extraordinary. He was over six feet high and had piercing light blue eyes. He towered over lesser mortals and in conversation he had the habit of turning up his eyes to heaven, so that they showed the whites. He was physically ungainly. His head was too large for his narrow shoulders. He had long legs but his arms were too short for his body, hanging like the fore-flappers of a dinosaur. When seated, his great bald dome dominated the table, and when he was plied with good wine his talk became lively and amusing, but he always boomed, and it was impossible to get a word in when his voice rang round the room. One of the Churchill stories, which is often told, was an occasion at number ten during the war when Dalton's voice was heard shouting in an ante-room when the Prime Minister came in. 'Who's that shouting?' he demanded. 'It's Dalton. He's speaking to Edinburgh.' 'Why on earth doesn't he use the telephone?' said Churchill.

Having been brought up in the pre-Russian Revolution era,

Hugh was no revolutionary socialist. He hated Marxism and could not bear the clever, theorising, Marxist intellectuals like Harold Laski. Dialectical materialism was beyond him. Hugh's socialism was derived from the innate sense of fair play which is fostered in the English public school. As a child he told his rich grandmother, who had a large Victorian house and grounds in South Wales, that her estate 'ought really to belong to the people of Neath'. In 1907, in his final term at Cambridge, he joined the Fabians and declared himself to be a socialist. Together with Rupert Brooke he founded the Cambridge Fabian Society. After listening to Keir Hardie, who came to lecture in Cambridge and was jeered at and almost mobbed by the upper-class 'rowdies', he became 'a quite-convinced socialist'. Having been a canon's son at Windsor and a day-boy at Eton – two species of animal which the aristocratic Etonian would love to tease – he had nurtured a strong dislike of the arrogant upper-class by whom he had been surrounded in his formative years.

What made Hugh Dalton such good company was his boyish romanticism, something which he retained throughout his life. He adored good-looking and gallant young men who were physically fit and strong and ready to fight for their country. His first great love was Rupert Brooke; his last was Anthony Crosland, although Tony was greatly embarrassed by this attention. In *Call Back Yesterday,* a letter from Rupert Brooke is quoted answering Hugh's invitation to what seemed like an erotic hiking holiday : 'I should love to sleep out with nothing on but a few extra socks'. Hugh was at that time keen on sleeping out, hiking, reciting, talking and arguing. One could imagine his fitting into a company of disputing, flagellating and erotic monks on a pilgrimage to Canterbury in Chaucer's day. When Rupert Brooke died in the First World War – pneumonia, not guns, carried him off – Hugh never forgave the Germans. My wife recalls that after the war, whenever she and Hugh used to discuss poetry, and Rupert Brooke's verses came into the conversation, as they inevitably did, tears used to come into his eyes as he recited them.

Hugh was very fond of my wife – his letters generally ended with 'Love to Olga – It's too long since I last saw her' – and in modern parlance he would be called 'bisexual'. After all, he married and had a child which unhappily died at the age of four.

I have a letter from him dated 27 October 1950 which exhibited this innocuous bi-sexuality.

> MY DEAR NICHOLAS,
> I would love to spend the week-end November 24th–26th with you at Hinton – I shall just have returned from Strasbourg – and to argue out with Dick Crossman some of his lively thoughts lately in debate. I have written to him about this and hope that you will be able to hook him for that weekend. Ruth will be in Derbyshire helping George Brown, one of our few still rising young Trade Unionists.
>   We shouldn't want, I think, too large a debating party that weekend, but you might like to get Tony Crosland and Roy Jenkins to look in. It would also be fun – wouldn't it? – to get Ian Little and his wife to come over for a meal, so that we could complete the Intellectual Comedy of Cat among the Pigeons. He is a very attractive little squirrel and I would like to get to know him better. I was astonished to hear that, with his social background, he had married a woman who wanted, being a married woman, to do a thesis on the Capital Market since the War! With such a woman you and I should clearly become more closely acquainted! Yours ever,
>
>   HUGH

Hugh was very attracted to the clever young economist of Nuffield, Ian Little, whom he insisted on calling 'Squirrel'. Ian's wife was called, less romantically I thought, 'Dobbs'. Ian wrote an abstruse book on *Welfare Economics* which I wrote up – with Tony Crosland's help – in the *Times Literary Supplement* to Hugh's great delight.

Hugh himself fought gallantly in the First World War, first in France and then on the Italian Front. He and Attlee were alone of the old Fabian leaders to carry their patriotism into action on the battlefield. Indeed, his sturdy patriotism made him unique among his socialist colleagues, most of whom were either open pacifists or underground Marxists. Even Attlee had suggested 'disbanding the national armies' in a speech in the House of Commons in March 1935. Hugh fought hard to prevent his party voting against rearmament in the late 1930s and only succeeded in 1938 when the Nazi menace had become really threatening.

He and Bevin in 1936 and 1937 were alone among the senior Labour leaders in demanding rearmament, but Hugh was supported by some of his younger friends, in particular, Hugh Gaitskell and Dick Crossman.

The intellectual Marxists were then exercising more and more influence upon Labour Party members. Richard Crossman, in his brilliant introduction to *New Fabian Essays,* singles out Tawney, Laski, Strachey and the Webbs as the writers who were dominating the thought of young socialists in the thirties :

> R. H. Tawney [he says] had long been studying Marxism and successfully assimilated its method of historical analysis into his Christian philosophy. Harold Laski, like the Webbs, imposed Marxism as a super-structure on his utilitarian principles and never succeeded in moulding the two into a consistent system. John Strachey swallowed it in a single heady draught and was the only Englishman who succeeded, not merely in translating Marxism but in re-thinking his system in Anglo-Saxon terms.

Eventually the Left Book Club, founded in 1936, replaced the Fabian Society as the home of the intellectual socialist *avant-garde.* John Strachey wrote for it the *Left News Bulletin* which became widely read. Such was the powerful stream of Marxist thought which Dalton and his colleagues had to withstand in the preparation of their policy memoranda. Dalton held firmly to the Fabian line of peaceful persuasion and was often the calm voice of sanity in the crescendo of wild revolutionary talk.

I was alarmed by this Marxist programme because the Labour Party was so ignorant of the workings of the financial system that it was bound to create havoc if it attempted to put it all under government control. The capital market where the savings of the people are converted into productive investment might well cease to function under ignorant socialist *dirigisme.* This would not only be the end of private enterprise but of the export trade as well. I discussed this possibility many times over morning coffee in City dives with Vaughan Berry (now Sir Vaughan Berry) who was then working as a bill-broker in the Union Discount Company. Berry was an ardent undercover Labour member. Knowing that I was a friend of Dalton he suggested one morning that we should form a private dining club where City men could meet the Labour leaders and instruct them in the mysteries of

City finance so that they would not make a hash of it when they came into power. 'Look, Nicholas', he said 'you know everyone in the City. Just canvass your friends and see if they would play'. I first consulted Dalton and obtained his blessing and support. He wrote in his *Fateful Years*:

> Early in 1932 I took some part in encouraging the formation of a small group of City people to advise the Party on questions of which they had practical knowledge. The membership and even the existence of this group was kept for some time a very close secret. I circulated papers which they sent to me to some of my colleagues but disclosed no names. The first, circulated in April 1932, was a description of the London money market with a number of suggestions for policy. Two of the founders of this group were H. V. Berry and Nicholas Davenport. Both knew a good deal about the City and its problems.

I went round the City and collected Bill Piercy (later Lord Piercy – at that time a stockbroker), Jimmy Lawrie, an Oxford man who had been recruited to the Bank of New Zealand, Francis Williams, then City editor of the *Daily Herald*, Douglas Jay who succeeded him as editor, Cecil Sprigge, then City editor of the *Manchester Guardian*, Hugh Quigley, then economic advisor of the Central Electricity Board, George Wansborough who had just left his wife and Benson's, the merchant bank, to become chairman of Reyrolle, the big electrical power company of the north east coast, and finally a director of Samuel Montagu, the gold bullion house, whose name had to remain a secret. Outside the City I recruited two economists – Evan Durbin and Hugh Gaitskell. Evan – a brilliant man – was tragically drowned off the Cornish coast in September 1948. He had been marked by Hugh Dalton for high office.

These were all my friends and they agreed to join with me and Berry in forming a private dining club which we called 'XYZ'. We invited the Labour leaders to meet us for dinner in quiet Soho restaurants where we could hire a small room and remain private and invisible to gossipy journalists. The leading politicians I brought in were Dalton, Morrison, Attlee and Cripps. They were all, except Cripps, sublimely ignorant of the City and suspicious of its institutions, especially the Stock Exchange which they regarded as a casino, where rich men gambled to make money regardless of the state of the economy. We City members did our best to enlighten them and exorcise the ghosts of Puritan bigotry and prejudice which haunted them. We wrote papers and produced statistics. Berry composed a draft for the nationalisation of the Bank of England while I wrote a paper on investment planning in which I advocated the setting up of a National Investment Board and an Industrial Finance Corporation. This was an enlargement of a paper I had written for one of the Liberal summer schools which followed on the publication of their *Yellow Book*.

I like to think that we did some good. Certainly Francis Williams thought so and wrote this account in his memoirs *Nothing So Strange* :

Over the years the XYZ Club drew up a blueprint for Labour's financial policy much of which, including detailed proposals for the nationalisation of the Bank of England, was adopted by the first post-war Labour government. It has indeed some claim to have exercised in a quiet sort of way more influence on future government policy than any other group of the time and to have done so in the most private manner without attracting publicity to itself.

Recently I came across, in a bundle of XYZ papers, the memorandum which must have been my first XYZ submission. It was the proposal for a National Investment Board and an Industrial Finance Corporation. The board was to be advisory and supervisory; the corporation was to be an active finance agency. It was strange that Dalton repudiated, in 1945, the first, and that Wilson took up the second in 1966. I reproduce my paper as an appendix at the end of the book. Dalton was given a copy of this memorandum and lifted parts of it bodily for the pamphlet he was preparing on *Currency, Banking and Finance* for submission to the Labour Party conference at Leicester in 1932. Maynard Keynes gave this pamphlet fine support in two articles which appeared in the *New Statesman* on 17 and 24 September 1932. In the second he said :

I welcome warmly the acceptance of the principle of setting up

a National Investment Board ... I should expect that its chief
problem would be to maintain the level of investment at a high
enough rate to ensure the optimum level of employment. ...
The grappling with these central controls is the rightly
conceived Socialism of the future.

I was grateful to Kingsley Martin for allowing me the space to
keep pushing the National Investment Board forward in the following years. The last and longest article I wrote on it appeared
in the *New Statesman* of 24 June 1939.

The Labour Party conference at Leicester in October 1932
found itself under great pressure from the Marxist left wing, led
by Frank Wise. Under his influence, the conference passed a
special resolution to nationalise the joint stock banks, stating that :

the enormous power exercised by the financial system cannot
continue to be left in private control and that the public
control of that system is essential for carrying out a planned
national development and to prevent a socialist policy from
being defeated from private financial interests.

The Executive proposed and the conference decided that the
Bank of England should be brought under public ownership and
control and that the Governor of the Bank should be appointed
by the Government and be subject to the general direction of the
Chancellor. It also proposed that a National Investment Board
should be set up 'to mobilise our financial resources and guide
them into the right channels' (my words). The object of the
board, it said, was to prevent waste and misdirection in the use of
long-term capital. The board should therefore have control over
all new public issues on the capital market and should be able to
refuse, if necessary, 'leave to deal' on the Stock Exchange for any
privately placed issue in order to secure priority for approved
State schemes of industrial reorganisation.

So part of what I had been urging upon Dalton for years had
at last become official Labour policy. What is more, the resolu-
tions of this Party conference of 1932 were reaffirmed and ex-
panded at the next Party conference, which not only again
attacked the Bank of England and redefined its role under
nationalisation but went on to specify how the control of short-

term credit as well as long-term credit should be administered when the joint stock banks were nationalised.

While I was delighted with my first success in political persuasion I was alarmed by what might happen if the wild Marxists succeeded in carrying the official Labour policy documents too far along destructive lines. To smash the financial system without putting anything comparable in its place would be an economic disaster and the end of free enterprise. I fervently desired to see a mixed economy work, even if the Fabians greatly enlarged the public sector, and I knew that it would not work unless the private enterprise side had the chance to make sufficient profits to finance industrial investment. But I always got the feeling that these Labour leaders did not really care what happened to private enterprise in the private sector. The Marxists, of course, wanted to kill it while the Fabians, I felt, were not sufficiently interested to keep it alive and kicking.

I raised this problem with Keynes but he was not prepared to waste his time discussing academic points with Fabian socialists at XYZ dinners. I therefore decided to try and clarify Dalton's ideas more than was possible at our brief little Soho dinner debates. Fortunately I had by this time acquired a new home in the country where I could entertain in a more comfortable and agreeable style. It was an historic manor house in Berkshire which I will describe in my next chapter.

Resignation from XYZ was eventually forced on me when its members were asked to become members of the New Fabian Research Bureau which Cole had founded. I sent for their articles of association and found that they subscribed to all the claptrap of Marxist Clause 4 socialism! It was not for me. I wrote to Vaughan Berry to explain why and he replied :

My Dear Davenport,

I agree the XYZ should confine itself to the purpose for which it was started, namely, financial planning, and as long as your acute mind is available for that purpose I do not ask any more – speaking, that is, as a socialist. As a friend, I shall miss you at the table – indeed it won't seem quite right for you not to be there.

Anyhow if we don't meet at XYZ we shall have to lunch

together sometimes in the City as a corrective to any growing fanaticism or extremism on my part. And I most genuinely reciprocate your warm personal regards. Yours ever,

H. V. Berry

I had another letter not long ago from H. V. B. expressing his great disgruntlement with Wilsonian socialism.

5
Hinton Manor and The First Puritan Revolution

It was in the summer of 1933 that I discovered and bought Hinton Manor, the Norman Honour of St Valery, some ten miles or more west of Oxford. It seemed a rash thing to do at the time, because the repair and upkeep of such a large place would tax my resources, but the price was temptingly low – it was in the middle of the slump – and my imagination had been fired by its long and fascinating history. From that moment I knew that I had to go on working in the City in order to pay for the restoration of a beautiful and historic house. Looking into the future I could see myself, if I ever retired, idling away the hours with nothing to do except create beautiful new vistas in the garden and perhaps write memoirs on the more famous owners of the manor. I was not aware at the time that the manor had been involved in the Puritan revolution of the seventeenth century and that one of my predecessors, the regicide Henry Marten, had been advising the Daltons of his time.

I shall never forget my first glimpse of it across the moat – a sprawling crenellated house with a large orangery on one side in the Regency style, the whole façade looking warm and friendly in a soft beige coat of old stucco. For a while I sat entranced on a large flat stone beside the moat – a fragment, I discovered later, of the Norman castle – conjuring up the centuries of English history it had survived. A feeling came over me that it was a haunted place, as indeed it turned out to be, but not unpleasantly haunted. It seemed to be happily dreaming of its past.

From the terrace of the north front you can see, framed between a Scots fir and a bog cypress, a distant view of the

Cotswolds reaching almost as far as Stow-on-the-Wold eighteen miles away. On this side, the house stands at the top of a steep hill, which is part of the escarpment running from Cumnor to Faringdon overlooking the Upper Thames Valley. In winter the stripling river often floods and presents the house with a startling water landscape. At the foot of the hill there is an ancient ford over the Thames, now called Duxford after a Saxon thane Duduc, which is still part of the manor estate. From an upper window on the east front, you can see Cumnor Church ten miles away with a wooded hill rising behind and shutting out the spires of Oxford from the view. From the south front you look out westwards up to the Berkshire downs and on a clear day you can just discern the hind-quarters of the White Horse which was cut out of the chalk by the Celtic British on the downs above Uffington. It is fifteen miles away and beyond it, further to the west, there is a clump of trees which hides the sarsen stones of a neolithic burial place called 'Wayland's Smithy'. This is in Wiltshire and so justifies our household claim to a glimpse of four counties. Not long ago, 'Wayland's Smithy' was dug up by the archaeologists of the Office of Works under the expert eye of Professor Stewart Pigott. They found two burial mounds, the lowest, the Professor told me, dating from before 2,500 BC. It must be the earliest building in England, contemporary with the first pyramids in Egypt. It is a thrill to feel that it is within sight of our house.

The oldest part of the house goes back over four hundred years. It is a large stone house in the Cotswold manner with two steeply pitched roofs in Stonefield tiles joined together in the middle by a little belfry – an architectural gem. The monastery-like bell in the belfry can still be rung, but to-day there will be no manorial servants to come running at the sound. This Tudor house was probably built in the late 1550s on the site of the old castle. There is a record in the Court Rolls that in 1549 Edward VI granted a Crown lease of the manor – it had become a royal manor at the time of Edward III – for forty-one years to George Owen, a fellow of Merton College. I knew nothing about George Owen until my friend, Dr Leslie Rowse, the great authority on the Tudor age, told me that he was the physican and confidant of Henry VIII. George Owen died in 1558, having acquired much land round Oxford, but whether he lived to see Hinton Manor completed I do not know. Two of the original fireplaces of his house remain in the hall and the library. I found them hidden behind Victorian plaster.

George Owen was followed in 1624 by Sir John Ramsey, the first Earl of Holderness, and after his death in 1627 Charles I assigned the Crown lease for the modest rent of £37 16s 8d a year to Sir Henry Marten, a judge of the Admiralty Court and of the Prerogative Court of Canterbury, and thrice Dean of the Arches. In the devious ways of a political judge, Sir Henry had amassed a fortune which he had invested wisely in land in north-west Berkshire where he had met his wife. He died full of riches and worldly honour in 1641 at the age of eighty-one. The two manors of Longworth and Hinton then came into the possession of his politician son Henry, republican and regicide, who held them until Cromwell assumed power and allowed him to be put away in the Rules for debt. Henry died in 1680 without money and without honour, a prisoner of State in Chepstow Castle.

None of these owners, as far as I can discover, made any alterations or improvements to the house. It was not until 1700 that Hinton Manor was 'modernised' – to quote the *Victoria County History* – by a Berkshire squire called John Loder who acquired the Marten properties when Henry was languishing in gaol as a convicted regicide.

I feel grateful to John Loder. By 1700 he had added the north wing, bringing the lovely view of the Cotswolds into the house. This is now our dining room, with a music room above. He also replaced the stone mullioned windows, except those in my bedroom on the east front, with the thick wooden sashes of the Renaissance. He panelled the large rooms with the heavy bolection mouldings of that period. Withal he made it a much more comfortable house to live in. Outside, on the south front he built a parapet over the upper windows, leaving the three dormers to peep over the top. This was the 'modernisation' of 1700 recorded in the *County History*. The orangery on the right of the front and the drawing room on the left were not added until 1830, the last year of George IV. These elevations were originally the same height and were crenellated in the prevailing fashion of the 1830 Gothic revival, but twenty years later bedrooms were added to the drawing room wing, raising its elevation and destroying the

D

architectural harmony of the south front. Happily the charm of it all remained.

A lot of restoration work had to be done before I opened the front door to Hugh Dalton in September 1934. I had no idea what the restoration would cost but I knew what I had to do. Back to John Loder's 'modernisation' of 1700 was my theme. This was the William and Mary style which strongly appealed to me, having lived three years in Hawksmoor's classical front quad of Queen's College, Oxford. I knew that I had to get rid of all the 1830 'Gothic' castellation from the parapets and the orangery. About a hundred pieces of stone were taken down and used to make walks and seats in the garden. I was also determined to recreate the great William-and-Mary door on the north front by removing a Victorian bow-window, and build a terrace to receive it with balustrading of the period. This I did after collecting cherubs and scrolls, which could be bought for a song at that time, in order to embellish the architrave of the door. The stone steps descended from the new terrace into a box garden of the 1700 period. I designed a box knot containing the letters W and M encrowned – for William and Mary – and transplanted a low box hedge to surround the existing fountain which sprayed above the heads of two cupids. I then planted a yew hedge with protruding screens shaped like pieces of green sculpture to enclose it all.

I was annoyed later on to find that in the *Shell Guide* for Berkshire, John Betjeman had written about an Elizabethan manor house at Hinton Waldrist which had been 'neo-Georgianised in the late 1930s'. He had never been to see the house but had, I suppose, heard about the restoration, though not about my concern for William and Mary. When the late Professor Joad was staying with us one summer weekend he insisted upon John Betjeman coming over to see for himself. The poet came, saw and was conquered. He handsomely apologised for his mistake. It was a lovely summer evening and when the moon was up we walked round the dry lower moat. Suddenly the nightingales burst into song in the wood below. The poet – now Poet Laureate – went home in a classical, if not a William-and-Mary, trance.

When I returned to London after my first enchanted visit I hurried to the Athenaeum Club library to look up the *Victoria*

County History of Berkshire. To my great joy it had a long account of the manor and it was packed with the royal history of medieval England. It began with St Valery. Those who fought with William in the field at Hastings were called the Conqueror's Companions of Honour. Among them was St Valery from Caux. I found the name of Bernard de St Valery on the bronze plaque erected to the memory of these Companions of Honour in the restored chapel of the Conqueror's castle at Falaise. The St Valerys were a powerful Norman family who had helped Duke William gain the suzerainty of Normandy and Brittany. Naturally they were singled out for favour on the conquest of England, and Bernard received a huge grant of land, stretching from Faringdon to the east side of Oxford, a distance of over twenty miles. This was the origin of Hinton Manor, the 'Honour of St Valery', as it was called in those days. Written in Latin, Valery becomes Walericus which the Berkshire dialect has corrupted into Waldrist.

What happened to the St Valerys at the beginning of the fourteenth century I have not been able to discover but when Hinton became a royal manor Edward III leased it to his relatives – the de Bohun family, Earls of Northampton, Hereford and Essex. Marie de Bohun married Bolingbroke but died before he became Henry IV in 1399. She was a talented and cultured girl. Her first son was Henry V and the last Duke Humphrey, benefactor of the Bodleian. She loved Hinton, having queened it there – at John of Gaunt's expense – for three quiet and happy years before the birth of Henry V. I believe she is the lady in red velvet who now haunts the place from time to time. I have not actually seen her, but an Irish friend of mine, Christopher Clarkson, a famous airman of the First World War, who had this psychic gift, saw her as I was showing him the music room in broad daylight. When I opened the door he told me that he saw a girl in red velvet sitting at the Italian table. This is the room on the north front with the wide view over the Thames Valley. When I first acquired the manor I used to dream at night that I was wandering through room after room in what seemed to be an old castle. There was one with an oriel window with a wide view, not unlike that from the music room. I wish I could have seen the lady in red velvet sitting at the table but I have heard her often at night walking past my bedroom. Once I awoke, on hearing steps in the passage, to find a light burning which I had never used for reading because it had too dark a shade. I can find no natural explanation for this strange phenomenon but I have come to feel that Marie de Bohun is still in love with Hinton and likes to wander in the castle. Who could wish a happy ghost to go away?

Although the St Valerys and the royal de Bohuns left few monuments behind them – apart from motte and moat and the large stone I sat on, which I discovered was part of the gate-house of the castle – they and their like left their mark on the national character of the English upper-class, as I found out when I went into the City and joined Rowe and Pitman. But the owner of the manor who left a deeper mark on the national character of the middle-class, and who helped to change the constitution from monarchical absolutism and feudalism to democracy – with even the promise of social democracy to come – was Henry Marten.

Henry was for me the most fascinating owner that Hinton Manor had ever had. He was born in 1602 at Oxford where his father – Sir Henry Marten, the crafty old Jacobean judge – was then living. In 1615 he became a gentleman commoner of University College. On 10 August 1618, he was admitted to Grays Inn. It was here that he met, and became intimate with the men who were later to become the leaders of the political revolution. One of the students was Oliver Cromwell. No less than twenty-one of the thirty-six who signed the death warrant, were at one time students of Gray's Inn. This is perhaps the first time in English history that we meet with a real students' revolt. And it ended in a bloody civil war.

One of my dottier friends who believes in the transmigration of souls suggested quite seriously that I was the re-incarnation of Henry Marten. Having done much research on his history I was not entirely flattered. Henry had twice been called a 'whore-master' – first by King Charles and then by Cromwell.

What I did discover about Henry, which I would be happy to claim as transmogrification, was his genuine sympathy for the poor and unprivileged, and his anger at the injustices they were made to suffer at the hands of the brutal Presbyterian ruling clique in Parliament. I was reminded of the compassion my father had felt for the poor, unprivileged and hard-driven coal miners of Leicestershire which had so deeply impressed me as a boy. The tortures suffered by the fanatical Colonel Lilburne, the leader of the Levellers, must have turned Henry towards the Leveller cause. Lilburne was once tied to a cart and whipped from St Paul's to Westminster Yard by order of the Star Chamber. How he endured two hundred lashes from a three-knotted whip is impossible to understand. He must have been made of the steel which was in his soul.

Another curious historical fact was produced by my friend in support of his far-fetched belief in the re-incarnation of souls. The Levellers were not represented in the House of Commons. They relied on Henry Marten to defend their cause in Parliament. He was the only politician they could trust. When the Leveller Walwyn's papers were discovered, it was found that the Levellers had given Marten a cypher number in their correspondence lest it should ever be disclosed that they had a friend and sympathiser in the House. 'Here are you,' said my friend, 'forming a secret club called XYZ to counsel and advise the Levellers of the 1930s. And you actually participated in the drafting of one of their pamphlets – on *Currency, Banking and Finance* – in 1932. Did not Henry Marten share in the drafting of some of the Leveller pamphlets of the 1640s?' Certainly in one – *England's Troublers Troubled* – published in 1648, in which the Levellers attacked the extortionately high money rents imposed by the Livery Companies in the City – land rents in the country as well as house and shop rents in the City – exploiting and impoverishing the poor through 'unconscionable, unreasonable, racked, oppressive and destructive rents'. 'Such Martenesque language inveighing against dear money, you have often used yourself,' said my friend, 'in your money columns in the *New Statesman*.'

There certainly were some extraordinary similarities between the Leveller movement of the 1640s and that of the 1930s. To begin with, they shared a fanatical Puritanism. There was always an element of envy, a desire to pull down what they did not possess or understand, in the Puritan soul. The new Levellers of the 1930s wanted to pull down private wealth and regarded the profit motive as immoral and wicked, just as the Levellers of the seventeenth century regarded the rich merchants and lawyers and the whole ruling clique as immoral and wicked. In fact, I feel justified in calling the subsequent socialist Government of

1945–51 the second Puritan revolution. So many of its members were ostentatiously Puritan in their mode of living and dressing. Their clothes were plain and ill-fitting. I have never seen anyone so shabbily dressed as Douglas Jay – before he held office. Their homes were bare and uncomfortable. Dalton's cottage at Aldbourne had no big soft-cushioned sofa or chair on which you could relax. Cripps had a gaunt, uncompromising face exactly like that of a Puritan saint. Dalton despised riches and once told me that England could be run on two-thousand-pounds-a-year men. I do not suppose he had ever had much more himself before he became a Minister. True, Nye Bevan enjoyed good food and champagne in the houses of the rich, but he was unique : he denounced not only the profiteering entrepreneur but the non-entrepreneurial middle-class. He was made of the stuff of the real proletarian revolutionary. Happily, however, his love of democracy was greater than his love of revolution.

Further, as in the 1640s, so in the 1930s there was a growing conviction among the Levellers that the wicked world of money was coming to an end. In 1640 some of the Puritan sects at the time believed in the doctrine of Christ's Second Coming. The Millenarians or Fifth Monarchy men were convinced that the time was at hand when the Kingdom of God would overthrow the kingdoms of the world and the militant Saints would prepare the world for the reign of the lowly and the poor. The soldiers became indoctrinated with the idea that they were the soldiers of Christ. In the 1930s the chapel folk of the Labour Party – Baptists, Methodists and Congregationalists, the rank and file Puritans who were to be found in the Labour lodges – were also convinced that the end of the capitalist world had come. The Marxists had fed them with the doctrine that capitalism carried within itself the seeds of its own destruction. They had witnessed the collapse of the American banking system after the Wall Street crash and they saw the rising tide of massive unemployment, sweeping through the western democracies, as proof that the capitalist world was disintegrating.

Even the intellectuals – Kingsley Martin, John Strachey, Harold Laski, Victor Gollancz and the rest of the Marxist élite – were caught up in this eschatological fever and began to preach the end of the capitalist world. Some of them – but not Dalton – saw in Stafford Cripps one of the militant 'saints' who would prepare the nation for the reign of the lowly, unprivileged workers. (Trade unions were not yet the bosses.) Cripps would no doubt have been prepared to play the part of Christ Resurgent if the Puritan rank and file had resorted to a general strike to overthrow the profit-making private enterprise system they regarded as so immoral. He had the same streak of fanaticism in his soul as they had in theirs. But fortunately, respect for Parliamentary democracy prevented thoughts of revolutionary action. The Puritan conscience – the driving force of the eschatological socialists of the thirties – made these potential revolutionaries feel that they could leave it all to God and the 'historical role' of the working-class – whatever that Marxist phrase means.

In the sixteenth century the 'historical role' of the working-class was not so evident. The Civil War was not a revolt of the left against the right. It was a political power struggle between an absolute monarch and a Parliamentary opposition consisting of rich City merchants and lawyers, and a landed gentry class – families like the Cromwells, the Pyms, the Eliots, the Hampdens and the Martens – some of whom had acquired their wealth in the corrupt ways of the time.

For eleven years up to 1640 King Charles had ruled absolutely without Parliament – imposing forced loans, exacting ship money, selling monopolies, allowing his chief minister, the Earl of Strafford, to do what he liked in foreign as well as home affairs. To make matters worse, Archbishop Laud, pig-headed and bad tempered, had tried to enforce conformity with his Anglican episcopal church upon a Presbyterian opposition. Not only did he levy heavy fines for non-conformity but he had the officers of the Star Chamber cut off the ears of the Puritan militants in public, as an example for the London crowds. Laud's final madness was to impose the service of the Anglican church on Presbyterian Scotland which brought the Scots into the struggle against the King as an ally of Puritan England. With a Scottish war on his hands, the King had to summon Parliament to raise more money. This brought Hinton Manor[1] also into the struggle, for Henry Marten in 1639 refused to contribute to the general loan which

---

[1] Cromwell apparently made use of the Manor house in his campaigns, for a request directed to the committee in London in May 1645 for money and arms 'to pursue the enemy' was despatched from Hinton Waldrist according to Antonia Fraser's *Cromwell- Our Chief of Men.*

the King was raising for the Scottish war. Henry became a hero in his county and he was returned as one of the members for Berkshire for the 'Short' Parliament in April 1640, and again for the 'Long' Parliament in the following November.

In Westminster Henry became leader of the group known as the Republican Lobby in the 'Long' Parliament from 1640 to 1648. What made Henry such an ardent republican I can only guess. According to Bishop Burnet, his republican ideas were founded 'upon the Roman and Greek principles'. Perhaps it was his erudite protest against the Hobbesian idea of absolutism which was then being practised by a devout and stubborn monarch suffering from the delusion of the Divine Right of kings.

The part which my predecessor at Hinton Manor played in the political revolution of the seventeenth century has been sadly underrated. The fact that he did not win battles like the master-general Cromwell, that he was not publicly whipped by order of the Star Chamber like the heroic Leveller, John Lilburne, served to keep him out of the headlines of the historians. But his influence in the House of Commons and behind the Parliamentary scenes in the long debates between the Army Grandees and the Levellers was profound. Brailsford writes of him in his book, *The Levellers and the English Revolution* :

> Colonel Henry Marten lives in history as the wit of the Long Parliament, an audacious pioneer of republicanism, a regicide and also a determined opponent of Cromwell's usurpation. . . . Marten was an intimate friend of the Leveller leaders and collaborated with them closely during the three critical years before the King's execution.

1647 was the most critical of these years. It saw in October the extraordinary debates at Putney when Cromwell and Ireton met the army rank and file to listen to their grievances and their ideas for a settlement of the kingdom. The army 'agitators' were led by Colonel Rainsborough, a confidant of Henry Marten, and they put forward the democratic programme of the Levellers – one man, one vote. Ireton was horrified. 'All the main thing that I speak for,' he said, 'is because I would have an eye to property'. Cromwell added : 'Without property a vote is anarchy'. The coleric Colonel Rainsborough shouted back : 'What have the soldiers been fighting for all this while – to become servile to men of property?' These were Henry Marten's sentiments.

The collaboration between Henry and the Levellers was closest in the drafting of the famous *Agreement of the People* earlier that year. Colonel Lilburne left a detailed account of how he and Henry Marten closeted themselves together in a room at Windsor to draft the articles when the negotiations between the Levellers and the Independents had broken down. The agreement may have struck the conservative Army Grandees as revolutionary at the time but it seems a very reasonable document today. It called for the dissolution of the disgraced Long Parliament and a new Parliament of four hundred, biennially elected through proportional representation, and manhood suffrage. This was defined as a vote by the 'natives or denizens of England . . . of one and twenty years old and upwards . . . not persons receiving alms, not servants to or receiving wages from any particular person . . . but *housekeepers* dwelling within the division for which the election is'. It also laid down fundamental rights which Parliament could not alter – the abolition of press gangs, freedom of conscience, equality before the law, trial by twelve jurymen, free trade, no 'usury' (six per cent interest on loans was the limit), no death penalty except for murder and treason, no privileges. It also created a Council of State (a cabinet) to manage the public affairs, and bound Parliament not to interfere in judicial affairs except to punish public officers for abusing their trust. It is good to see that Henry Marten insisted *inter alia* on cheaper money, which as a Keynesian I have always upheld.

The *Agreement of the People* was the climax of the Puritan revolution – the charter of liberties which these brave freedom fighters had won after years of struggle and the spilling of much blood. To their fight and to their victory we owe the very existence of democracy on both sides of the Atlantic. When we British and Americans thank God for the amazing constitutional liberties we enjoy today, let us not forget the heroic Levellers whom Cromwell crushed – and throw a penny in the fountain for their eccentric counsellor – Henry Marten of Hinton Manor.

The leaders of the Labour Party, who were so fond of quoting the revolution of the 1640s, did not seem to realise what Cromwell had done. He had done away with Parliament; he had restored the nobility and gentry to what he deemed to be their

D*

rightful place in English society. I quote from Christopher Hill's recent book *God's Englishman*:

> To his first Parliament of the Republic Cromwell proclaimed his support for the existing social order: 'A nobleman, a gentleman, a yeoman: that is a good interest of the nation and a great one. The magistracy of the nation, was it not almost trampled underfoot under despite and contempt, by men of Levelling principles?... Did not the Levelling principle tend to reducing all to an equality?... I tell you, Sir, you have no other way to deal with these men [the Levellers] but to break them or they will break you.'

Oliver again declared to his second Parliament in 1650: 'We would keep up the nobility and gentry'. Major Attlee followed his advice to the letter when he promptly secured for himself and his family an hereditary earldom as soon as his 'Levellers' lost office in 1951.

The intelligentsia of the Labour Party, who were to be my guests in Henry Marten's home, may well have fancied that they could re-write history and achieve the real power which the Levellers had been denied in the 1640s. It was perhaps significant that Nye Bevan, when he was writing anti-Churchill articles in *Tribune* during the war, assumed the pseudonym of 'Colonel Rainsborough', the fiery Leveller and agitator who had been Henry Marten's friend. He was fond of quoting Rainsborough's outburst at the Putney debates: 'For really I think that the poorest he that is in England hath a life to live as the greatest he.' However, when Nye came to lunch at Hinton Manor and saw the plaque on the terrace to the memory of the regicide, he told me that he was quite unaware of Henry Marten's existence and of the realistic advice which he had given to the Levellers. I tried to explain to him that if the Levellers had listened more to his advice they might have won over the moderate Independents, the practical Army Grandees who were suspicious of Cromwell, and have circumvented the fascist-style dictatorship of the Lord Protector.

I could not help thinking that if the new Levellers of the 1930s had listened more to the advice of Henry Marten's successor at Hinton Manor they might have carried through a more practical and economically more viable 'second Puritan revolution'. Henry and I had both been sceptical of egalitarianism, that 'doctrinaire abstraction'. Henry did not believe in the Second Coming of Christ. I did not believe in the Second Coming of Marx. We both believed in democratic and social reform from within. I passionately believed that under the beneficent influence of Keynes the capitalist system could be more humane, more respectable and more efficient – with a sufficient extension of public ownership, and a sufficient dose of redistributive taxation to satisfy the more reasonable Levellers – and that both free enterprise and public enterprise could combine and flourish in a mixed economy. But were the new Levellers prepared to accept the middle way?

6

New Levellers at Hinton Manor

When the first stage of the restoration work was done, and I stood on the circular steps gazing out over the moat, waiting for Hugh Dalton to arrive, I had a strange sense that I had experienced all this before. Was the haunting of the past, which I always felt in the old Tudor house, beginning to take hold of me? Was I beginning to feel the presence of my predecessor, Henry Marten? The suspicion began to grow upon me that the egalitarian Labour leaders, in particular, Hugh Dalton and Stafford Cripps, were in fact re-enacting the part of the Levellers and that I too might be playing unconsciously the role of Henry Marten who had been their friend and counsellor.

Of course the second Puritan revolution, which I sensed was coming, was not likely to be bloody like the first. The old Fabian socialists like Dalton, who were in firm control of the Labour Party, would only proceed on their nationalisation course step by step – consensus by consensus – by attempting to persuade the managerial élite and the floating voters of the middle-class. The Marxists like Laski and Strachey and Kingsley Martin, who expected that they would have to use force against desperate Tories fiercely resisting a too rapid nationalisation of industry or a confiscation of private property, were happily not in power, and were never likely, in my view, to gain power.

I had arranged the weekend party for Dalton on 22 September 1934, primarily to discuss the future of XYZ and see whether we could be of more help to the leaders of the centre in their constant disputes with the Marxist socialists at the party conferences. For this end I had invited Vaughan Berry, co-founder of the XYZ Club, to join us. He was as fearful as I was that Labour might wreck the whole financial system of a mixed economy through its ignorance of the working of City institutions. As Berry was rather a dear, serious character I invited also Aylmer Vallance, a sub-editor of the *New Statesman,* who had a lively mind and a sharp dry wit and could be relied upon to rescue the conversation if it fell flat.

I cannot remember whether this weekend of debate did any good for my cause, that is, whether it persuaded our 'Leveller' guest that it was essential to preserve the financial system in the City during the first instalment of Fabian socialism which they were planning. Educating politicians in subjects uncongenial to them is an arduous job. It was clear that Hugh had not lost his old bias against the City. He was fond of quoting Lloyd George's memorable remark about the 'flapping penguins' of the Square Mile. He did not share the starry idealism of the Marxists about the destruction of the capitalist order but he remained convinced that the profit motive was immoral and that capitalism in the City was the enemy whose head would have to be cut off one day, just as his predecessors in the first Puritan revolution had – in the end – to cut off the head of King Charles. What worried me, as we argued that weekend, was the thought that he might cut off the wrong head – namely, the head of honest private enterprise, on which depended the growth of the economy and the expansion of the export trade. The head he ought to have had designs on was that of international finance-capitalism. But that is another story which remains to be told in chapters 11 and 12.

The most authentic egalitarian of the Levellers who came to Hinton was Stafford Cripps. I gave up trying to bring Stafford into a saner understanding of the useful part played by the City in the working of the capital market. Having joined the Socialist League in 1932 he was utterly opposed to the capitalism of a mixed economy. I began to look on him as the Colonel Lilburne in the coming Puritan revolution. He had the glint of the Leveller in his eye. I can see him now, tall, erect, rigid, and grim. Here was a man, you would feel, who is perfectly controlled, co-ordinated in mind and body, absolutely sure of his destiny, mentally and physically a distinguished and superior person. There was nothing of the untidy left-wing intellectual about his appearance, no round shoulders, no long hair, no slovenly dress. He was neat and well-groomed. He was not stiffly erect like a guardsman but he carried his head forward and up from a remarkably straight spine. There was a particular reason for this upstanding characteristic. Stafford, like Bernard Shaw, was a firm believer in the system of psycho-physical re-education, taught by Mathias Alexander and expounded at Notting Hill by his disciple Charles Neil.[1] He had, in fact, mastered the technique of holding his head and spinal column in a correct line and performing his bodily movements without putting tension on his spine, even when sitting on his lavatory seat. It did him no apparent good. He did not enjoy robust health. At the beginning of the First World War he had picked up some intestinal bug – while lorry-driving, I believe, in France – and the conquest of it caused him to turn to vegetarianism and soft drinks. That was quite enough to eliminate all *joie de vivre*. Not that he loved the austerity of living for its own sake. Whenever my wife offered him a special vegetarian lunch he would enjoy every course of it and, at the end, would light a cigar and take obvious pleasure in every pull and puff. But it did not last long. His guilt complex would quickly regain control and his face would resume its haunted, saint-like appearance as he expounded his egalitarian gospel.

I remember calling on him one day in the Inner Temple after he had given up his practice. He was at his typewriter, tapping out a letter. I remarked how strange it was to see a rich barrister doing the work of a secretary. He smiled with delight : 'Yesterday I had thirty thousand pounds a year – today I have no income at all'. He said it with puritan relish. I did not like to remind him that he could always fall back on his wife's capital. Isobel Cripps came from the family of Eno's Fruit Salts and was well endowed.

Stafford lived in the not far off Cotswold village of Filkins and was often invited to lunch at Hinton. I thought it would be fun to arrange a meeting between Maynard Keynes and a Marxist socialist as fanatical as Stafford Cripps. Maynard had always pretended that he had never studied Marx and had no use for such ignorant socialists as the Labour leaders. So when Maynard and Lydia Lopokova came to spend the weekend at Hinton in June 1935 I suggested that we should motor over to see Stafford at Filkins. Maynard jumped at the idea. The other guests at the weekend included Lord Listowel, a moderate socialist, and his

[1] After his death Isobel Cripps helped the Neil consulting rooms to turn into a clinic for the study and propagation of the Alexander method of psycho-physical co-ordination.

first wife Judith who had accompanied me to Munich in 1932 when we met Hitler and I had exposed Dr Schacht as a Nazi (this tale is told in Chapter 7). So one Sunday afternoon we called. Cripps was then a rich man and had transformed Filkins by building some splendid new cottages for farm workers complete with bathrooms. He showed them to us with evident pride. Cripps told the great economist that when he came into political power he would build up-to-date cottages for the farm workers throughout the entire country, however much the Treasury objected to the cost and whatever the economists said about the inflationary consequences. He said they presently lived in hovels – fit for the beasts they looked after, but not for men with living souls. Maynard was delighted. He drew Stafford on about his spending schemes and finally got him to admit that under his regime the budget would be hopelessly unbalanced and perpetually in deficit. The conversation flew back and forth with delightful gusto. On the way home Maynard said to me that Cripps was a man after his own heart for he despised conventional economics, he hated bankers and he believed in deficit spending. What Stafford thought of Keynes I never discovered. Probably he wrote him off as lacking in political *gravitas*. Stafford, for me, had too much of it. I can still see the horror on his face when, after a lunch party at Hinton, in which he had expounded his revolutionary socialism and his belief in the destruction of our social and economic system, I had asked him whether he was really serious. It was as if Henry Marten had asked Colonel Lilburne whether he really believed in the Second Coming of Christ.

A very different Wykehamist egalitarian who visited Hinton was Hugh Gaitskell. He was the cleverest and most self-contained of the young men whom Hugh Dalton advanced. He was actually discovered by the Coles at Oxford, about 1925, and as a professional economist he edited for a time the quarterly journal of the New Fabian Research Bureau which they founded. But it was the General Strike of 1926 which made him a Labour activist. This, and his later experience in Vienna, while working on a Rockefeller grant, when he saw the fascists smash the socialists in street fighting, brought him emotionally as well as intellectually on the side of the working-class. But he was never a believer in the class war. He rejected Marxist economics and, like his friend

Evan Durbin, he detested the medievally cruel Soviet dictatorship. It was under the guidance of R. H. Tawney that he
embraced Fabian socialism.

I had many economic talks with Hugh Gaitskell over lunches
at the Athenaeum Club and was always impressed by his grasp of
technical money details, something which Dalton never had.
When he and Dora, his charming and highly intelligent wife,
came down to Hinton one weekend to join an evening party at
the near-by house of Ian Little, the Nuffield economist, I was
struck by his gaiety and *joie de vivre*. He loved parties and he
adored dancing. He would dance away until the early hours of
the morning. It was ridiculous to call him, as Nye did, a 'desic-
cated calculating machine'. He was a highly emotional man and
deadly serious about politics. What made him unique among
contemporary politicians was his honesty and his obstinacy.
When he saw what he believed to be the truth he would not
budge from it or compromise. This led him into two great fights
with his party – the first over Clause 4, the second over unilateral
disarmament.

Hugh Gaitskell believed almost passionately in the pragmatic
Fabian socialism which the Social Democratic parties in Continental Europe eventually adopted after the war. The Socialist
International in Frankfurt in 1951 passed this resolution : 'Socialist planning does not presuppose the ownership of all the means of
production. It is compatible with private ownership in important
fields'. That was Gaitskell's view and he tried to persuade his
party to accept it. He regarded nationalisation as a means, not an
end. He sought to remove the nationalisation threats of the 1918
and 1945 policy memoranda which had been losing the good will
of the floating voter and alarming and upsetting the private sector
of the economy. In fact, he wanted the Marxist Clause 4
abolished altogether from the Labour Party's constitution. But in
this frontal attack upon Labour dogma he was badly defeated.
The party simply refused to remove or amend Clause 4. Tony
Crosland in *The Conservative Enemy* blamed 'the extreme con-
servatism of the British working-class movement' for this defeat.

After much heated debate, a compromise was reached on 16
March 1960 between the root-and-branch Gaitskellites, the
sentimentalists who wanted to retain Clause 4 as a sacred cow for
worship and the revolutionaries who really believed in it as

Marxist socialists. A new *Statement of Aims* was drawn up with much lofty phrasing in the preamble about the 'fundamental dignity of man,' 'the classless society' and 'social justice', and with much righteous condemnation of the 'selfish, acquisitive doctrines of capitalism' and 'the pursuit of material wealth'. The party now stands, it said, 'for the protection of workers, consumers and all citizens against any exercise of arbitrary power, whether by the State, by private or by public authorities'. (They might have added 'or by trade unions'.) It went on :

> It is convinced that these social and economic objectives can be achieved only through an expansion of common ownership substantial enough to give the community power over the commanding heights of the economy. Common ownership takes varying forms, including state-owned industries and firms, producer and consumer co-operation, municipal owner-ship and public participation in private concerns. Recognising that both public and private enterprise have a place in the economy, it believes that further extension of common owner-ship should be decided from time to time in the light of these objectives and according to circumstances with due regard for the view of the workers and consumers concerned.

Subsequently I wrote to Harold Wilson for an elucidation of this amendment and on 6 December 1963 he replied : 'You are right in thinking that the Statement of March 1960 was only a statement of aims and not a technical amendment of Clause 4.' Nevertheless I believe this new statement of aims should have made the Labour Party stand firmly on the social democracy of a mixed economy in which private enterprise could work happily along with public enterprise. This is how Hugh Gaitskell wanted it to be, but the majority of his party thought otherwise.

His second fight with his party – over unilateral disarmament – followed at the Scarborough conference in the autumn of 1960. He was actually defeated – the trade unions sided with the pacifists – but he bravely declared that he would 'fight and fight again' until they reversed their ridiculous decision. Here was the stuff of real leadership. And he won his battle at the conference of 1961, when the unilateral disarmament decision was reversed. It required the courage of the lion to face the possibility of a second defeat which would have meant his immediate resignation.

If Hugh Gaitskell had lived to win the 1964 election he would, I feel, have had the 1918 Constitution revised, as he intended it to be, without Clause 4. This, of course, would have split the Labour movement. The ramshackle coalition would have broken up and the extreme left wing and Marxists elements would have been driven out to form once again another Independent Labour Party. But Hugh would have continued to reign as an honest social democrat, backed not only by the right wing and centre social reformers of the Labour movement but by the great middle-class floating vote. His was the sort of socialism which appealed to a much wider public. He defined it at the conference of 1955 in these appealing words :

> I became a socialist quite candidly, not so much because I was a passionate advocate of public ownership but because I came to hate and loathe social injustice, because I disliked the class structure of our society, because I could not tolerate the indefensible difference of status and income which disfigures our society.

It was interesting to read in George Wigg's autobiography a passage of violent criticism of Hugh Gaitskell. This was understandable because George Wigg and his great friend 'Manny' Shinwell derived from the red 'grass roots' of the Clydeside revolutionaries. I do not suppose that his Lordship Wigg ever intended to smash up our sporting social structure and bring in State jockeys in a nationalised racing industry, but he had an instinctive dislike for an intellectual like Hugh Gaitskell who saw more clearly than he did where our civil liberties would end if revolutionary Clydeside hot-heads took over 10 Downing Street.

Hugh Gaitskell's death in 1963 was a national tragedy. He would have been a great Prime Minister. In my view, if he had been spared, he would have remained in power at number ten to this day. My heart went out to his loyal and clever wife Dora when he died so untimely and so mysteriously that I have often wondered whether he had been attacked by some malevolent supernatural power.

One of Hugh Dalton's great contributions to the Labour cause was to encourage and advance young men of promise. One of these, who became a close friend and came often to Hinton was John Wilmot – not so young, not so handsome, for he had an

owlish face which made him appear wiser than, in fact, he was –
but a warm, companionable man who loved, like Hugh, good
food and wine and talk at Hinton. He was no austere Leveller, for
he collaborated in business life with millionaires in order to pay
for the comforts which his urbane way of life demanded, but he
had a rare quality in a Labour politician – a feeling for art which
endeared him to me and my artist wife. He was descended, he
told me, from the famous Victorian clown Grimaldi, so that he
had artistry in his blood. He took up painting in his later life,
having been taught and inspired by a close woman friend who
was a professional artist.

At the start of his political career John was a poor man, an ex-
clerk of Lloyds Bank. A leftish stockbroker called Chance, a
friend of mine, gave him a job in his office and to provide him
with an extra £500 a year he and an LCC friend, later Lord
Latham, set up a Shareholders Protection Association, so that
John could attend shareholders' meetings and attack the directors
if they had committed some outrage on their equity owners. His
political career began when he won the famous bye-election at
Fulham in October 1933. Baldwin claimed that this proved the
people's aversion to rearmament – the Conservative candidate
had advocated increased spending on armaments – but this was
far from the truth. John told me that the campaign was not
fought on rearmament – he had not stressed foreign affairs at
all – but was concentrated on social policy and decent housing for
the poor. His opponent had been a landlord and a telling picture
was published in the *Evening Standard* of a Fulham slum of
delapidated terraced houses with a common pump for water in
the centre. That turned the scale of floating votes but John owed
much also to the hard and devoted canvassing of his wife Elsa, a
charming woman who called on every door. Without Elsa, John
would never have made the count. But he was a good speaker and
was able to make a crowd feel his innate honesty and deep
concern for social reform.

Having been a bank clerk and now a Labour MP – and a
friend of Hugh Dalton – John Wilmot was seized upon as a useful recruit to any company board whose owners or managing-
directors saw Labour coming into power. He was invited by a
Dutch millionaire called Tresfon to become chairman of his
Norwich company Boulton & Paul. He was also invited to the

chair of West Cumberland Silk Mills which was formed by that genius of a textile designer, the late Miki Seckers. After the war he became chairman of Illingworth Morris, a large wool textile firm in Yorkshire, whose President, Isidore Ostrer, was a maverick reformer of the money system. He thus became rich.

John frankly enjoyed dining out with the rich – not for snobbish reasons but for the good food and wine he loved. I introduced him to Alexander Korda and, dining together once in Alex's penthouse at the top of Claridges, John told us that he was going to New York for the first time. 'Tell me,' said Alex, 'what you would most enjoy doing when you arrive?' 'I would like,' said John, 'to dine with an American millionaire in his penthouse on top of a skyscraper and ride on a fire-engine of the New York fire brigade.' At that time John was chairman of the London Fire Brigade. You shall do both, said Alex, and so it was miraculously arranged. I have never seen a man so transported with childish pleasure. In later life John became chairman of the Trustees of Glyndebourne, which was near his farm house in Sussex. He invited me to his box in the theatre and it was a pleasure to see him exuding happiness over his social success and cultural good living. He died suddenly dining at the Hyde Park Hotel where he invited a poor constituent each year for a modest feast. That was typical of the good man he was. When his political career ended and he was made a life peer, the College of Heralds delighted him by giving him the arms of the first Lord Wilmot, Earl of Rochester whose son John (1647–80) had been a minor poet and a major libertine. As long as status and style are held in public esteem, which may not be for long, who would deny John Wilmot's innocent pleasure in their possession? He died worth a little over £200,000 – to his wife's immense tax disadvantage. I am sure he just wanted to show how a poor bank clerk had made good.

One of the young men whom Hugh Dalton pushed forward began his career in the Labour Party during a weekend at Hinton Manor. This was Douglas Jay, who had been invited down for tennis and XYZ talk. Douglas was a fanatical tennis player and always played to win – even if it involved some doubtful decisions. I suggested that he should meet Hugh Dalton, whom he did not know. I arranged a rendez-vous at a Wiltshire pub, so that we could walk back to Hugh's cottage. We met and strode forth, and when Douglas beat the older man to the top of the down – he was almost a professional walker, having done a record hike from Oxford to Hampstead – Hugh was so delighted that I knew Douglas's career in the Labour Party had begun and was assured. This is how Hugh Dalton described it in *The Fateful Years* :

> On leaving the pub we walked along a road on one side of which rose a steep bank of grassy chalk, leading up to the Downs. Crying 'Come on!' I led the way up this steep bank. Only Douglas Jay followed and he outpaced me to the top. This founded our friendship and my physical respect for this young Fellow of All Souls.

Douglas Jay is an extraordinary mixture of serious political thinker and economist, and a frivolous-minded eccentric. His eccentricities used to fascinate me. It was because they were not put on, but were real and obsessional. For example, he hates draughts. As soon as he enters a room he will look round to see if a window is open and will immediately close it if it is. Once he was staying at the British embassy in Paris, when the Hayters were in occupation, and complained to the ambassador of a draught in his bedroom. Lady Hayter told me that when the guests had gone upstairs to change for dinner she saw in a corridor a stumbling figure carrying a large mattress. It was Douglas. He had found a still-room without windows, where the linen was kept, and was transferring his bed to get out of a draught.

Douglas also has an aversion to foreign ways of eating. When he has to go abroad he puts in his luggage a packet of cereals for breakfast. Foreigners, he said, do not understand what the human body needs at breakfast – cereals and cream covered copiously with sugar. He himself required a lot of sugar and cups and cups of coffee. When he came to stay at Hinton and the breakfast coffee was exhausted he would go into the kitchen, without a word to my wife, and make some more. I used to be worried because his tall body always looked thin and starved but it had amazing vital force and this was shown in his attraction to women. When he could be persuaded at dinner to be serious he could quote endlessly from Houseman and Shakespeare – his memory was prodigious – and develop fascinating trains of thought. But the facetiousness of a school-boy would intervene before long and upset the flow. I remember my embarrassment when I first dined with him at All Souls. In the common room over port and dessert he aimed shots at the eminent Isaiah Berlin with cherry stones.

During the war Hugh Dalton brought Douglas into the Board of Trade when he was President and a great administrative partnership was developed. In spite of his eccentricity in food and other peculiar habits Douglas was a first-class, down-to-earth, practical administrator and did the ground work for Hugh's policy of bringing work to the distressed areas of high unemployment – now called the 'Development Areas'. It was Douglas who thought of the Industrial Development Certificate which was one of the main instruments of economic control in the second Labour government. No company could build a factory without first securing an IDC and Douglas would only issue one if the company agreed to go to a distressed area. Dalton and Jay should go down in the history books as the pioneers of regional aid.

Tony Crosland's career in the Labour Party may also be said to have been launched at Hinton Manor during a dinner party I will describe in chapter nine. Tony Crosland and Douglas Jay were the only two 'Levellers' I knew who translated their levelling ideas into political and economic terms. Each wrote an excellent book on modern socialism but Tony's *The Future of Socialism* was the more impressive and forward-looking. In this really important work Tony developed his idea of social democracy to the great annoyance of the Clause 4 Marxists in his party. Unfortunately he denounced equity shares as a useless anachronism because company ownership had been divorced from control which was now vested in the managerial élite. This was not the whole truth. The equity share is the legal device invented to enable the entrepreneur to raise 'risk' capital on the Stock Exchange. No one would subscribe, certainly no investment institution, to a 'risk' equity unless he was entitled to all the surplus, if there was any, because in the event of failure he would lose all his money. The equity shareholder is now at last taking much more notice of the important part he plays in the capitalist scheme of things. On the initiative of the Bank of England the institutional owner of equity shares is being encouraged to keep in closer touch with the management, to interfere if it goes wrong and to turn up at the company's general meeting to voice his dissatisfaction if it is called for.

Both Tony Crosland and Douglas Jay in their revisionist books on socialism tended to be led astray, I thought, by their Party's passion for equality. Tony Crosland in his *Future of Socialism* argued the case for 'equality' not on class war grounds but on the pragmatic grounds of social justice and the more efficient use of the national resources. So he advocated more severe measures of direct taxation of incomes and capital to bring about a wider distribution of wealth and to increase social contentment. Being a sound economist I am sure he attributed more importance to the latter, than to the former. Douglas Jay in his *Socialism in the New Society* (published in 1962) took an even more pragmatic line. Equality, he said, was a natural socialist aim but if one took the superfluous incomes of the rich and spread them out over everyone less rich, the latter would only receive a few farthings from the rich man's table. Equality, he added, was not as important as the aim of basic human and political rights. The objective of modern socialism, in his view, was 'the minimum practicable inequality'. Like Tony Crosland he advocated direct taxation of capital gains as a redistributive agency, but since such a tax has been imposed we have seen little redistributive effect. I do not suppose either believed the nonsense that you can achieve equality of wealth by tax legislation.

In the late thirties I had an angry correspondence in the *New Statesman* on this point with Dick Acland, who had flirted with a new 'Commonwealth Party' (*pace* Cromwell) in company with Cripps. In the final letter I wrote: 'egalitarianism will be the death of modern socialism'. Any democracy which allows the rich to pursue their acquisitive habits will benefit because employment and the standard of living of the workers will rise as a result. Any socialist democracy which taxes them so severely as to interfere with their pursuit of profit, kill their initiative and drive them out of the country, will suffer. There is, of course, only one way to level wealth and that is to have a bloody revolution, confiscate the property not only of the rich, but of every humble householder, and end up with a centralised authoritarian communist dictatorship denying all freedom to the working men as well as to the intelligentsia and bourgeoisie. Our domestic Fabians just refused to face these unpleasant facts.

Tony Crosland used to get so heated in these debates about egalitarianism that he once told my wife and myself that in any event we would be on different sides of the barricades and he would be able to shoot us first because we had had no war experience as he had, and would not be able to handle a gun. Tony is much more mellow and mild today after his trials as a minister in the Wilson administration. I am sure he owes much to his second marriage to the charming Susan Barnes. He was certainly the most brilliant of the young politicians discovered and helped by Hugh Dalton.

Of the intellectual Levellers who visited Hinton in this period, the most stimulating talkers were Nye Bevan, Roy Jenkins and Dick Crossman. We did not know Nye Bevan well but used to meet him and Jennie Lee dining with our friend Gavin (Lord) Faringdon at Buscot Park over the famous gold plate. We generally avoided political discussion but were always captivated by Nye's witty and brilliant talk and we always felt the warmth of their extrovert personalities. If Nye had lived to work with Gaitskell in a social democrat government the dangerous industrial conflicts of today might have been avoided.

Roy and Jennifer Jenkins were among our favourite political guests because they were free from the compulsion to talk politics and really enjoyed talking about art and literature. When politics came up Roy would always have interesting historical analogies to bring into the argument, for his scholarship was profound and in consequence his political ideas never partisan.

Dick Crossman was the self-appointed philosopher and confessor of the Labour Party. He became a not too-far-off farming neighbour when he married the charming Anne MacDougal of Prescot Manor near Banbury. She was the daughter of an agricultural expert who had run a model dairy farm and had started the Banbury cattle mart. The acquisition of this profitable and extensive farming land made Dick into the most incongruous member of the landed-gentry class one could imagine.

I saw in Dick the reincarnation of James Harrington, the philosopher of the Puritan revolution of the seventeenth century. Harrington was a very learned man. He took no part in the Civil War, but pursued his reading and writing while the fighting went on. He was a convinced republican, yet he remained a sincere friend of the King, having been a Groom of the Bedchamber when Charles was under house arrest, first at Holmby House and later in Carisbrooke Castle. Dick Crossman was also an avowed republican but had to wait upon the Queen when he became Lord President of the Council in 1968. What a bizarre appointment it was to make a republican Lord President of the Council! On one occasion when Dick declared his theoretical republicanism to a noble earl with whom he was dining after some local function, his host revealed that he was perhaps one of the Queen's closest friends. At the next meeting of the Privy Council the Queen remarked pleasantly to Dick : 'I hear, Mr Crossman, that you dined with my friend Lord – ' 'So he told you all?' replied Dick. The Queen returned an enigmatic smile.

Harrington was famous for his *Oceana*, a book in which he constructed the ideal constitution for England. He had the strange idea that a distribution of property would achieve the correct balance of power provided landed estates were limited to £3000 a year. He proposed a senate with this property qualification which would prepare laws to be voted upon by the people. (A horrified Cromwell seized the manuscript). Dick Crossman, now justly famous for his brilliant introduction to the 1964 edition of Bagehot's *English Constitution*, revised the Harrington thesis by proposing a House of Lords which would remove the last vestige of power from the hereditary land-owning peers, and give all patronage to the ruling Prime Minister. If Harrington's republic was, in effect, a moderated aristocracy, Dick Crossman's ideal republic was intended to be based on a meritocracy. But alas! he made the fatal mistake of retaining the power of selection – within limits – to the Prime Minister of the day. It only needed a disreputable Premier to have a House of Lords composed of the duds and dregs of political life. His bill was happily killed by the opposition of two opposites – Michael Foot and Enoch Powell.

Dick Crossman was not easy for the non-intellectual to understand. His detractors have called him 'double Crossman', treacherous, irresponsible and unreliable. He was none of these things, but as a searcher after the absolute truth which evaded him, he sometimes gave these wrong impressions. When he took up a cause he became its staunchest crusader. One of the good causes of his life was to fight Bevin's attempt, as he saw it, to destroy Israel, to help in its birth as a nation and to stand up for it whenever it got into trouble. Incidentally, this cost him the loss of a job in the Attlee Government. As I visualised him he was the fundamentally loyal disciple of the Greek school of Socratic philosophical debate. When I was motoring him and Zeta (his second wife) across France one summer he used to say : 'Now, Nicholas, choose a subject for debate'. When I opened up a thesis he would proceed to demolish it bit by bit. But if the last bit brought him round to a new thesis which stood for the opposite of what he had first been arguing he would not be in the least disturbed. It was the final rational truth which mattered, even if it meant standing on your head. I found him always great fun, a perpetual intellectual stimulant and a loyal friend.

The only Marxist intellectual who was a frequent visitor to Hinton in what Dalton called *The Fateful Years* was Kingsley Martin, and that was because I was writing the financial page in the *New Statesman* and he was my editor. He was irritating, lovable, talkative and extremely vain. He really believed that his diary in the *New Statesman* was better than Pepys' : it certainly was not. I remember one weekend, when my wife, then a distinguished actress, and I were entertaining Robert Donat and Deborah Kerr. Kingsley suggested charades. One of the words to be acted was 'editor'. Naturally he played the editor but it was amusing to watch his refusal to allow these professional artistes to speak a line. He monopolised the entire dialogue with evident delight. He made the two girls play a dumb secretary and a char and Robert Donat an office boy. On another occasion he swelled with visible pride when my friend Gabriel Pascal, the film pro- ducer, offered to cast Kingsley in the role of Stogumber in the film he proposed to make of St Joan. Alas ! it was never made, but Kingsley, I am sure, would have been superb as Stogumber and would have jumped at the chance of being hailed as a great film star as well as a great editor. His vanity never flagged.

As I contributed weekly to the *New Statesman* I came to know Kingsley well as an editor. He was an inspired left-wing opposi- tion journalist. He sat on so many fences that he gathered round him an immense following. The circulation of the *New Statesman* soared with the membership of the Left Book Club. Kingsley appealed to the pacifists, to the communists, to the Labour leftists, to the liberals who stood for free love and the League of Nations, to the dissenters, to the agnostics, to the atheists, to the cranks of every walk of life. Dalton fittingly called the *New Statesman* 'The Belly-achers Bulletin'. Kingsley was in fact the weekly voice of dissenting, bloody-minded England. He was a quite ruthless and unscrupulous editor. He would occasionally refuse to print letters which corrected his inaccuracies or put the points of view he detested. He was so terrified of war that he would not print anything that might enrage Hitler and provoke war. My friend the late Commander Stephen King-Hall told me that Kingsley had actually refused to print an article he had written exposing the brutal treatment of Jews in the Nazi concentration camps in the 1930s.

Maddening as Kingsley was in refusing to face unpleasant political or economic facts, putting forth the frightened rabbit or the pacifist or the communist point of view week after week, he was a delightful weekend guest. What I loved about him was his great sense of fun. I remember on one occasion when he was playing Chinker Chequers with Deborah Kerr at Hinton, he twice dropped a marble down her bosom to her great indignation. He would never have turned her upside down to extract the marble but the imagination of a topsy-turvy with this beautiful actress moved him to quiet chuckles of delight.

Kingsley never lost his faith in a British brand of communism although he eventually lost his faith in Soviet Russia. How he ever imagined that Britain could run a centralised communist economy without concentration camps or lunatic asylums for dissident socialists and workers – of which he would have been the first inmate – I never understood.

The pro-communist and pacifist line of the *New Statesman* in the late 1930s so enraged Keynes that he finally retired from the board and refused to have the paper in his house. When war broke out he wrote a letter to *The Times*, saying in effect 'Thank God for Colonel Blimp'. I quote the following passage :

The intelligentsia of the left were the loudest in demanding that the Nazi aggression should be resisted at all costs. When it comes to a showdown, scarce four weeks have passed before they remember that they are pacifists and write defeatist letters to your columns, leaving the defence of freedom and of civilisation to Colonel Blimp and the Old School Tie, for whom Three Cheers.

Of the descent to war, which postponed the second Puritan revolution by six years, I will now tell as I saw it in the City and in the film studios where I was involved for a time.

7
Descent into War: the City and Films

The City was a depressing place to work in during the thirties. I was glad to take on extra journalistic work for a time with the *Economist*. Walter Layton, its editor, asked me to help Hargreaves Parkinson start a Stock Exchange section in the weekly paper. It was fun to attend the Monday editorial conferences and listen to Arnold Toynbee, who was then their foreign correspondent, range over world affairs. Once started on his monologue he would never stop until he had reached some dead end like the Falkland Islands. We listened to him spellbound.

My *Economist* work brought me new friends. I became close for a time with Graham Hutton, whose then Swiss wife Madl, beautiful and rich, was enchanting, if moody. Graham is now living happily with his fourth wife. Dear Hargreaves Parkinson wrote a classically dull book on ordinary shares, became an excellent editor of the *Financial Times* after the war and wore himself out to an untimely death. His heart could not stand the pace of Brendan Bracken. I was very fond of him and wrote occasionally for him when he was editor of the *Financial Times*.

My liaison with the *Economist* led me later on to write the leaders for the *Investor's Chronicle*, which they owned, under the pseudonym 'Candidus'. This again was fun because it brought me more into contact with Brendan Bracken, and his young colleague Garrett Moore, now Lord Drogheda and managing director of the *Financial Times*. To Garrett we owe the superb arts page in the *Financial Times* which he conveniently keeps loose so that one can hand it over to one's wife at breakfast. Lunches with Brendan and Garrett to discuss my leaders were a delight. Whenever Brendan opened his mouth a stream of slander and wit would pour out. He was always full of provocative ideas and the best backer any leader writer could want. 'Say what you like', he told me. 'Go for him : he'll never come into court.' Later on I handed over this leader writing in the *Investor's Chronicle* to Harold Wincott who was told to imitate the racy style of my Candidus. He did it admirably, but played down, I thought, to a lower intellectual level of reader-ship. I could not stand his conversational articles which began 'Hello Son' – 'Hello Dad'. But he won journalistic fame as the simple, honest guy who stood up against the nonsense of socialism in the City.

It must be conceded that Neville Chamberlain did his best to cheer up the Stock Exchange when he was Chancellor. Tariffs were laid on to protect British industry and as a result of the floating exchange rate for the pound, money was made cheaper and industrial growth followed. This was reflected in a rise of nearly one hundred per cent in industrial shares between July 1931 and July 1935. Cheaper money also brought a revival in housing. Bank rate had been lowered from 6% to 5% on 18 February 1932 and then in rapid degrees it slipped down to 2% on 30 June 1932 where it stayed until August 1939. Neville Chamberlain was able to take a mean advantage of the boom in the gilt-edged market which these Bank rate cuts had fired, for in December 1932, he persuaded the holders of around £2000 million of 5% War Loan to accept a 3½% coupon. As the stock had touched 115, the holders responded with alacrity, glad to help 'the dear old country' out of its depression. If they could have foreseen that the stock would fall to 23½ in 1974 they might have had second thoughts.

During this phenomenal boom in the gilt-edged market, which allowed the market traders to make a lot of safe money, 2½% Consols rose to 77 in 1933, to 93 in 1934 and to 94 in 1935. We Keynesians were delighted, but again the unpleasant side of the City stirred one's conscience. While the quite innocent investors were making a lot of money out of their shares and bonds, the wretched unemployed and half-starved workers were having a miserable time. As George Orwell remarked in his *Road to Wigan Pier*, thousands of people settled down to living on the dole. Millions were on the poverty line even when at work. In the 'distressed areas' it was a nightmare of misery. Our massive unemployment was never, in fact, eliminated until the Government began to spend hundreds of millions on rearmament. Hitler was the first to show us how it could be done. He cured German unemployment in a few years by heavy deficit spending on rearmament.

At the *New Statesman* we went on pressing for more spending and more employment. Our hopes rose when the master in 1936 published his *General Theory of Employment, Interest and Money*. Hubert Henderson was the first to pick holes in it, and to my great sorrow a coolness developed between the two who had been such close colleagues in my *Nation* days.

Here I must digress for a moment to defend my *guru*. Keynes revolutionised economic theory by showing that the key to full employment was maximising aggregate demand made up of consumption demand and investment demand. If the two fractions added up to more than one, there would be demand-induced inflation with rising prices. If they added up to less than one there would be unemployment and falling prices. Here he destroyed the classical economic view of savings and investment. Harrod rightly pointed out that the theory did not take into account the relationship between the various rates of growth of the different elements in the economy. If consumption demand were growing faster than investment demand – through an inordinate rise in wages – there would be cost-inflation and rising prices. Keynes, of course, knew all this but not long after the publication of the *General Theory* he fell ill. Then the war came and he was overworked at the Treasury and at Bretton Woods. He had no time and no energy to develop or revise his theories but he would have been the first to recognise that as soon as the American and British governments had adopted the Keynesian White Paper of 1944 on Full Employment as their official economic policy after the war, giving full employment the priority over any other policy, bargaining-power passed to the trade unions in all future wage negotiations. He would have said immediately that cost-inflation would follow and his remedy for it would have been forced savings. I had no opportunity to discuss with him my own scheme for forced savings – by deducting so much from pay packets for investment in a public unit trust – which I put before Harold Wilson at a later date, but I have not the slightest doubt that he would have approved of it. Unfortunately he was killing himself over the 1945–6 negotiations for the American and Canadian loans. He died in 1946 before he had time to prove that Keynesian economic theories do not collapse but develop.

Incidentally I have found a letter from Keynes dated 17 April 1945 which was in answer to an article I had written on the post-war monetary settlement :

> MY DEAR NICHOLAS,
> Thank you for your letter. I had been on the point of writing to you today that the implication of your whole article was that nothing could be more improbable than my wanting to tie sterling to gold! Why, therefore, believe something so preposterous? Yours,
> MAYNARD KEYNES

But the IMF compromise he had to agree to – a gold exchange standard based on the gold dollar – was not one he really believed in. The world clearing union with a super world bank was his ideal solution, which the Americans refused to consider.

Ever since a curious and sinister encounter I had in Munich in the summer of 1932 I had felt that war with Germany was inevitable. I was going for a holiday in Austria with a girl friend and had arranged to meet in Munich Graham Hutton, his wife Madl, and Judith Marffy-Mantuano, who became the first Lady Listowel. (It was Judith who had brought Graham and Madl together when they were all three at the London School of Economics.) It was on 3 July 1932, the day of a German general election. I had asked Walter Layton, who was then chairman of the *News Chronicle*, whether he would like an article on Hitler's financial policy. He agreed, but doubted whether I could see anyone who mattered. After we had arrived in Munich Graham, Madl, Judith and I went to a *Bierhalle* to watch the people and listen to the election news. They all looked very glum, drinking hard and talking little. For the first time the Nazis had won more votes than any other party, but not an absolute majority. This they never got. I have kept in a drawer a copy of the *Volkischer Beobachter* 1–2 August 1932, which gave the Nazi party 13,732,777 votes out of a total of 36,560,000 and 229 seats out of 617. Late in the night we went to the Brown House to see what was going on. The place was in tumult because the Nazis

(*previous page*) Keynes as seen by David Low.

(*above and below*) Two views of Hinton Manor.

NEW LEVELLERS AT HINTON

From left to right Anthony Crosland, Nicholas Davenport, 'Dobbs' Little, Hugh Dalton, Ian Little.

(below) From left to right Douglas Jay, Margaret Jay, Anthony Quinton, Olga, Nicholas.

FRIENDS AT
HINTON IN
THE FIFTIES

Sir Matthew Smith.

Enid Starkie on the
terrace.

The Yogi, not the
Commissar – Arthur
Koestler sunbathing.

Jennifer and Roy
Jenkins with their son.

(*left*) Stephen Potter
and Richard Crossman.
(*below left*) *From left to
right* Olga, Deborah's
daughters 'Frankie' and
Melanie, Deborah Kerr.

(*above*) Olga Edwardes
the actress.

(*right*) Olga Davenport
the painter.

(*following page*) Olga and
Nicholas at an Oxford
'Commem' ball.

expected raids from the police at any moment. Ugly-looking uniformed despatch riders darted in and out of the forecourt as if a civil war was on, which in a way, was indeed the case.

Next morning we went to the Brown House to seek an interview. As we were arguing with a storm trooper, who denied our entry, 'Putzi' Hanfstaengl, Hitler's press chief, came into the hall. He had met Judith in London and with an eye always to a pretty girl he invited us to his room, unlocking doors as he went. Judith explained that I was an economist interested in the Nazi financial and economic policy, especially their attitude to the German 'Dawes' and 'Young' loans. Would the Nazis repudiate them if they came to power? 'Those filthy Jewish loans?' he shouted, 'Extorted by those swinish Jewish usurers?' He walked round the room, spluttering with rage. 'Of course we shall repudiate them', he went on. 'Is that the Führer's policy?' I asked. 'The Führer does not understand these financial things', he replied 'but he knows who knows, and I will get you the answers if you will write out your questions and hand them in'. I asked: 'Who is it who knows?' Putzi put his fingers to his lips as if telling a top secret: 'Dr Schacht!' he said. As Dr Schacht was regarded as a respectable and non-political German banker, head of the Deutsche Bank, I was greatly surprised and shocked. 'If you like,' he added, 'you can hand the questions to me tonight: I shall be at the Opera House with the Führer'.

We rushed back to our hotel and I dictated ten questions to Judith who typed them out in German. (She described them in her book *This I Have Seen* as 'the most tricky lot of economic traps I have ever read'). We were late for the opera and arrived as the audience was coming out into the foyer after the first act. I saw Putzi, Hitler and two nondescript women slowly emerging and then an extraordinary thing happened. There was a sudden silence as Hitler entered the foyer. Everyone had turned their backs on the Hitler entourage and had stopped talking. Although the election had gone in the Nazi favour the people of Munich were obviously dumbfounded and determined to show their disapproval and disgust. It was a dramatic moment which I shall never forget.

I advanced towards Hitler with my paper in my hand. He stared at me with that peculiar look of a stage hypnotist. The Chaplin moustache and the forelock drooping down over his fore-

E

head gave him a musical hall appearance. He was correctly dressed in a dinner-jacket with a gold swastika emblem on his lapel. Putzi, imaging that I was going to confound Hitler with some rude journalist question, stepped in front and refused to let me hand the questions to Hitler personally. Judith then described the scene as follows : 'Then we shook hands with Hitler. He had well-shaped sensitive hands, quite out of keeping with the rest of his appearance. Hitler did not speak a word. We who felt very superior also remained silent.' Personally I cannot remember shaking hands with Hitler. If I had done so I am sure I would have felt the shiver of the cold hand of death.

Next day Graham and I were back at the Brown House to get the answers. Judith had gone on to Budapest. 'Why did you let that Calypso go,' asked Putzi angrily, 'when she was in your grasp?' (I hasten to add that Judith was never in my grasp.) We were then given the answers – presumably from Dr Schacht. The Nazis would default on these Jewish loans 'for good and compelling reason' was the substance of the reply. I went back to the hotel, wrote my notes, rang the *News Chronicle* to dictate my dispatch, exposing Dr Schacht as Hitler's financial adviser, and retired discreetly to a hotel in the mountains above Munich with my charming companion.

There was a curious sequel. The news editor of the *News Chronicle* must have thought that my dispatch was rather dull and technical. To give it more life he had inscribed across the front page in bold letters: 'Our special Correspondent's Interview with Herr Hitler.' I was unaware of the great sensation this 'interview' and exposure of Dr Schacht had caused until I got back to London. The Brown House indignantly denied the interview and demanded a correction which they never got.

I went on from Munich to visit the Brown House in Vienna. I was there shown over the whole office by a proud Austrian Nazi. He took me into the board room where a huge map of the city was displayed, with Nazi flags stuck into the factories where there were Nazi cells. 'Are you a branch of the Brown House in Munich?' I asked. 'A branch! We are one! We are one body and Hitler is our Führer.' 'Where do you keep your arms?' I asked, with an innocent expression. 'Do not ask', he smiled. On the way out he pointed to the names of Jewish tenants in the neighbouring apartment house. 'You will see those filthy names disappear when we get into power', he added. He made a noise like 'phut' with his tongue, and passed his hand across his throat. It was not many years afterwards that Dollfus was assassinated and these Austrian Nazis came into power.

What must have angered Hitler was that an English journalist had exposed on 30 August 1932, Dr Schacht, a respectable German banker, as a Nazi and an active ally. Without Dr Schacht's ingenuity as a financier – he invented the bilateral agreements which enabled the Nazis to secure enough foreign exchange for their rearmament – Hitler could never have gone to war. Although, before the end of the war, Dr Schacht fell foul of the Führer and was found in a concentration camp by the advancing Americans, I thought he was extremely lucky to be reprieved at the Nuremberg trial.

I never went back to Germany. Judith, having a diplomatic passport, did so but was always watched and followed. She was put on the Nazi black list. There was a further extraordinary sequel to this story. Putzi Hanfstaengl fell into disfavour with Hitler, having come up against Dr Goebbels. When the Spanish Civil War was raging, Putzi received an order from Hitler to fly to Spain on some public relations matter. The aeroplane touched down in an airport near Leipzig for refuelling and the flight captain, who was a friend, said to Putzi: 'You know what my mission is? Drop you behind the Republican lines!' 'Thank you', said Putzi. He took to his heels and ran off the aerodrome.

He found his way to Switzerland and then to London where he was received by the Anglo-German Fellowship with great cordiality and of course invited to the Cliveden parties. In the course of his gay life in London he got some rude publicity in the *Daily Express* and the *Evening Standard*. Both papers quoted some heated words at a party between him and Lady Listowel about the famous interview in Munich. The next day the 'Londoner's Diary' in the *Evening Standard* published an account of his cocktail row and said that Lady Listowel protested when Putzi called some Oxford professors, who had made some adverse remarks about Nazi justice, 'a lot of *Schweinhund*'. Putzi sued both papers for libel. When the case came into court Putzi's counsel said that Lady Listowel's words could not be believed because 'She and a Mr Nicholas Davenport were responsible in August 1932 for the greatest journalistic fraud of all time – a faked interview with Herr Hitler'. The judge made some facetious remarks about journalists in general and Mr Davenport in particular and the jury found for Putzi, awarding him £2,000 damages. When war broke out Putzi was interned. Exploiting the fact that he had once been a Harvard graduate he wrote to the State Department in Washington and asked for a job as an adviser. Having been an intimate friend of Hitler he claimed that he could explain and uncover the Nazi mind. I believe he was actually employed in Washington for the rest of the war. Afterwards, he wrote a mendacious book saying 'I warned Hitler'. Not a word of remorse for the persecution of the Jews which had begun long before he fell foul of Dr Goebbels.

As the grim feeling of the certainty of war grew upon us in the late thirties, the City became divided. A section of it, which hated communism much more than fascism, clung to the hope, as Neville Chamberlain did, that the mad dog in Germany would attack Russia and leave us in peace. *Mein Kampf* had suggested it. Some were even prepared to do a deal with Hitler. Not only the reactionary Tory set but also some of the faint-hearted liberals became willing to compromise. I heard that during the weeks before war was actually declared, a party of City right-wingers flew to Potsdam to meet Goering to see if it was not possible to make a deal with Hitler even at the eleventh hour. Strict secrecy was observed and the truth about this appeasement party will never be told. Its leader's name was revealed to me but I was pledged to silence.

My City partner John Tennant had a cousin, Lord Glenconner, who ran the great chemical firm of C. Tennant and Sons which did a large trade with Germany. One day John said to me that he would like to introduce me to Ernest Tennant, who often went on business to Germany and met the top people of the Nazi Party. He invited me to a lunch at the Great Eastern Hotel to meet him. Ernest had just spent the previous weekend in Germany with Ribbentrop. He spoke enthusiastically about Ribbentrop and of the wonderful things which the Nazi Government was doing for the German people. Unemployment had disappeared. Naturally, I remarked, through rearmament. He had met, he said, a man named Himmler who struck him as a quiet, intellectual sort of schoolmaster, and to his surprise he had discovered that he was head of the secret police. The next weekend,

30 June 1934 turned out to be 'the night of the long knives', when Hitler, Goering and Himmler murdered in cold blood Colonel Roehm and the other leaders of the SA army.

In the City I was active in the opposite camp to the appeasers and joined a committee chaired by Arthur Salter (now Lord Salter) set up to consider the practical issues involved in the mobilisation of shipping and the accumulation of stocks of consumer goods. Vickers, a First World War VC, held meetings in the City to warn people of the Nazi menace and to get them prepared for war. Bob Boothby was also active in public speeches and behind the scenes, as indeed were all the friends of Churchill, who was leading the opposition to appeasement.

I was busy writing in the *New Statesman* exposing the bilateral agreements of Dr Schacht and the finance of German rearmament in 1936 when I had a serious accident which might have put me on crutches for the rest of my life. Douglas Jay had brought down to Hinton a glamorous actress for a gay weekend party, and in a wild dance on the lawn after dinner I took a flying leap over a rose bush, fell and tore my Achilles tendon so badly that it was doubtful whether it could be sewn up, but a clever South African surgeon at the Nuffield Home in Oxford managed to do a miracle. Among the letters of sympathy from my friends I treasure this one from Lydia Keynes :

Tilton,
Firle, Sussex.
2 August 1936

MY DEAR NICHOLAS,

Maynard told me about your Achilles, and I was upset, but he also told me that in a week's time you turned around thread and needle street and that the foot was mending.

Won't you come to us for a weekend on August the 15th? It will be lovely to have you.

What a splendid thing you wrote in the N.S. So wise, so clear, so strong. M. was delighted with it. Yours,

LYDIA KEYNES

I remember going to a dinner in the House of Commons which Bob Boothby gave for a few friends to meet Churchill. It was after Hitler's march into the Rhineland in March 1936. Chase was there with Walter Elliott and another Member of Parliament, whose name I cannot remember. Churchill came in late, moody and ill-tempered. He tucked into his food without saying a word. It was slightly embarrassing until the brandy and cigars came round. Then, while we were all silent, he began to speak, telling us of the secret preparations for war which were being made in Germany and of the ferocity and brutality of the aggressive Nazis. We were all shocked and alarmed. Chase went away firmly convinced that when war was declared there would be fifty thousand casualties in London on the first night of bombing. 'You won't be able to motor down to your beautiful Hinton Manor;' he said, 'the roads will be blocked by the debris and the stampeding refugees. I'll tell you what we must do. You and I will buy a motor boat and moor it at Westminster Pier. It will be the only way to escape out of London. We'll take Bob with us, as he will know exactly what the Government is up to over the evacuation.' The boat, thank Heaven, was never purchased.

Looking back on the grand climacterics of history most of us will blush at the memory of how we failed to live up to the dramatic moment. On 3 September 1939 – how flat Neville Chamberlain made that historic declaration of war sound! – the group listening to the radio at Hinton Manor included Gabriel Pascal, the Hungarian film impresario, his American secretary and girl friend, Marion Baldwin, his art director, Lawrence Irving, grandson of the great actor, and an actress friend of mine, Leslie Brook, whose brother had won the first airman VC in the First World War. We were all silent and then we muttered that war must not interfere with the shooting of *Major Barbara* at Denham Studios! Gabriel proudly wrote in the house book: 'This war will be the Renaissance of English culture and art, and I will do my best for my part in it.' Alas! Poor Gabriel did not live to see what strange things happened to English culture in the late 1960s. The American girl briefly scribbled: 'I am proud to be an American. I'm proud to be in England.' That properly expressed the feeling abroad – a mixture of amazement and admiration at Britain's quixotic stand against the gathering forces of evil.

I must explain how this curious film gathering came about. In 1938 I had been mad enough to invest £3000 – eventually £3800 – in a syndicate of angels to finance a film starring Pola Negri and directed by Dr Czinner, the husband of the famous

German actress, Elizabeth Bergner. It was a dreadful film, and we lost all our money, but it convinced me that I really knew how not to produce British films. My only consolation was that it gave me some comic relief from City life. My holiday job was to be bodyguard for Pola who was besieged by the holiday crowds whenever she left the hotel in St Ives. Once in the car, she would pull up her skirt and pull out a brandy flask which she had tucked inside the top of her stocking. 'Guard this, Nicholas, with your life', she said. I have never seen anyone drink so much – champagne, brandy and absinthe were the usual round – yet I never found her drunk. Her acting was dynamic, but I was often called in to stop her walking out. 'Is he vealthy?' was her usual question if I brought a friend to watch the shooting. Her appearance was so striking – blue-black hair, enormous dark eyes and a white skin covered in thick make-up – that if we walked into a restaurant there would be a deadly silence; everyone would stop eating to stare. It was this film which brought me into touch with the most remarkable impresario of the film world – Gabriel Pascal – for it was he who miraculously sold the European rights of the film for us creditors.

In the summer of 1938 I was standing on the platform at Oxford Station waiting for the London train to arrive. As it drew in I saw the window of a first class carriage open and a dark head with sleek black hair shouted out in Continental English : '*Nikolas, komm here!*' It was Gabriel Pascal. He was in a great fever of excitement. He had been to the Malvern festival, had captivated Bernard Shaw, and produced from his pocket a letter with Shaw's unmistakable signature giving him the sole right to make a film version of *Pygmalion*. Shaw loved flamboyant rogues, impostors, *flaneurs* – provided they had an inner spark of truth and humour. The tales Gabriel told him might have come from a character in a Shavian play – how he had been a member of the Imperial Company of Actors at the Court of the Emperor Francis Joseph, how he had got into trouble by telling a naughty story which had convulsed the Emperor's mistress in her villa on the very afternoon, decreed by protocol, for the Emperor's visit, how he had read every Shaw play while he was incarcerated in the guard-room, and how he had been convinced by a vision of the Virgin Mary that it was his destiny to make a film version of *Pygmalion*, the world's greatest comedy. 'That's all very well,' said Shaw, 'I've had many people after it from Hollywood. How much money have you got?' Gabriel put his hand in his pocket and produced half-a-crown. 'That is all, *maestro,* but I get more.' 'Good heavens,' replied Shaw, 'you are the first honest man I have met in the film business. You shall have the *Pygmalion* contract.'

'This will make a fortune', said Gabriel to me in the train, 'but I cannot do it unless you help. I am broke and you must raise five thousand pounds immediately to get the scenario written for the maestro's approval.' Before the train had reached Paddington I had agreed. I was a devoted Shavian; *Pygmalion* was Shaw's greatest comedy; it could not fail on the screen because it was essentially a Cinderella story. So I went the round of my friends in the City and got four of them to put up with me £1000 each. Wendy Hillier was signed as Eliza, Leslie Howard as Higgins, and Anthony Asquith as co-director with Leslie. The money soon vanished and I canvassed a second time for another £5000, one of the new subscribers being Henry Andrews, the husband of Rebecca West. Then we got C. M. Woolf, the distributor for Rank, to give us a distributor's guarantee for £50,000 which was discountable at the bank. Woolf was sceptical when we first went to see him. '*Pygmalion?* A Greek story? Never'. 'But it's Bernard Shaw's greatest comedy' we cried. 'Too highbrow. We'll lose the lot.' But we convinced him, and in the end he went to see a try-out at Huddersfield before a mainly working-class audience who had not been advised of it beforehand. They laughed their heads off. Some stayed in their seats to hear 'not bloody likely' come a second time round. Woolf came home astonished. 'It's a box office clean up', he said.

Pygmalion was surely one of the greatest pre-war British films ever screened. It made film history by bringing good English and meaningful dialogue for the first time to the mass audience. Leslie Howard was the ideal Higgins; he did not have the vulgarity which Rex Harrison brought to *My Fair Lady*. Wendy Hillier was the ideal Eliza. Curiously, the bourgeois Birmingham accent she had was a help; she translated it into Cockney superbly. As I watched her outside the church in Covent Garden, where the first exterior scenes were shot, I saw Shaw's Eliza come vividly to life. The tea-party scene with its 'not bloody likely', was comedy of the classic order and never failed to bring the house down in convulsive laughter.

As usual with Pascal's enterprises there was a constant stream of financial crises. We had budgeted for £80,000 but had heavily over-spent. It was necessary to raise another £10,000 to enable Pascal to go to Hollywood and get an advance and a release from Metro-Goldwyn. I had to go again to Henry Andrews, who was the richest of my promoters. None the less, it was the most successful independent film to emerge from the British studios. Although we were fleeced by the distributors at home and abroad, who took much too high a percentage of the 'gross' box office receipts, although Pascal's extravangances were terrible, the company which Pascal and I owned (80%–20%) netted £50,000. We put it all in the next production of *Major Barbara* and lost the lot!

So this explains the film gathering at Hinton Manor when war was declared. But before I go on I must record the tragic end of poor Leslie Howard. During the 'phoney' war it was arranged for him to fly out to Gibraltar to do a show for the garrison, and he took with him our accountant, Chenhalls, who had an extraordinary likeness to Winston Churchill. A Nazi agent on the rock reported to the German High Command that Churchill had arrived in Gibraltar. They had Chenhalls shadowed, and when he took off with Leslie Howard in a non-military plane for Lisbon, a German fighter shot it down in the Bay of Biscay. This is the true story of the tragedy which Malcolm Muggeridge described, not quite accurately in his fascinating memoirs.

Major Barbara was the only film being shot in England on the outbreak of the war. Apart from this rash enterprise the film industry had closed down. We were the only company at work at Denham studios, and we had a man on the roof with a whistle to sound the alarm when the German fighter planes came over. As soon as the Polish fighter squadron took off from Northolt to chase them away, the whistle blew again and we came up from the underground shelter to start work again. Wendy Hillier was Major Barbara. Robert Morley was Undershaft and Rex Harrison played the Greek professor, Cusins (in love with Barbara). During the shooting of the film I had to see Bernard Shaw several times to report on progress. He had been disquietened by the tales he had heard of trouble on the set. On one

E*

occasion he had said to me : 'Davenport, have you ever directed a film'? 'No, never.' I replied. 'Good,' he said. 'Then you are just the man for the job. You go on the set with a stop-watch. When the camera has taken in the dialogue you call out : "Time Gentlemen! Next shot please!" It will come out just the same. After all, it's my dialogue which makes the film.'

After the film had been released I went to see Shaw on various financial matters. He was always worried about his surtax – he claimed that he paid 21s in the pound which was impossible – and we had made use of some part of his ten percent royalties on *Pygmalion* for the finance of *Major Barbara*. One day I mentioned to him that I had written a play called *And So To Wed*. It was about a young man (Stephen) and a girl (Diana) who were having a love affair and a great row because Stephen did not believe in marriage, while Diana was longing to get married. The row came to a crisis when the father of the girl (Lilo) from Stephen's past love-life intervened to insist on Stephen's marrying Lilo. 'Can I read it?' Shaw asked. 'I would not dare to show it to you', I replied. 'Besides, my hero, Stephen, wanted to live with his girl, Diana, on a contract based on the wording of the lease of a flat – it is very funny when you substitute "bodies" for "premises" in a lease – and I found out that you had suggested a marriage contract in your *Getting Married* which I confess I had never read when I wrote my play.' 'Oh don't worry about that,' he said. 'I would like to read it because I take a professional's interest.' So I sent him the manuscript, and in due course I had it returned with the following delightful letter on how to write a play :

FROM BERNARD SHAW
                    TELEGRAMS : SOCIALIST-PARL LONDON
                                        4, Whitehall Ct,
                                        London S.W.1
                                        25 August 1943

DEAR DAVENPORT,
It was unlucky our both hitting on the same comedy of an attempt to draft an up-to-date marriage contract. The same thing happened to me once when I read the script of Jerome's *Passing of the Third Floor Back*, and found in it word for word, a scene which I had invented myself and intended to use.

There is a speech in one of my published plays which is also in one of Oscar Wilde's.

I have been trying to think of an alternative point of honor for Stephen, but have not succeeded so far. You might have a try; for the critics will accuse you of plagiarism if they have seen my *Getting Married* lately; and, besides, there are one or two laughs that the word 'premises' will raise which are all right for Hollywood but not quite on your level as a sociologist. There is a third reason for a change. It is very important that a first act should not only introduce the characters, but rouse and maintain expectancy. Without this the cleverest dialogue or the liveliest incident will not get the play going. Dialogue gives you no trouble; but you must not depend on it : it becomes wearisome unless the audience has a sense that it is leading somewhere, and are curious to find out where.

This is the only useful criticism I can make. The characterization is good : in fact it is almost too good, as the audience will want some more of Vardy and one or two others, and be disappointed at their having so little to do.

Just try for a fresh conscientious objection for Stephen, and consequently a fresh title for the play. It will not be very troublesome; and if you don't, the play will leave an impression that there is something against you long after everyone has forgotten what it is. Faithfully,

G. Bernard Shaw

PS I forgot to say that it is very dangerous to let the players laugh at the play or at their own or each other's witticisms. As a good working rule you may take it that if the players laugh the audience doesn't. Sheridan's ha ha has are now unbearable.

I re-wrote the final act to meet his criticism and sent it back with some trepidation. To my delight it was returned with some of my dialogue corrected by him in red ink and a few extra lines of his own added. His postcard ran :

I have made a few changes, partly mechanically through habit, but chiefly because the Lord Chamberlain may object to the reference to living persons (he sometimes does); but if you can say that I wrote them myself it will be alright.

GBS

The 'living persons' referred to himself and a French dramatist. The play was published in book form by Jonathan Cape with a postscript on marriage and procreation in the Shavian manner. The postscript began : ' It needs no Gallup Poll, no mass Observation, no Social Survey, or any other clever way of counting up the banalities of human thought, to decide that marriage can be everything – from legalised prostitution to a spiritual union of souls. But what should it be?' The book sold well, and several frustrated wives I knew telephoned to ask for a heart-to-heart talk.

Shaw never told me which of his plays had a sentence which is also in one of Oscar Wilde's but an American professor of drama, Martin Meisel, gave me this interpretation:

Wilde, *Lady Windermere's Fan* (1892) Act III.
Dumby: I congratulate you, my dear fellow. In this world there are only two tragedies. One is not getting what one wants, and the other is getting it. The last is much the worst; the last is a real tragedy!

Shaw, *Man and Superman* (1903) Act IV.
Mendoza: Sir: there are two tragedies in life. One is to lose your heart's desire. The other is to gain it. Mine and yours, sir.

One curious result of *Major Barbara* was my playing Pygmalion to Deborah Kerr. When we were casting Jenny – the Salvation Army girl who is slapped in the face by the drunken bruiser, who was Robert Newton – a film agent sent along a girl of eighteen with auburn hair to see Gabby and me in his room at the Mayfair Hotel for a test. 'Recite the Lord's Prayer' thundered Gabby to the terrified girl. After a moment's concentration she recited the prayer in the most moving fashion. We had found our Jenny! Everyone on the set acclaimed her scene with Robert Newton, especially as her lip was swollen from his clout. When the film was finished her aunt, who was a professional drama teacher in Bristol, asked me to keep an eye on Deborah and manage her contracts. The first star role I signed for her was *Love on the Dole*, the famous play by Walter Greenwood. She was superb. Then followed *Hatters Castle* with Robert Newton – again she got slapped, which enhanced her reputation for sensitivity – and finally she reached the top as the star in *Colonel Blimp* which was directed and produced by Michael Powell, in whose hands I left her. It was certainly a diversion from City life to play Pygmalion to such a talented actress. She was living at the YWCA hostel in London when she came to me; I had her fitted out – with the help of one of the editors of *Vogue* – with a complete wardrobe before the clothes rationing scheme overtook us; and I introduced her at a ball to the Berkshire county. It was, in its way a Cinderella story, for she finally went to Hollywood at £1000 a week under a contract to MGM, which I had arranged when I was with Korda.

8

War-time: The Board of Trade and the Vested Interests

The Stock Exchange remained open during the war – there was never a day when the capital market ceased to function – but turnover was a small fraction of the normal and the broking houses were kept going by a few elderly members while the younger ones were away in the services. The leading equity shares dropped in price by about a third, but never went down to the 1931 disaster levels. By the end of 1941 they had begun to rise again. By the end of 1944 the *Financial Times* index had reached 140 against 88 in 1941. Capitalism had survived another devastating crisis. But again Keynes had intervened to help. His advice and influence at the Treasury caused money to remain strictly controlled and cheap. We fought the greatest war in world history on a three per cent basis.

On the outbreak of war I offered Hinton Manor to the Oxford hospital authorities. It was refused. At that time there was no piped water in the village and no main drainage. It was still regarded as a remote and medieval part of the world. Before long some soldiery appeared and inspected it for a take-over. I then consulted a friend who happened to be second-in-command of MI5 – Brigadier Jasper Harker, late of the Indian police. (He had married Sidney Russell Cooke's sister). When the MI5 office at Wormwood Scrubs had been bombed and the staff had been removed to Blenheim Palace, which was sixteen miles away from Hinton, he served a billeting order on the manor on behalf of MI5. For him no doubt it was a wise precaution; for me it was a stroke of luck. He and his wife motored down every Friday night and brought me with them. The remoteness and secrecy of

Hinton Manor doubtless appealed to an officer in charge of MI5. It also appealed to the Ministry of Food who came and stored emergency rations for the village in the saddle-room of the stable block, where the rats quickly got to work.

In 1940, when the German air force held undisputed sway over our skies, everyone expected a Nazi airborne division to land on the Berkshire downs ten miles away. So I joined the Home Guard for the defence of the village. For a long time the only weapon we possessed was my sporting gun, for which I had provided heavy buckshot. I was proud of the fact that the manor could produce its own 'Molotov cocktails'. I had a huge stack of empty Gordon's gin bottles which we filled with petrol. One shot from my sporting gun sent a gin bottle ablaze. The stock of bottles was enlarged after a visit from Hugh Dalton who had been appointed Minister of Economic Warfare. This is how he described it in *The Fateful Years*:

> On June 22 1940 for the first time since I became a Minister I spent a night out of London. I drove down with John and Elsa Wilmot to Nicholas Davenport's most agreeable house at Hinton Waldrist near Faringdon. The Home Guard were out and when we asked the way at a rural road crossing they demanded our identity cards. 'What's the game?' they cried in tones of menace and suspicion. Next day I inspected and addressed a detachment of them in Davenport's stable yard. I had nearly created a local crisis earlier by inadvertently ringing an outside bell in the garden. The order was that no outside bells and no church bells were to be rung any more except if German parachutists should appear. Fortunately the bell was not heard save by the household.

It was, in fact, heard by the whole village, but by this time the arrival of the Minister of Economic Warfare was local talk.

I took my turn at night sentry duty and remember on bright moonlight nights jumping into the ditch whenever a German bomber passed unmolested overhead. I surveyed the manor grounds with a view to its defence, imagining that I was back in the civil war between King Stephen and the Queen Mother Matilda when Hinton was in the centre of the fighting. After Dunkirk, we had for a short time a detachment of 'regular' machine gun men who bivouacked in the park and dug a trench which was immediately filled with water. They were soon bored to death and I was relieved when they departed. We had arranged two elaborate fire posts – one at the east and the other at the west approach to the village. On the west, where the road comes up from the Berkshire downs, we posted a man behind the hedge who was to throw my 'Molotov cocktails' at the approaching German cars. He was in the direct line of fire of our rifles on the other side of the road. Clearly, the first casualty of the war, if it came to Berkshire, would be a gallant Hinton man gloriously falling victim to the sharp-shooting of our own Home Guard. It was all in the finest traditions of *Dad's Army*.

I well remember the night in August 1940 when the Commanding Officer at Faringdon rang me up at midnight to say that the Germans had set sail from the Dutch ports for the invasion. 'Get your men out and man your posts', he ordered. I went into the Brigadier's bedroom to warn him. 'Jasper, the balloon has gone up', I said. 'The Germans are on their way across the Channel'. 'Don't be a fool,' he replied, 'MI5 hasn't telephoned'. And he turned over and went to sleep. We all looked pretty foolish when the dawn came with no order from headquarters. Some of the men became restive, as they had cows to milk, so I dismissed them on my own authority. Finally I was left alone feeling cold, forlorn and forgotten. When my ex-farm hand motored past me in his own car on the way to the motor factories at Cowley I called it off and went back to a late breakfast. But we never received any orders from Faringdon to dismiss.

The brief training I received at the Home Guard headquarters at Coleshill, near Faringdon, was designed, I discovered later, to fit me and my squad for infiltration behind the German lines if they really landed on the Berkshire downs. It was a training in dirty warfare for the Berkshire Maquis. I was shown how to derail a train. For that dark purpose you must have a sharp curve in the railway line (which we had at Faringdon) and a tin of oil to put on the rails. I was assured that an engine would then topple over when it came hurtling round the bend. I was also taught how to dispose of a German sentry. You had to creep up behind him silently, pull his tunic back over his shoulders, drop his trousers down his legs, and kick him in the balls. This legerdemain would have defeated me. I would obviously have been the first casualty.

How many local tragedies and scandals were avoided when Hitler refused to sign the order for invasion and Britain remained free! The Commanding Officer of the Home Guard at Faringdon came one day to ask me whether I had carefully examined the men in my squad to satisfy myself that they would all turn up in the hour of danger. I had to answer that I suspected one or two would be trading briskly with the Germans on the black market and selling our local pheasants as soon as they had arrived. An Oxford friend, the late Enid Starkie, a fellow of Somerville College, told me that she had heard of at least one Latin oration which had been composed to welcome Hitler should he come to Oxford to receive his honorary degree in the Humanities.

The danger of invasion passed and the manor happily survived the sporadic local bombing. On 19 March 1941, eighteen bombs were dropped by a German aircraft returning home after bombarding the aerodrome at Stanton Harcourt, and the last four landed on my land, destroying one apple tree in the lower orchard. I showed a piece of the shrapnel from the bomb crater to Air Marshall 'Bomber' Harris who came one night to dine and play bridge with Brigadier Harker. I remember this occasion well, because in the middle of a rubber the telephone rang. It was 'Bomber' Harris's headquarters at High Wycombe. There was a dead silence while he took up the receiver in the ante-room. We gathered from the conversation that there had been a drastic change in weather conditions over the German target of the night. A long pause and then we heard the Air Marshall saying 'Then make it – ' Presumably a new target had been chosen, a few thousand Germans had been spared, and a few thousand others been marked for annihilation. I thought of Browning's lines in *Caliban upon Setebos*:

> Am strong myself compared to yonder crabs
> That march now from the mountain to the sea;
> Let twenty pass and stone the twenty-first,
> Loving not, hating not, just choosing so.

Among the letters I kept of the war period at Hinton, I came across one from the Commanding Officer of the Faringdon Home Guard, Colonel T. Allen Stevens, dated 30 May 1941 :

Thanks for your letter. I quite appreciate your present position and that resignation seems the only alternative. I am very sorry that you are going. If the invasion does come and you are at Hinton I hope you will join the party! Will you please return your equipment.

I resigned from the local Home Guard because I had been appointed by the Board of Trade as Public Relations Officer for the war-time Clothes Rationing Scheme, on 30 December 1941. This was a fascinating experience in psychological warfare. The people resented the bureaucrats – the bureaucrats resented the people. The main opposition came from the Woman Editor of the *Daily Mirror*, the wife of Ernest Betts, but finally I won her over. She saw I was doing my best to make the bureaucrats human and reasonable. I forced that stuffy department, the Board of Trade, to permit – for the first time I believe – 'off-the-record' press conferences, where the officials could speak freely to journalists who were, of course, under obligation not to reveal State secrets. I found myself often fighting the bureaucrats harder than I fought the press. For example, I objected strongly to Sir Francis Meynell's slogan 'Fair Shares for All'. The same number of coupons which a poor woman required to buy a cloth coat would enable a rich woman to buy a mink coat. I told them that in our present social *mélange* of inequality there was no such thing as 'Fair Shares for All'! But they insisted on propagating this outrageous social lie.

My work at the Board of Trade opened my eyes to the nature of the British Civil Service. It is an enclosed monastic order. Clever young men from Oxford and Cambridge who pass top in the examinations go immediately into the Whitehall cloisters and thereafter are shut off from the outside world. They have no experience of life, much less of business life, no knowledge of manufacturing or of trading or of finance. They do not pass through technical or business colleges as they do in America and even in France. They become isolated from the main stream of our natural thought, and the isolation makes them blind, bigoted and opinionated. They also become obsessed with the power game of status – how to climb the Civil Service ladder from clerk to assistant secretary and secretary of their departments.

The monasticism of the Civil Service had some hilariously funny results in the Clothes Rationing Scheme. Secrecy was the order of the day and the committee which drew up the 'loading' code for the coupons attaching to each garment were not able to consult the outside world. They made the egregious mistake of loading French panties with a much larger number of coupons than those assigned to a legless pantie, not knowing that French panties were virtually legless. When the mistake was discovered another order under the Emergency Powers Act was solemnly issued to give French panties their rightful place in a rationed – but irrational – world.

The corridor of the Millbank office of the Board of Trade in which I worked – now the head office of ICI – was dark and cavernous and depressing for anyone who had been accustomed to the free air and talk of Hinton. The monotonous minutes mounting on the files which passed from room to room were deadening to the mind. I imagined that I was living in an underground cave where the monastic order of civil servants had been turned into stalactites and stalagmites. The stalactites were the temporary civil servants who kept dripping minutes on the stalagmites, who were the permanent civil servants. The effect of the dripping was that the stalagmites grew higher and higher until they reached the roof of the cavern and became unapproachable. It was a nightmarish experience, brought on by the frustration I felt at never being able to see the head of my department except after weeks of meaningless minuting. My incarceration at the Board of Trade lasted about eighteen months. It had two important results for me and Hinton Manor. The first was the writing of another book – *The Vested Interests or Common Pool* – which had some relevance for the coming 'Puritan' revolution – and the second was a chance meeting with a beautiful young actress, a most unusual personality, Olga Edwardes, who became my wife. This meeting came about in an amusing way.

To educate the public on the Clothes Rationaing Scheme in 1940–1, I gave popular radio talks on the BBC and was fortunate to secure as partner in the act Elizabeth Cowell the famous wartime broadcaster – the girl with a honeyed voice, jet black hair and a beautiful classical face. (She is now the wife of Alistair Balfour of Dawyk in Peebleshire.) She acted as my stooge, whose role it was to misunderstand or abuse the clothes coupon code of the Board of Trade and receive angry correction from me. The

start of the broadcasts was somewhat frigid and I asked my talks
director, who happened to be Guy Burgess – he was always
extremely helpful this side of the Iron Curtain – if I could take
Elizabeth out to lunch and break down the ice barrier. We
became great friends and she kept asking me to meet her girl
friends saying that it was about time I got married again. At one
of her cocktail parties, when I was supposed to meet a desirable
blonde from the War Cabinet Office, I saw across the room a
beautiful brunette talking to a guest animatedly. She had a
retroussé nose, the high cheekbones of the Slav, long dark eye-
lashes, the heavy lidded eyes of an infant Buddha, and a very
clear, cultured English voice. She was unique. I went over to
intervene in the conversation, in the rude way tolerated at
cocktail parties and was immediately, but with charm and
humour, put in my place. This made me determined to take her
out to dinner and after the party, emboldened by many gins, I
pushed aside a man who was actually getting her into a taxi and
before she had time to protest I told the driver to go to *L'Ecu de
France*, a restaurant where I was well known and could be sure of
a table. There over the dinner I proposed. She raised a quizzical
eyebrow and said : 'Perhaps you will ask me again when you are
sober'. I did.

Olga Edwardes, I discovered, was born in South Africa with
Russian, French, Irish and Scottish blood in her veins. Her father,
who died tragically young, was a distinguished architect and
portrait painter. Her mother had acted successfully on the
London stage and after her marriage had produced plays in Cape
Town and had gathered round her an interesting circle of artists
and intellectuals. Olga must have inherited talents from both
parents. Sometimes as a child she was in her mother's plays and
she had exhibited a painting in the South African Academy when
she was fifteen. She had intended to make painting her career but
in her teens the family came back to England and a change in
their fortunes obliged her to earn her living. Chance led her to
ballet dancing – she worked for a while with Anton Dolin – and
then she went on to be a straight actress. In her first leading role,
opposite Frances Sullivan at the Apollo theatre in London, the
press headlined her as a new star. She was a fine Shavian actress,
playing opposite Esme Percy for the Macdonagh Players. When
she played Eliza in *Pygmalion* at the Manchester Opera House

the *Guardian* critic, an elderly man who remembered Mrs Patrick Campbell, compared her favourably with that great actress. And on her performance as Mrs Dubedat in *The Doctor's Dilemma* he wrote: 'In her, there is not only charm and grace, but a spirit of intelligence which animates the whole of her playing.' After our marriage she continued her very successful stage and film career, and when eventually she decided to return to her painting, Sir John Gielgud in a letter to her said that he thought it a great pity that she had given up the theatre. Personally I was not sorry, for she went on to make a success of her painting. Her first one-man show at the Piccadilly Gallery in 1969 was a sell-out, and, what pleased her most, was praised by the artists she most admired.

And she could cook! I therefore counted myself lucky when, after much talk and exchange of books and coming and going at Hinton, I was eventually accepted. We were married one day at the Henley Register Office on our way down to Hinton and our best man was her soldier brother, Paul Edwardes, who had won the MC at the storming of Walcheren Island. The registrar seemed much more concerned about my getting Olga's food ration card than about our future happiness.

Olga's introduction to some of my more conservative neighbours in north-west Berkshire proved dramatic. 'But I hate the common people, don't you?' said a local baronet at a Hinton lunch party. 'I am afraid I cannot remain in the room with anyone who makes a remark like that,' she replied and rose from the table. She became known as my 'bolshie' chatelaine. I should add that she was a war widow when we met. Her first marriage had been to a promising young writer, Anthony Baerlein, who had been killed on a bombing raid over Germany. His first novel *Daze the Magician* had been highly praised.

Olga, being a sensitive, intellectual girl, always seemed to inspire writers to write and poets to compose. As a young actress she was going to catch a train one day to play in a theatre at Frinton-on-Sea when she met A. P. Herbert in Piccadilly. As she had no time to stop and chat he said he would travel down to Frinton with her and catch the next train back. The following day she received this poem which he had written in the train on the way home:

> Is he so mad who travels to the shore
> Then back at once to where he was before?
> Does not the Ocean, under Olga's sway,
> Commit the same sweet folly twice a day?
> Thus the mad fish pursue the Moon in vain,
> But will, as happily, pursue again.
> Thus climbers, having made the steep ascent,
> Salute the stars, and then return – content.

If only APH had lived to write another poem in the train –
with matching inspiration – on Princess Anne's marriage!

I settled down at Hinton to write my book *The Vested Interests*
late in 1940. I tried out my ideas first in some articles in the *New
Statesman* and got an encouraging letter from Maynard Keynes:

46 Gordon Square,
Bloomsbury,
1 November 1940

My Dear Nicholas,

I thought your articles most brilliant, particularly the last but
one, which is one of the best things you have ever done. I am in
agreement with nearly all your destructive criticisms, but am,
of course, not so happy about your constructive ideas.

I understand quite well what happens with those activities
which you forthwith socialise. But I do not exactly comprehend
what the difference will be between your system and the
present state of affairs in the case of those which you lease. I
wish you would write another article taking four leading
typical cases and exhibit in exact detail in what respects the
new arrangements differ from the old and in what respects they
would be the same. Yours,

J.M.K.

What stirred my indignation and had moved me to write, was
the sight of the 'vested interests' at work in the corridors of power
at the Board of Trade. I was convinced that if the war-time
coalition of big business and organised labour carried on into the
peace there would be a grave danger of a British corporate state.
The Churchill Government had taken over the entire national
resources of capital and labour for the duration of the war and
had invited the leaders of 'big business' into the Board of Trade

and the Ministry of Production to control the supplies and direct the output of the munitions of war. It never occurred to them to appoint 'national men' to control the output of big business. To the consternation of some of my friends, I disclosed in the book the names of the big business controllers who were 'inside' the department, controlling their own industries. As for Labour, the great trade union leader, Ernest Bevin, had been put in charge of the Ministry of Labour and could answer for the unions. Monopolism, I said, was as much the breath of trade unionism as it was of the new feudalism of big business. It seemed to me that if Britain was to be managed after the war by the employer associations and the trade unions joined together in an unholy alliance, practising a form of state capitalism, then prices and wages would have a free run, the consumer would be exploited and freedom of consumer choice would disappear. I consulted Bernard Shaw, and received a postcard from him expressing his agreement and saying: 'State aided capitalism is fascism. We invented it, Mussolini pioneered it and Hitler adulterated it with Jew-baiting and chosen-people egomania.'

The threat of a corporate state did not, in fact, pass away until Attlee refused to join a Churchill coalition after the war. But seven years later Richard Crossman still thought it necessary to write in *New Fabian Essays*: 'Today the enemy of freedom is the managerial society and the central coercive power which goes with it'.

After leaving the Board of Trade I had been invited by Alex Korda to join him in a personal advisory role after he had read a provocative article I had written for the *Evening Standard* on how to run the British film industry. Naturally I had been keeping in touch as far as I could with the political 'Levellers' who had been privy to our Hinton debates. Dalton at the Ministry of Economic Warfare was incommunicado until he went to the Board of Trade, but with Cripps I kept up a correspondence. At the beginning of the war he had been sent as ambassador to Moscow where he was extremely bored. Stalin at first refused to meet a member of the English upper-class who had become a socialist. I wrote to Cripps about my fears of the corporate state and again about the need to keep in mind the main object of the financial reforms which we had been debating at XYZ. I sent him two articles I had written on the post-war financial reforms for the *New Statesman*. The first letter I received was dated 7 December 1940 :

British Embassy,
Moscow.

DEAR NICHOLAS,
Thank you very much indeed for sending me the two articles out of the *N.S.* which I have read with great interest (as have also my staff here!) I think that there is a good deal in what you say and I suspect something along those lines may be the sort of compromise at which we shall arrive. It is all to the good that these things should be discussed now with a view to forming and crystallising public opinion. All good wishes in which my wife joins sincerely. Yours very sincerely,

STAFFORD

His second letter is dated 10 January 1941 :

British Embassy,
Moscow.

DEAR NICHOLAS,
I was very glad to get your third article which I have not only read but have translated into French for the benefit of some of my more intimate French speaking colleagues. . . . I wish I could see some signs of realisation of the need for a new world in our political directors. I see none and I fear more and more that we shall enter on the next 'Armistice period' as fatally as we did the last in 1918, with a repetition of all the follies and stupidities. I hope your work at least will serve to wake up the sleepers! Yours ever,

STAFFORD

When the *Vested Interests* had been sent to the printers, Stafford Cripps was back in England. He had asked to be recalled and returned in January 1942 to become Lord Privy Seal and Leader of the Commons. I have another letter from him – from Gwydyr House – which said :

28 April 1942

DEAR NICHOLAS,
I have just read the papers you sent to Lady Cripps including

the two reprints from the *New Statesman* which are most interesting and convincing. We are trying to get on to lines such as these in at least one direction at present – and I wish it were possible to go further – but we must bide our time for any great change – though the chance may come sooner than some of us suspect. Your book at any rate, will be very timely and interesting. Yours sincerely,

STAFFORD

At that time, Stafford was going through a period of intense strain and was losing his confidence in victory. He had begun to question Churchill's direction of the war. Everything indeed had gone wrong. Malaya and Singapore had been lost; two of our battleships had been ignominiously destroyed; and Rommel was on the frontiers of Egypt. It was the eve of the Battle of Alamein (October 1942). I heard the following story from Brendan Bracken who often used to come in for a post-midnight supper in Alexander Korda's penthouse in Claridges where my wife and I were frequent guests. One night, while he was waiting for the scrambled eggs and bacon Brendan suddenly burst out : 'I have never seen the old man so angry. He was pacing round and round the room in his boiler suit spluttering with rage. I knew what had happened. Stafford Cripps, against my strong advice, had been to see him.' Beginning to imitate Churchill's speech Bracken went on : 'This man [Stafford Cripps] had the hardihood – the hardihood – to come and tell me that he was dissatisfied with the conduct of the war. I thought of having him arrested on the spot. He dared to tell me that he had harboured the intention to resign and move a motion in the Commons for the appointment of a Committee of Public Safety. Like another bloody French Revolution ! I told him that we were on the eve of one of the decisive battles of world history – a battle which could turn the tide of war in our favour. I ordered him to remain silent until the battle had been fought and won. He gave me his word. Of course, he will have to go. I can't have him in the War Cabinet any longer.'

The sequel to the story was told to us by Brendan Bracken days later during another midnight supper. 'I have just been discussing with the old man', he said, 'the future of Stafford Cripps.' Again he began imitating Churchill. ' "I don't want to sack him",' [the PM said], ' "he had the decency to come and apologise to me after the battle had been won. Of course, he can't stay in the War Cabinet. Where do you think we can put him?" ' [Dead silence from me]. ' "Wait",' said Churchill, ' "wasn't he a manager of some factory at one time? Yes, of course, a munition factory in the First World War. . . . Then he can go to the Ministry of Aircraft and Production. The post is vacant and we need a good factory manager".'

Churchill never liked Stafford Cripps. He once said of him: 'He has all the virtues I dislike and none of the vices I admire'. But according to Brendan, he never bore Stafford any grudge for this extraordinary outburst in a moment of national danger. He never even referred to it in his memoirs. As far as I know this is the first time the story has been told.

Stafford was really happier in his new and less exalted office. I went to see him not long after he had taken over and found him grinning as I entered the room. 'Nicholas,' he said, 'I have just discovered the painless way to nationalise private enterprise. You simply negotiate a price and buy the equity shares'. He was referring to the State purchase of the Whittle jet engine company which had been financed and developed by O. T. Falk and Partners, as I have told. He had squeezed Foxy over the sharer, exacting a miserably low price of 63s 6d by the exercise of his ministerial *force majeure*. Stafford was no doubt preparing for the socialist takeover which he expected to come after the war.

The Vested Interests or Common Pool was published by Victor Gollancz in August 1942 and quickly ran through four impressions, the last being in March 1943. The book was extremely radical and shocked some of my Conservative friends, but it was written in the heat of wartime patriotism, roused in me by the extraordinary sacrifice of the fighting and working people. It had an ecstatic reception from the left. I received a postcard from Bernard Shaw which ran:

> The book is thoroughly deserving of its success. It takes its subject out of the morass of abstractions and Joseph Surface sentiments . . . and brings it into the practical world. A most useful set of suggestions and a good example to the abstraction merchants. And, for a wonder, a good book had a good press.

The best appraisal of the book was given by Harold Laski who wrote rather an embarrassing 'rave' review in the *New Statesman* of 15 August 1942 :

> If I had the power I would make Mr Davenport's book compulsory reading not only for every member of the House of Commons (above all for Mr Churchill and Mr Attlee), but also for every person who discusses the social and economic issues of the war. Sir Stafford Cripps, who has been painting pictures for us of the post-war Utopia that awaits us, if only nobody raises inconvenient questions now, ought to examine in these pages Mr Davenport's superb dissection of the foundations which are being prepared for the superstructure. Above all, I could wish that it could be read by that elusive animal the general reader. There might follow one of those bursts of public indignation which drives even coalition governments to mend their ways.
>
> Effectively, Mr Davenport shows that what has happened is that the vested interests of monopoly capitalism have, for all practical purposes, taken over the government of this country. Behind the façade of political democracy they are preparing the economic foundations of the corporate State; and, to no small extent, they are being aided and abetted in this task by the powerful trade unions. This part of Mr Davenport's book, written with precision, with clarity, and the expert knowledge of one who has seen the system from the inside, is worthy – and I am measuring my words – of the great Cobbett at his best. Among living economists only Lord Keynes could rival its superb pungency. . . .

What I was striving for in *The Vested Interests*, was first to expose the threat of a post-war corporate state, second, to point the way to a reconstruction of capitalist society which would avoid the risks of a violent conflict between capital and labour. I thought that if the capital resources of the nation, which had been mobilised for war, could be *de jure* nationalised and *leased back* to private enterprise, to work on payment of a royalty (like a special corporation tax), and in accordance with a national investment plan worked out by my National Investments Board, labour would be satisfied, the class war would be averted and British industry would be forced to bring itself up to date. It was certainly not a plan which I would advocate today seeing that

Fabian socialism has been replaced by revolutionary Marxism on the left.

Laski was never convinced that such a revolutionary change could ever be carried out without force, and Kingsley Martin agreed with him. Indeed, Kingsley actually expected revolution to break out throughout the Continent as soon as hostilities had ended. I argued with him on several weekends at Hinton, but he would not shift his opinion. Where Harold Laski and Kingsley Martin went wrong was to believe that their own revolutionary Marxist friends would actually come into power in England or attempt to seize it. The Labour leaders and the trade union bosses, like Ernest Bevin, who supported them, were no revolutionaries and were not in a revolutionary mood. They were merely waiting for the powers, privileges and 'perks' of the ruling Establishment to fall into their hands on the post-war election.

Two more years of fighting had to be endured before this forecast was proved correct. After the opening of the 'second front', in France, we all knew that victory was only a matter of time, but time seemed to stand still as horror followed upon horror. The house book of Hinton records that on 17 September 1944, when my guests and I were having breakfast on the north terrace, on a sunny but misty morning we suddenly heard the droning of many planes which became louder and louder until it reached a crescendo – the crescendo of a mighty aerial armada. There, over the Thames Valley, suddenly appeared hundreds and hundreds of planes towing the great Horsa gliders. It was an incredible and fearful sight : it made one feel that we were witness to some Wellsian war of the worlds. For several minutes the tugs and gliders darted in and out of the mist, roaring loudly, and then gradually the noise died away and they were gone. What we were in fact witnessing was an episode in the ill-fated Arnhem aerial invasion – Montgomery's ingenious plan to get at Berlin through Holland before the Russians arrived. A half-hour went by and we were still sitting spell-bound by the apparition when suddenly the front bell rang. I went to the door and found an airman in full flying kit in an agitated state of mind. Behind him stood a white horse quietly nibbling at the grass. He was, he said, Pilot Sergeant Brody, the captain of a Horsa glider which had been obliged to uncouple his machine from the tug plane because it had been obscured by fog for more than two or three minutes. He had borrowed the horse from the farmer and could he telephone his aerodrome in Gloucestershire to inform them of the mishap? This done, he explained his mission and I went down to Duxford farm where his Horsa glider, miraculously missing the overhead cable wires of the Central Electricity Board in its forced descent, had landed in the stubble of a corn field. There in the glider was a machine gun and a detachment of the Border regiment who were amazed that they were not in Holland. The mishap had probably saved their lives.

My son, Antony, who had joined the Grenadiers, was caught up in the fighting of 1944–5. On 31 October 1944, he left Victoria Station to join the armoured brigade of Guards under the direct control of Montgomery. He was engaged in battle first in Holland and finally crossed the Rhine with the brigade in March 1945. Then began the exciting armoured strike into the heart of Germany. American commandos were sitting on the back of the huge Churchill tanks ready to deploy and mop up any resistance if they ran into trouble. And indeed they did. The house book records that on 22 April 1945, Antony was wounded when a sniper's bullet hit the turret of his Churchill tank as he popped out his head to reconnoitre. His Commanding Officer Major G. E. Pike, of the 4th Battalion, Grenadier Guards, wrote to me : 'He was hit on Saturday last a few miles short of the Elbe, just north of Dannenberg, when his tank was leading the advance. He really has done most magnificently well. Particularly so in the last few days. And we all miss him most terribly here'.

It was Dannenberg where Montgomery received the surrender of the German armies in the West on 5 May 1945. The Norman Lords of Hinton would have considered it only proper that a son of their manor should have helped to defend on the Continent the Anglo-Norman heritage of nine hundred years.

9

The Second Puritan Revolution–
Song in his Heart

In July 1945 the 'Leveller' party was voted into power with the huge overall majority – to its great astonishment – of 152. When Attlee was summoned to Buckingham Palace to form a government on behalf of 'Us' (the ruled) instead of 'Them' (the ruling clique) Hartley Shawcross was moved to exclaim 'We are the rulers now'. His lordship, now a business tycoon and head of the City 'Takeover Panel', must surely regret allowing his heart to run away with his head – perhaps for the first and only time in his life.

The advent of a socialist government in power greatly upset the dispossessed ruling clique. I remember going with my wife to a grand party given by Edward Hulton in Hyde Park Gate – decor by Oliver Messel and complete with fun fair, swings and cabaret – and meeting Duff Cooper at the champagne bar in a tent. He had just caught sight of Hartley Shawcross, who had become Labour's Attorney-General, and was shouting at the top of his voice 'Good God! A socialist here! I'm not staying here if they let in bloody socialists'. 'That's good,' I said, 'I'm rather on the left myself'. He turned to me in an alcoholic rage and shouted: 'Left of what, you bloody fool?' He turned and went unsteadily out of the tent.

I confess I felt myself a certain uneasiness because of the new Levellers extreme fanaticism and ignorance of the capitalist money system. The seventeenth-century Levellers were at least prepared for their modest social and economic revolution, while those of 1945, who on paper were far more revolutionary, were not. This was made evident to me when Hugh Dalton came to stay the weekend at Hinton on his way to take up the high office of Chancellor of the Exchequer.

Labour had fought the 1945 election on a revolutionary socialist ticket. The election manifesto *Let Us Face The Future* boldly declared that it was 'a socialist party and proud of it'. Its ultimate purpose at home, it said, was the establishment of the 'socialist Commonwealth of Great Britain'. The manifesto, true to its Fabian principles, also advised their followers : 'socialism cannot come overnight as the product of a weekend revolution. There are basic industries ripe and over-ripe for public ownership. There are big industries not yet ripe'. They published the names of the 'ripe' ones – coal, gas, electricity, railways, airlines, road transport, civil aviation, cables and wireless, iron and steel and the Bank of England – a formidable list. These were to be the first instalment of the revolutionary Marxist clause 4 – the 'socialisation of *all* the means of production, distribution and exchange'. To leave the electorate in no doubt that this was an instalment, not the end, they added : 'Labour believes in land nationalisation and will work towards it'. At that time, and before the war, I foolishly believed that the Fabians meant what they said. I had reduced the acreage of Hinton Manor from 1250 acres to just under 400, thinking that this was about the level below which nationalisation would not be applied to farmers. The memory of this cautionary step still reduces me to laughter – and a few inflationary tears.

I knew from the intimate talks I had had with Dalton in the late thirties that the 'big five' Labour leaders were no social revolutionaries, except Stafford Cripps, but by this time Cripps had lost his revolutionary fervour and was tired out. Attlee, Morrison, Dalton and Bevin were gradualists – orthodox Fabians who would be content to carry out their election package of nationalisation but no more, regarding it as a measure of social reform. They were not even united on the nationalisation of the steel industry. Herbert Morrison had always been against it and Attlee lukewarm. Dalton told me, one day at Hinton, that it was he who forced them to include it in the election manifesto. He always saw things, as public schoolboys did, in black and white, and for him the steel-masters, like the coal owners, were fascist reactionaries. The arch 'Leveller agitator' Aneurin Bevan – 'Colonel Rainsborough' as he had called himself when writing in

Tribune during the war – was thought to be a dangerous revolutionary, but he was tarred with the same Leveller brush – a Puritan hatred of wealth and profit-making – although he enjoyed dining and wining with Lord Beaverbrook. As a dedicated proletarian he looked on private enterprise in pursuit of profit as immoral and degrading. He was even 'holier' than the others for he regarded the middle-class as foul as the upper-class of capitalists.

I have always thought that if Nye Bevan had ever attained power at 10 Downing Street, he would have become a Cromwell and would have put the trade unions in their place. His book *In Place of Fear* certainly gave me that impression. But he was not allowed by Attlee a position where he could influence policy. He was relegated to the minor office of Minister of Health. Yet he was the only minister who carried through a real and lasting socialist revolution – the National Health Service. His tragic death in 1960 removed one of the few politicians who could have altered the course of British history.

The academic Marxists like Harold Laski were not brought into consultation with the new ministers. In fact, Laski who had just been elected chairman of the National Executive, had become a thorn in the flesh of Attlee, Dalton and Bevin, for he had been intriguing against Attlee, hoping to get Morrison as Premier. He had actually advised Attlee not to accept the King's invitation until the Parliamentary party had met and decided.

Laski and Attlee really hated each other. I have a letter from Laski dated 9 December 1943 which revealed that he had no confidence in any of the Labour leaders. It ran : 'And if you ask me whether the Labour Party will learn its danger in time my answer is emphatically No. It will remain faithful to Winston until victory and then ask him to put brass handles on its coffin. Attlee will attend as a weeper.'

These Marxist intellectuals always got the mood of people wrong.

After the 1945 election Laski rapidly lost his prestige as a potential left-wing revolutionary leader. It had been reported in the press that in a campaign speech he had declared that Labour might have 'to use force' against its political opponents as he had always believed. He lost the libel action which he subsequently brought against the newspapers. I contributed to the fund raised to help him pay his damages in the libel action, for I thought that an old friend had been unfairly treated. I was agreeably surprised to find that he died a comparatively rich man.

The personal wealth of the new Levellers was a conundrum which intrigued Lord Beaverbrook. He had been greatly annoyed by an article I had written in the *Evening Standard* – on the instigation of Michael Foot – in which I crowed over the 1945 election as the first time the moneyed ruling-class of England had been displaced by the 'working-class of villeins and labourers, aided by a few landless and rootless intellectuals from the universities'. He suddenly asked me to lunch with him alone at his flat in Park Lane. He kindly complimented me on my writing – I had written several times for the *Evening Standard* – but expressed extreme dislike of my election whoopee. Then he frankly expressed his sense of being out of touch with the new ruling set-up apart from Attlee, Cripps, Bevin and Bevan. 'Tell me,' he asked, 'how much money have they got? You are a friend of Dalton and John Wilmot. Are they poor or are they rich? Have they got any investments?' I was not willing to disclose these details, being a financial adviser of my friends, and the conversation dropped. At the beginning of lunch he had asked whether I liked drinking champagne. I said I did. However, no champagne ever appeared. He had obviously thought that it was not worthwhile wasting his good champagne on too reticent a financial writer.

The important political fact in 1945 was that although the Labour Party had campaigned on a revolutionary, Marxist ticket, the mass of the electorate were not in a revolutionary mood at all. The troops wanted to get back into 'civvies' and enjoy happy civilian life. The soldiers' vote, which had been cleverly canvassed for Labour by Colonel Wigg (now Lord Wigg), of the Army educational branch, had been solidly anti-Churchill for that sole reason. They regarded Churchill as a warlord who might keep them in khaki for some European power game. My wife and I had been to watch the election campaign in John Wilmot's constituency in Battersea. We were listening to a speech in some drab street when word went round that the great man was coming. He arrived, standing up in a car, looking bored and bewildered. When he started to address the gathering, some Labour hack began to mount a rival meeting on the other side of the street. It

F

became a shouting match and Churchill's ire was roused. Turning to a seedy looking heckler he said : 'Yes, and yours is the sort of ugly mug we would have when the socialist Gestapo takes over'. He really saw a Marxist revolution coming and Laski as the head of the socialist Gestapo. It was pathetic to see a great man, enraged and confused as a bull blooded in a Spanish arena, really believing in an Attlee terror. John Wilmot told me that he had never banked on his own electoral triumph until he saw the soldiers' vote from overseas rolling in on an anti-Churchill tidal wave.

I felt some misgivings over Dalton's appointment as Chancellor. He was excellent on simple financial principles – witness his concise but elementary book on public finance – but he was ill-equipped to handle the complicated details of currency and banking of which he had no practical experience. I knew he wanted to be Foreign Minister and I could see him standing up valiantly for Britain in the confused post-war world, for he was a great patriot. The fateful switching of offices by Attlee on 26 July 1945 – in the lunch interval after his audience with the King – has never been properly explained. Dalton records in *The Fateful Years*, that when he saw Attlee before lunch, the P.M. had said in his clipped manner : 'Almost certainly the Foreign Office. Advise you to pack in readiness to leave for Potsdam the next day'.

It is recorded that King George VI expressed a wish to Attlee that Bevin should be Foreign Secretary and not Dalton, but Attlee in an article in the *Observer* on 23 August 1959 wrote that the King's views were not the decisive factor. He had felt that 'Ernie and Herbert wouldn't have worked well together on the Home Front'. I do not find this explanation convincing. If Bevin and Morrison did not get on well together, neither did Dalton and Morrison. In fact, Dalton loathed Morrison. He quoted with relish in his memoirs Attlee's curt opinion of Morrison : 'He never knew the difference between a big thing and a small thing.' A better explanation came to me from a friend who had been working in the Foreign Office and was still close to the senior civil servants there. Bridges, I was told, came to Attlee in the lunch interval and said that certain Foreign Office officials would resign rather than serve under Dalton. This probably persuaded Attlee, who had his doubts after his audience with the King, that the offices should be switched. Having had experience of the power of the Civil Service bureaucracy under Bridges I find this story the most convincing.

When Hugh Dalton arrived for the weekend at Hinton on 5 August 1945 on his way up to the Treasury, my misgivings deepened. We had a long conversation in the drawing-room after dinner. I had to explain to him the functions of the Government broker and handed him a note about the inconsistencies of this office, the holder of which was a partner in a leading firm of stockbrokers. I had also to explain the difference between jobbers and brokers on the Stock Exchange, about which he knew nothing. I had to expound, among many other things, the techniques for the management of the Government debt in the gilt-edged market and how the rate of interest could be manipulated when the money supply was under firm control. Here was one of the big men in the Labour Party taking up high office who seemed to be utterly ignorant of the workings of the monetary system. Yet his party was coming into office to 'seize' the 'commanding heights of the economy' and to carry out a financial revolution. If they ever appreciated the private sector's vital role in the economy they did not bother to consider what made it 'tick', which was profit. For them profit was a dirty word. They despised the pursuit of profit and the whole business of profit-making. To them the profit-motive was immoral, making money out of money was the sin of usury, the City was parasitic, the Stock Exchange was a casino, business speculation was one of the deadly sins. All they were really interested in was 'levelling wealth', which meant taking from the rich and giving to the poor.

I was never able to convince these Levellers that business men who had a genius for making money should be encouraged, for their enterprise would mean more jobs, higher wages, and greater economic growth. There were a number of rich men who voted Labour – I was surprised once at a party given by Hugh Gaitskell in his Hampstead home to find several millionaires in the room – but they were never called in to help the mixed economy expand. It was probably assumed that these millionaires had supported Labour merely to secure their peerages. But Labour should have learned from them, should have made use of their business acumen, instead of looking upon their profit-making as something reprehensible, if not immoral. The normal business drive to maximise profits should have been harnessed for the good of the economy. After all, the Labour leaders had no immediate intention or desire to establish a completely socialised State.

Dalton, for example, never learned from Harold Lever, a rich and highly intelligent barrister and banker, who later became a close friend of mine, as I will tell. Whenever he happened to meet Harold Lever in the lobbies of the House he used to call out: 'Hello! Harold! the money-lenders' friend!'. Later on Harold became the best Financial Secretary the Treasury had ever seen.

Surely, as I have said, I am right to call this 'Levelling crew', obsessed as they were, with hatred of the profit-motive and suspicion of all private enterprise, the 'second Puritan revolution'. I was driven gradually to the conclusion that it would end in disaster because the new Levellers did not seem to appreciate that they were utterly dependent on the 'profit-makers' they were attacking for the growth of the economy and a surplus on our overseas trading account.

On the Monday morning my wife and I motored Hugh Dalton from Hinton up to the Treasury for his first day in office. It was an uncomfortable journey because the silencer had broken down and the noise was deafening but Hugh did not appear to notice. He was in fine shouting form. He boomed away about his job and when we got to Great George Street he said to me: 'I have got your XYZ papers in my bag and I am going to put them on my desk, press the button for my new slaves and ask them why we should not put them into practice.' I knew that the slaves would soon become his masters. 'Come and see me,' he shouted, 'whenever you like'. But I knew that would be impossible: the monastery guards would bar the way. Agnostic as he was, Hugh before long would be taking the monastic vows of an office whose high priests were ordained to worship the pound sterling and the Crown as the twin pillars of the British Establishment. Their worship of the pound sterling in its convertibility holiness in August 1947 was to be the beginning of Hugh's downfall.

My fears about the business acumen of the new Levellers were confirmed by John Wilmot who came to Hinton for the weekend of 17 August 1945. John had been in banking and in business before the war, and thanks to Dalton pushing, had now been appointed Minister of Supply and Aircraft Production – two huge ministries he had to amalgamate. We called him 'Pooh-Bah' and his wife, Elsa, who had a fine sense of humour, wrote in our house-book :

> Our privilege and pleasure
> Which we cherish beyond measure
> Is of running little errands
> For the Minister of State.

Elsa was typical of Labour ministerial wives who still devotedly waited on their husbands and did the household chores in spite of their newly acquired affluence.

John Wilmot was responsible for the official 'take-over' of the steel industry and knew as a business man that this Leveller government was incapable of running it. He had a difficult position. As a protégé of Dalton he had to appear keen to nationalise iron and steel but he knew that the tough 'steel-masters' – public enemy number one in the eyes of public-schoolboy Dalton – would never co-operate with a Labour government in the nationalisation and obliteration of the individual steel companies. At Steel House, where Sir Andrew Duncan presided, no socialist minister was allowed to enter and take a sight of the facts and figures which were needed for the control of this complicated industry. On 12 April 1946, when he came down to Hinton for another weekend, John Wilmot told me privately that he was prepared to do a deal with Sir Andrew Duncan. The deal was that the Government should allow the individual steel companies to continue operating separately under their own name subject to 'overall' direction from the new national Steel Board, over which Sir Andrew would then be willing to preside. When this became known there was a Cabinet row – Attlee and Morrison being for, and Cripps and Dalton against the deal. Later, when Dalton had to resign in late 1947 from the Treasury and Cripps took over, Wilmot was immediately sacked by the new Chancellor.

One of the odd episodes of the passing of the Steel Act was the appointment of an amateur Steel Board in which no one had any confidence; in fact, it aroused derision in the business world. The chairman was not a steel man – no steel man would serve – and one of the members was my old friend Vaughan Berry of the XYZ club. As Berry had been made one of the post-war Commissioners in Germany – as compensation for not being made a member of the Court of the Bank of England by Dalton – and as he had been in this capacity titular head of the Ruhr steel board he had been hailed as a 'steel man' and appointed to the Steel Board as finance director. He knew nothing about steel and came to me to seek advice as to what to do with the steel companies' money. I replied that as a Labour 'revolutionary' he should immediately seize the companies' cash and Government bonds and set up a central finance department. In the end the Government was never able to operate State steel as a going concern.

In November 1947 John Wilmot told me at Hinton one weekend, the curious story of his sacking. The Prime Minister sent for him at number 10, and when they were seated Attlee began, as his habit was, to doodle on a piece of paper without raising his eyes to look at his colleague. 'You know, John,' he said, 'that I have to make some changes now that Hugh has left the Treasury.' Pause. The doodling went on. 'Well, I want you to leave the Ministry of Supply and go to the Lords.' John was astonished. 'Why, have I done anything wrong?', he asked. 'Oh dear no!', replied Attlee, 'I wish your colleagues had been half as efficient as you have been'. Pause. More doodling. 'But I don't really want to go to the Lords', said John. 'Oh,' said Attlee, 'then I'm afraid there is no more to be said.' He rose from his desk and John withdrew, feeling that he had been caned by the headmaster for something he had not done. But he was wise not to accept his life peerage at that point. He took it with more dignity later on when the Party wanted his seat.

This story reminds me of another Attlee interview, which was even more bizarre. Dick Crossman had been a member of the Anglo-American Commission on Palestine, set up in 1945, and had gone to Palestine during the troubles to make an independent survey in company with an American diplomat and report back to the Foreign Secretary. He went, and both observers were convinced that withdrawal and partition was the only solution. Dick made a brilliant report, sent it to Ernest Bevin the Foreign Secretary and heard no more. Disgruntled he asked for an interview with the Prime Minister as the Foreign Secretary had refused to see him. The same sort of encounter took place. Attlee sat down, said nothing and began as usual to doodle. Dick allowed himself twenty minutes to state his case for partition which he did in his concise and donnish manner. It was no doubt a brilliant exposition but Attlee said nothing. A pause and more doodling. 'Well,' said Dick, 'if I may summarise our conclusions in a few words . . . .' He went on for another five minutes and stopped. Attlee then got up and as they moved in silence to the door he said pleasantly : 'Did you know, Dick, I met your mother last week?' Not a word did he say about Palestine.

Some historians still regard Attlee as a great man but he was, in fact, a small man, suddenly jacked up, like Truman, into a position of great power and responsibility. But he was a fine level-headed chairman for a disputatious coalition, and, withal, a business-like administrator. He will be remembered primarily as the Prime Minister who gave freedom to India – not because he particularly loved the Indians – but because he was trained in the fine democratic traditions of the British liberal-left. Compared with Hugh Dalton I found him as cold as a fish. We were both members of the Athenaeum, but in line with club tradition he would never smile or open his mouth when we met.

Like many other social reformers I had high hopes that in changing the old capitalism into a mixed economy with an enlarged public sector the new Labour Government might make the private sector more efficient as well as more prosperous with better planned investment through a National Investment Board. Dalton began gaily with a song in his heart, bringing in an autumn budget and the bill for the nationalisation of the Bank of England. We had given him some apples from our orchard and he replied on 6 November 1945: 'My dear Nicholas, thank you very much indeed for the most agreeable gift of Blenheims. Eating apples night and morning is one of the foundations of health and happiness. I hope you like my Budget and my Bank Bill. And there's more fun coming! With every good wish, Yours ever, Hugh Dalton.'

In point of fact I did not like his budget. It played down to the popular idea of 'levelling', which just meant taking from the rich and giving (if possible) to the poor by the conventional means of taxation. Dalton in the autumn budget took 1s off income tax – from 10s to 9s – but increased surtax by steeply graduated steps until it reached 10s 6d in the pound on all incomes in excess of £20,000. This made it absurd for any ambitious, clever man to aspire to reach the top positions in big industry. An extra £10,000 gross might only mean an extra £250 net. Dalton realised in the end that he had made a mistake over the surtax increase, which simply destroyed the incentives of the ablest business men in the country without contributing anything worthwhile to the Exchequer. Even in 1972-3 surtax brought in only about £350 million.

My next disappointment came when Hugh refused to set up the National Investment Board which we had discussed so often and agreed upon during our Hinton debates. Bridges, the head of the Treasury, talked him out of it because the great utility industries – coal, railways, electricity, gas and road transport – which were being nationalised, accounted for so much of the national investment. But to placate his left-wing, in 1946 Dalton set up instead a consultative National Investment Council on which he invited me to serve. He wrote to me at Hinton :

> Treasury Chambers,
> Great George Street,
> S.W.1.
> 24 January 1946

MY DEAR NICHOLAS,

As you will have seen, I have just introduced the Investment (Control and Guarantees) Bill. You may like to have the enclosed copy, together with a copy of the Command Paper which was presented simultaneously.

The Command Paper sets out fully the functions of the National Investment Council, which I intend to create, and you will see that the Council will have an important job to do. I have been giving a good deal of thought to its construction, which I want to be as widely representative as possible, and I should like you to take this letter as a definite invitation to be one of its members. Will you give me great pleasure by writing to say 'Yes'? I would like very much, on personal grounds, to have you on the Council. Yours ever,

> HUGH DALTON

Alas! The National Investment Council was really a waste of time. It was denied by the Treasury all power, all information, all staff and all dignity. It was never even given a Government Paper to study. We used to meet in the Chancellor's room for tea and a pleasant chat. Bridges and his bureaucrats would sit behind the Chancellor in rows, their poker faces alert to see that we did not propose anything revolutionary that might upset the Treasury

Establishment. The thing was a farce and everyone knew it except Dalton. No planning of the national investment was ever discussed. Members were invited to air their opinions about any subject that entered their heads – provided it was not about the actual business of planning investment. As soon as Cripps became Chancellor in October 1947 the council was abolished. I wrote to Stafford saying that he had severed his only link with the outside world of business. He never replied. The Treasury had always been determined to kill an outside body which might poke its nose into the affairs of their sacred Establishment.

Dalton in his *High Tide and After* said that the National Investment Council was 'a fine body of high-powered collective wisdom' and that he found its occasional meetings valuable. He referred to an excellent paper by Sir Clarence Sadd, the general manager of the Midland Bank, on cheap money. This incident showed how flattery could so easily lead dear Hugh astray. Sir Clarence had got the Midland Bank to support the cheap money policy by having a streamlined bank portfolio, including medium-dated and long-dated stocks, which banks conventionally never held, as well as 'shorts'. He would always preface his remarks at the Council meetings with such back-slapping as : 'Of course, Mr Chancellor, I bow to your superior wisdom, which has been so evident in your handling of the market' and so on. I regret to say that Hugh loved all this flattery.

My second disappointment was over cheap money. I always had the misgiving that Hugh would not know how to carry it through or would over-do it and crash. Of course, cheap money was essential for a post-war government which had to service a heavily swollen debt of £24,000 million and was committed to a vast programme of social investment. The fact that Hugh got the banks to accept a $\frac{1}{2}\%$ on Treasury bills, so that the service of the floating debt cost the country only £25 million a year, was a remarkable achievement. It is to Hugh's credit that he fully appreciated the economics of cheap money. Even at that time, a difference of 1% on the borrowing rate meant an increase of 12s a week on a council house rent which the worker could ill afford. Indeed, he would have demanded a rise in wages to pay for it, so that dear money would have been inflationary in its immediate impact.

It must be remembered that the war had been fought on cheap

money – thanks to Keynes – only because of strict monetary and physical controls which could not be continued indefinitely in peacetime. During the war the Bank of England simply saw to it – through purchases of Treasury bills – that the joint stock banks had a sufficient cash base to support each day the total of their advances. This perpetually increasing money supply was kept cheap because each day the Government broker had to buy Government bonds in the market if they fell below the desired yield level of around three per cent. Dalton did not seem to appreciate that the advances of the banks might be used not only to transact the essential business of the country but to finance speculation, in particular, the speculators who would buy government bonds in the booming gilt-edged market for a quick money gain. What is more, if the banks themselves joined in the market gamble and bought Government stock for their own port-folios, the Bank of England would be increasing the money supply in a highly inflationary manner. A monetary inflation did, in fact, erupt when Hugh decided to convert 3% Local Loans into an undated $2\frac{1}{2}$% Treasury stock, and threw Government funds, in addition to the banking funds, into the gilt-edged market to sup-port the issue.

In his *High Tide and After* Hugh devoted a whole chapter to the defence of his cheap money policy and it left the impression on me that the flattery and encouragement of his Treasury advisers had carried him on to a position he could not maintain. He wanted to out-Goschen Goschen. In the epoch-making issue of 1888 the then Chancellor Goschen had converted $2\frac{3}{4}$% Consols to $2\frac{1}{2}$% Consols but Hugh out-did him by converting a 3% stock to $2\frac{1}{2}$% undated and even securing for a short time a price above par which Goschen never did. Hugh quoted at length in his book from articles in the *Sunday Times*, the *Financial Times* and the *Economist* which said in effect that he had performed miracles. But the *Sunday Times* made it clear how the miracle had been performed – by the rigid control of new issues (through a New Issues Committee on which I was very thankful Hugh never asked me to serve), by the restriction of trustee funds to a limited list of gilt-edged securities, by the use on a vast scale of physical and price controls and finally by using Government money to support the market. The City fathers regarded these measures as worthy of a 'bucket' shop which usually supports its dubious issues in the market by manipulated buying. But Hugh's 'rigging' did the trick. He got $2\frac{1}{2}\%$ (old) Consols up to $99\frac{1}{2}$ in 1946 and $3\frac{1}{2}\%$ War loan up to $108\frac{1}{4}\%$ in January 1947 and Local Loans over par.

There is no doubt that Dalton acted with commendable gusto in his market drive to $2\frac{1}{2}\%$ but unfortunately none of his colleagues counselled caution. Hugh records that 'I was getting much encouragement from Keynes and from the "top brass" both at the Bank and the Treasury.' Only his PPS Evan Durbin, a professional economist, disagreed with his policy and tactics. When he announced the coming issue of a $2\frac{1}{2}\%$ undated Treasury stock, now called 'Daltons', he told Attlee that there might be a row in the City but that his advisers were in full agreement. The Prime Minister simply said 'Go ahead'.

When $2\frac{1}{2}\%$ 'Daltons' were finally floated on the market in January 1947 the price held only for a short time – it touched 100.22 on 13 January an unlucky day – but selling grew and finally a gigantic bear raid was launched. Dalton ordered the National Insurance fund to support the market and encouraged bankers, like Sir Clarence Sadd, to do the same. In fact, he threw in about £570 million of public money in support but private and institutional sellers unloaded £630 million. So the 'bears' won the battle.

With this fatal collapse in the gilt-edged market, Hugh's cheap money policy was doomed. One cannot blame him personally for the disaster. The layman had to do what his professional experts advised, for he himself knew nothing about operations in the bond market. It is true that Keynes had encouraged Dalton in his cheap money drive whenever they met, but Keynes alas had died on 21 April 1946, and cannot be blamed for the subsequent tactical mistakes of the Treasury Knights. It was they who unanimously told Dalton to issue an undated stock. When the terms were announced I told Hugh that I doubted very much whether he could get away with a $2\frac{1}{2}\%$ coupon undated.

Geoffrey Crowther, the editor of the *Economist*, was the fiercest critic of Hugh's cheap money policy and wrote blistering articles against it. Hugh hated him and used to call him 'Little Piggy Crowther' because he looked at that time rather like a well-fed porker. Some years later I had occasion to attack Crowther for his unfair campaign against the Chancellor and I sent Hugh a copy of the letter. I received back the following reply :

House of Commons,
S.W.1.
4 November 1950

My Dear Nicholas,
Many thanks for your admirable letter to Little Piggy Crowther. I hope he'll have the decency to publish it next week. It is a perfect rebuke. Thank you too for your most interesting Memo on the future of the rate of interest. I think it very good. I certainly had bad – unanimous but bad – advice on the $2\frac{1}{2}\%$ undated. I should have kept to $2\frac{1}{2}\%$, but given it a fairly distant date. If you are going to write anything more on my cheap money policy, let us discuss it before you write. I am sure that, broadly, I was right, that there was no real inflationary argument the other way (several anti-Labour economists can be quoted here!), that the interest reductions were very salutary (there is a good summary of them in my first Budget speech of 1947) and that what I really lacked – and what my successor should acquire – was a power to direct a prescribed minimum – to be varied from time to time by order – of large holdings (institutional and individual) into gilt-edged. I put down this thought in an article in the *New Statesman*, soon after I resigned, at the end of 1947. The 'euthanasia of the rentier' must still be one of our aims. Love to Olga, Yours ever,

Hugh

Three months later I received another, and even more revealing letter on the technical point of the undated issue.

My Dear Nicholas,
It may amuse you to see a copy of a note I sent to the Editor of the Prig's Weekly with my letter on Keynes which he prints this week. One reference in the third paragraph is to Keynes' private advice to me to replace Local Loans 3% undated by a Dalton 2% *dated*, with a term as long as a well massaged market could stand – up to, say, 15 years. He was dead, of course, before I got the final advice of Bank and Treasury to make it $2\frac{1}{2}\%$ undated. Looking back, Keynes was right again !

Looking forward to lunching with you next Friday. Love to Olga.

HUGH

This surely proves conclusively that Dalton must not be blamed for the fiasco of his undated $2\frac{1}{2}\%$ Treasury stock. The blame lies at the door of the Treasury Knights. Looking back I suspect that the Treasury Knights played on Hugh's vanity and made him feel too cock-sure about his policy. A story I was told in Montreal, on my American trip in 1947, confirms my suspicion. Hugh, who proceeded me on this trip, had called on the chairman of the Bank of Montreal who warned him against pushing cheap money too far. 'My dear George,' replied Dalton, patting the little man on his shoulder, 'you need not worry yourself. The rate of interest is just what I choose to make it. I've chosen $2\frac{1}{2}\%$.' So a certain amount of pride went before the fall.

On a much later date I discussed the tragedy with Hugh Gaitskell when he visited Hinton. I subsequently sent him a copy of an article I had written on cheap money and he replied :

DEAR NICHOLAS,

I entirely agree with all that you say. In particular, that Hugh was absolutely right to go out for cheap money, that he went too far but that was definitely on the advice of the Treasury experts. It is perhaps worth pointing out that even by 1951 interest rates were still comparatively low although I was prepared to let the long-term rate go up to 4%. The really crucial change came with the removal of the peg which the Bank wanted to do, which I had refused to do, and which the Tories did almost immediately after they came into power. Yours ever,

HUGH

The 'peg' in the gilt-edged market was the rule under which the Government Broker had to buy Government bonds whenever they had fallen to yield a little over 3%. The big slide in the market began when Bank rate, which had remained fixed at 2% since October 1939, was raised by Rab Butler to $2\frac{1}{2}\%$ on 26 October 1951, and 4% on 11 March 1952. 'Daltons' touched bottom (I hope) at under 17 in the spring of 1974. Some of the stock which Dalton had bought at par in January 1947 for the

National Insurance Fund had to be sold at under 30 when the Fund ran out of money in an influenza crisis in the late sixties. So this foolish 'undated' issue cost the nation hundreds of millions in hard cash.

My third disappointment was over the Bill to nationalise the Bank of England. Here was another XYZ matter on which Dalton left many others, beside Berry and myself, sadly disillusioned. We had found Labour politicians before 1945 constantly talking of how they would seize 'the commanding heights of the economy'. This was a Leninist phrase, and sounded well when suitably intoned on political platforms before an audience of 'comrades'. We had tried to explain to them that 'the commanding heights of the economy' were all to be found within the square mile of the City clustered round and about the Bank of England. We of the XYZ Club fondly imagined that when they had got control of the Bank they would appoint a technocrat Governor outside politics who was experienced in the monetary management of a mixed economy, that they would restrict the Court of the Bank to technical experts and that they would remove the part-time merchant bank directors who, later on, were to give their amateur selves away at the Bank Rate Tribunal of 1961. We also expected that they would take power for the Bank to issue and enforce clear directives to the directors of other banks, perhaps requiring Government representation on the boards of the banks so 'directed'. This was our conception of the practical way in which the money system of the country could be brought under proper public control.

But what Dalton did was really a great non-event. First, he asked the existing Governor of the Bank, Lord Catto of Morgan Grenfell, to stay on because he was such a nice friendly chap who had risen up from the ranks. Then he reduced the Court from twenty-four to sixteen and took power to appoint only four of them each year. He retained the prominent directors who had been associated with the worst disasters of Montagu Norman. Of the four 'Labour' men he appointed, the one from the trade unions had to retire over an 'indiscretion' and the one from the City had to retire also over another sort of 'indiscretion'. Later, when Dalton had gone, Cripps gave up trying to appoint four Labour supporters each year and accepted as a matter of course the nominations put up to him by the Governor. They were mainly old Etonians. And the Governor he chose, Cobbold, was the protégé of Montagu Norman, the very man who had given Dalton wrong advice over the convertibility of sterling in 1947.

It is obvious that poor Hugh was led astray partly by ignorance of the way in which the City Establishment worked, partly by conceit over his success in the nationalisation debate, partly by hatred of the left-wing intellectuals like Laski. In his autobiography he wrote : 'Once in some Left Book Club circles I had listened to the tedious theory that the capitalists would resist, if necessary by force, a socialist government which would try to nationalise the Bank of England or anything else. Impatiently I had replied: "Make me Chancellor of the Exchequer and give me a good Labour majority in Parliament and I will undertake the nationalisation of the Bank of England over a dinner party. And now no dinner party had been necessary: only tea for two".' Of course Lord Catto would not resist, or any of his capitalist friends, because they knew that Dalton planned no real change in the management of the Bank and had no real wish to upset the financial Establishment or undermine the subtle power it exercised through its interlocking bank directorships. Nationalisation of the Bank would have had a very different reception if a real revolution had been intended.

The Act of Nationalisation of the Bank of England was the first of the great measures of socialisation intended to implement Clause 4 – and the worst drafted. Dalton called it a 'streamlined socialist statute' but it was streamlined with ambiguities. As a result of its own obscure Clause 4, the Governor and his new Court regarded themselves as an autonomous public board, managing their own affairs independently of Parliament and Treasury and changing Bank rate on their own initiative and judgement without prior consultation with the Treasury. Under this clause, no direction could be given to the Bank except after consultation with the Governor, who would of course, be opposed to any direction. As for directions to the joint stock banks these were to emanate from the Bank, not from the Treasury, and therefore were not likely to emanate at all. As no sanctions were attached to them they could in any case be safely ignored. In fact no directions have ever been given to this day, partly because, as Cobbold explained at the Radcliffe inquiry, no one was able legally to define a bank.

The Radcliffe Committee was later to report that the Bank had laid 'mistaken stress' upon those provisions of the Act which concerned 'the affairs of the Bank.' The Bank witnesses had told them that in the Governor's opinion these were 'the affairs of Bank rate, the management of the money market and the management of the issue department's portfolio'. The Radcliffe Committee did not agree. They rejected the view expressed by more than one official witness that the public interest required that the central bank should be assured complete political independence. I well remember Macmillan saying to Robert Boothby and myself, when he was Chancellor of the Exchequer in 1956 – this was in an interview he gave us on a memorandum I had written on monetary policy for a Boothby committee – that the Bank of England had become far more independent since it had been nationalised. Nobody, he said, could now sack the Governor or his officials, being civil servants, and the Governor was no longer amenable to political influence. In the old days, he added, you could always influence Montagu Norman if you got him to dine alone and locked all the doors.

The Second Puritan Revolution—Decline and Fall

I had another disappointment which I must mention in passing. It was over films. When the Labour Government was installed, with Harold Wilson at the Board of Trade, Alex Korda had called me in as political as well as financial adviser. The case I made out for government help for the British film industry was based on Alex's sound arguments. First, the British screen was dominated by the Americans, to whom we were paying royalties in dollars to the detriment of our balance of payments. Second, film distribution was controlled by the two big circuits – Odeon and AB Pictures – which had tie-ups with American film companies. No British film could hope for more than a showing of a week or two in any one theatre of these two big circuits. Alex rightly insisted that to maximise revenue from good films you would have to take over a theatre for as long as the run met with public support, which is exactly what the American companies do now when they spend $5 million or more on a 'super' film. These arguments I put both to Hugh Dalton, who was greatly concerned about the dollar film drain, and to Harold Wilson, as the minister responsible for the British film industry. One night I brought Harold Wilson and Mary to dine with Alex in his penthouse at Claridges. Dining there was always an occasion – brilliant talk, marvellous food and wine on the table, fine Impressionist pictures on the walls. The other guests were my wife, Vivien Leigh and Lawrence Olivier. My wife was then one of Korda's young 'stars' – she had played a lead in his fine film *The Angel and the Trumpet* – and the conversation about films sparkled away. Harold seemed to agree upon the need to help British film production. On the way home Olga said to me : 'Tell me about Harold Wilson. He says he is the youngest minister since Pitt. He seems full of Yorkshire confidence. I have a hunch he will be Prime Minister one day.' I pooh-poohed her fanciful suggestion.

In due course the Treasury and the Board of Trade came to the conclusion that something would have to be done to help British film makers. Dalton was still fussing about the dollar drain but he could not legally discriminate against the American film trade. So he agreed with Harold Wilson that if more British films were made, we would have to import fewer American films. This, of course, was a *non sequitur*, because if the British films were so bad that they would empty the house, the two big circuits would still import the same number of American films. I was not, however, surprised when Harold Wilson telephoned to me one day to say that he had decided to create a National Film Finance Company and wanted me to become a member. 'Don't let me down', he added. Although he had said nothing about the chairman or the set-up of the Company I felt I ought to accept the appointment in view of what I had written in the press and the fact that I had submitted to Wilson's predecessor at the Board of Trade, Oliver Lyttleton, a memorandum on a State film bank. What I did not know at the time was that Sir Wilfred Eady at the Treasury (a man I had never met) had persuaded Wilson that British Lion, a company created to organise and finance independent producers, was the proper instrument for channelling public money into the film production industry. 'Good heavens', I thought, 'did they not know that British Lion was controlled by Alex Korda and was already in financial trouble?'

I went to Alex to resign my lucrative advisory job with him, and found him in an elated mood. He was so effusive in his congratulations on my becoming a member of the NFFC that I became suspicious. After all I had done nothing but argue the film case on national grounds in the national press, and was giving up a large income to take the pittance offered by the State to its servants. I discovered the truth the next day when I was invited to meet Sir Wilfred Eady at the Treasury. Another new member of the NFFC and myself waited in Sir Wilfred's ante-room for about fifteen minutes. Then the door opened and Sir Wilfred and my friend Jimmie Laurie, who had been made the managing director of the NFFC on leaving the ICFC (the

Industrial and Commercial Finance Corporation), appeared with a two-page foolscap letter addressed to British Lion offering to lend them £3 million – with an immediate advance of £1 million – to enable them to carry on their finance of British independent producers. Jimmie signed as managing-director and passed the letter to us. My colleague looked at me, questioning, but I said : 'We've got to sign. We've foolishly agreed to serve on the NFFC, a Government body, and we are now merely Government stooges'. So we signed. I learned afterwards that Sir Arthur Jarratt, the managing-director of British Lion, was waiting in a room downstairs, trembling like a leaf. He knew that if he did not get an immediate grant, British Lion was 'bust'.

I had an uneasy night. British Lion was controlled by Korda's private family company, London Films, and I knew what was tacked on to the film budgets by way of Korda's family overheads. If the House of Commons got to know they would be horrified. So I went to have breakfast with Alex in his penthouse to tell him my misgivings. Breakfast with Alex was always a bizarre occasion. He would start with *pâté de foie gras* and toast and then light up an enormous cigar while he drank black coffee. When I had managed to secure some normal food I told him that the House of Commons would never agree to vote public money to be spent *ad lib* by a company privately controlled and managed by a Hungarian film impresario who had been in financial trouble. Always a patriot, Alex asked what I proposed. I said I would like him to announce that he would hand over his controlling shares in British Lion to a trust and deposit them at the Treasury while the public funds were being spent. 'If you think that is the right course, Nicholas, I will agree', he said. He always did the big thing if it was right for his beloved adopted country. Yet when I reported this wonderful gesture to Sir Wilfred Eady at the Treasury I was sharply told to forget it. Parliament, he said, would never accept ownership of a speculative film producing company. In the end this was exactly what they had to accept. The £3 million loan was before long exhausted, and some of the films financed made appalling losses. British Lion became hopelessly insolvent. This should have been a lesson to Treasury Knights who lack business and common sense.

I did not stay long on the board of the NFFC. I was sure the Board would lose all the public money given to them to lend to

British film makers because the borrowers would be the less successful or untried producers whom no one else would finance. Of course, it kept alive some British film production, which might otherwise have collapsed altogether, but it also kept alive a lot of producers who ought to have been dead. And in so doing it drove crowds away from the cinemas exhibiting their trash. The film-going habit began to lose its popularity just as television was gaining it.

I do not think that Harold Wilson was at all pleased with my resigning from his NFFC. Later on, he and his charming wife Mary motored down one Sunday in November 1947 to Hinton to meet Alex Korda for lunch and a film talk but I felt that Harold had lost interest in British film production. When a minister sets up the wrong sort of public body to do a job on the wrong lines he tends to put it out of his mind. From that moment I had no further meeting with Harold about film finance. If he had been a real socialist, he would, of course, have nationalised or municipal-ised the two great cinema circuits which were later shown up by the Monopolies Commission in 1966 to be riddled with restrictive and monopolistic practices.

1947 opened with a gay New Year's eve party at Hinton and our guests had included Frank Soskice (the Solicitor-General) and his wife Susan, (now Lord and Lady Stow Hill), the Wilmots, Lord Faringdon, Maria Carras (a Greek ship-owner's lively and attractive wife), MacDonald Hastings and his wife Anne Scott James (now the wife of Osbert Lancaster) and Air Marshall Sir Arthur Harris. We made many cheerful New Year predictions which proved hopelessly wrong, for 1947 turned out to be the *annus horrendus* of Hugh Dalton. To begin with, Shinwell told the nation in February that we had run out of coal and that there would be no electricity from 9–12 am and 2–4 pm each day.

In March, my wife and I sailed for the USA. Hinton was ice-bound in the worst of the post-war cold winters. Our car could not reach the manor gates and we had to walk the last three hundred yards through great snow drifts. I was glad to get away from the debacle in the gilt-edged market. In New York I was hailed as 'the adviser' to the Chancellor of the Exchequer because I was on the National Investment Council. It was always necessary for an English visitor to have some definite personal label so that he could be shown off on appropriate social occasions. Those were the days when visitors of any importance from socialistic Britain were seized upon by New York hostesses as a prize exhibit at their cocktail and dinner parties. And what wealth these occasions displayed! Dining with dollar millionaires I was amazed to find footmen behind the chairs serving the guests. But the wine was never comparable with that served in more humble homes in Europe and the champagne was often undrinkable.

The Americans really thought that Britain under a socialist government had gone communist and mad. The bankers and business men were all shocked and dismayed. I was called upon to address the New York State Chamber of Commerce, and about forty bankers came to listen. A diplomat was sent as a spy from the British Embassy in Washington to see that I did not talk socialist propaganda. I assured the bankers that with the Iron and Steel Bill, which had just been introduced into the House of Commons, socialism in Britain had shot its bolt. The effect on the audience and on the Foreign Office spy was electrifying. 'Can this be true?' they cried, 'Oh my God! What a relief! How wonderful if it is true!' They came and hit me on the back with joy. When I told this story to Hugh Dalton on my return he laughed and remarked how stupid American bankers were.

Our New York visit was wonderfully managed by the Government's public relations officer, Sir Barclay Ormerod. He knew everyone, and his tactful introductions were superb. He arranged two press conferences for me, one in New York, the other in Washington. I was struck by the warm sympathy which these tough financial journalists showed for us British, living under harsh rationing schemes. 'Tell us,' they asked, 'do you think the British working man is getting enough to eat under these rationing schemes?' 'No, I don't' I replied, mentioning the size of the meat ration. 'Then what are we asking questions for?' they replied. 'We should send food ships to Britain – we should give them all they want.' There was a chorus of approval.

One afternoon we were taken to have tea with the Misses Peabody, elderly relics of the Morgan empire, on the top floor of a skyscraper which they owned. A private lift shot us at rocket speed up to the thirty-third floor and into the hall of the Peabody flat where a butler escorted us into their presence. 'I hear you are an adviser, Mr Davenport, to the socialist Chancellor Mr Dalton. I want to let you know that we Americans don't like socialism in England. When are you going to stop it?' I was slightly startled by her vehemence, and feebly tried to reassure her about the Iron and Steel Bill.

We went on to stay a week or so with Deborah Kerr in Hollywood. The film stars had fortunately never heard of socialism in England. In fact, they never heard any European news at all. The only newsprint they read was that of the Hollywood gossip columnists. If they did not find themselves personally mentioned, they would telephone their agents to ask if they were slipping in news value. Deborah's husband warned us at the station that film stars in America were treated as royalty. It was true. We got the impression that we had arrived at a great lunatic asylum where the inmates really believed they were important royal celebrities. On being introduced to Rita Hayworth at a lunch party *chez* David Niven I felt it was the Empress Josephine who murmured about her coming trip to Europe 'I am so enthused.' David was, of course, down to earth, and showed me his new bathing pool where he had contrived mirrors in the changing rooms so that the men could see the girls disrobing. Douglas Fairbanks and his charming wife gave us a grand dinner party. The women were gorgeously dressed and bejewelled : the men, being the inferior sex in America, wore slacks. The Ronald Colmans were then the reigning monarchs and Mrs Colman, having been told I was an English intellectual, assured me that she had found Aldous Huxley an 'absolute pet'. Douglas made a formal speech to welcome the Davenports and to praise gallant England, and I dropped the awful brick of making light of the whole business in my reply. We said goodbye to Deborah in a daze. Our clearest recollection of this journey to a make-believe colony was that the charming Clark Gable looked exactly like Clark Gable, flapping ears and all.

When we returned home in May we found a sterling crisis approaching over the worsening balance of payments which proved to be Hugh Dalton's undoing. Hugh had sent a curt note to Attlee asking what was the good of spending £1000 million a year on arms if there was to be an economic crash within a year. He was entirely without blame for the sterling crisis. He had continually urged his colleagues to cut down their spending and warned them that the American and Canadian loans would be exhausted before the balance of payments had been restored to surplus. A clause in the American loan agreement compelled us to make the pound convertible by 1947 unless it was considered impracticable. Hugh's advice from the Bank of England – he blamed, of course, Cobbold for it – was that it was entirely practicable. As soon as it was tried out, there was a wild flight from sterling. In a letter which I wrote to *The Times* of 2 August I protested strongly. It ran as follows:

> Sir. Only $1,000,000,000 of the American loan is left. The accelerated rate of drawings – $700,000,000 this month – points to only one thing – a flight from 'free' sterling. This must be stopped at once. We did not borrow from America to provide foreign countries with dollars but our workpeople with food and our factories with raw materials. If we are to survive as a great trading nation we cannot allow our last reserves of gold and dollars to disappear down the drain of a convertibility clause in the American Financial Agreement of December 1945.... A flight from 'free' sterling at the rate of £750,000,000 a year is unthinkable.... I venture to suggest that the Prime Minister should immediately declare that we find the convertibility clause to be unworkable and that we must immediately restrict the conversion of 'free' sterling in order to protect our vital dollar reserves, which must be strengthened by drawing the balance of the American loan. In this connection it would be pertinent for him to point out that the rise in American prices had reduced by about $1,000,000,000 the value of the original loan which we never regarded as adequate to see us through the post-war difficulties.
>
> NICHOLAS DAVENPORT

The next day I received this letter from Hubert Henderson.

ALL SOULS

3 August 1947

MY DEAR NICHOLAS,

Congratulations on your really admirable letter in *The Times*. Many things that badly needed saying excellently put! I think *The Times* are going to publish two articles by me on Tuesday and Wednesday and you may be inclined to suspect plagiarism.

In fact, however, they were written before your letter appeared. So it is an instance of great minds thinking alike.

The really key question today is – when we will move ourselves to repudiate convertibility? Yours ever,

HUBERT HENDERSON

Convertibility was suspended on 20 August and in the following week, at a meeting of the National Investment Council, Hugh growled: 'I see some of you have been writing to the Press!' He was very cross and petulant.

Christopher Hollis MP also wrote me a letter saying that he had tabled a motion in the house – weeks before my letter to *The Times* had appeared – demanding that we invoke the 'special circumstance reservation' clause in the loan agreement:

> You will doubtless be shocked [he added] at the insane complacency of Glenvill Hall in saying that the situation was still under control and that it was a matter of opinion whether the present circumstances were exceptional. But what frightens me is that there seems a complete lack of understanding either on the front Government or on the front Opposition bench of the urgency of the situation. Dalton exudes a beaming optimism that is merely fatuous.

Twice Hugh came down to Hinton nervously exhausted after this ordeal and twice my wife and I brought him back to a working balance. Hugh recorded in his diary:

> After another infinitely wearisome Cabinet meeting at which a number of restrictive decisions were taken, e.g. to stop the basic petrol ration and holidays abroad, I leave by car with Nicholas Davenport for Hinton. A large crowd in Downing Street cheers loudly as we leave. I say to Nicholas: 'They are cheering because they see that the National Investment Council has been in action' (a poor joke I thought). Nicholas and Olga are perfect hosts at such a time. I stay with them until Friday, the 29th and celebrate on the day after my arrival my sixtieth birthday. I am, indeed, now an Elder Statesman. I sleep a great deal and we visit one or two places of interest, including Kelmscott. Tony Crosland comes one evening to dinner. He is a very attractive and promising young man.

I well remember the occasion. Hugh had asked me specially to invite his young friend who was the economics Fellow of Trinity College. 'I want to see how he behaves when he is drunk', he said. Tony came in his bright red sports car, wearing the red beret of the Parachute Regiment. We had an entertaining evening of drink and talk and Tony drove back to Oxford as steadily as he had come. He could obviously hold his drink. As he drove away I could see in Hugh's eyes the rekindling of his romantic love for gallant and handsome young men. After another weekend occasion, when Tony had left abruptly to catch a train with a girl to London, leaving Hugh and me alone to dine, Hugh actually refused to eat or speak. He paced about the room as if he had been jilted as a lover.

On leaving Hinton on 29 August, Hugh had written in the house book : 'Dead to the world ! As dead as sterling into dollars ! But soon revived. Nicholas and Olga are tops as hosts.'

This was the first time I began to be anxious about Hugh's health. The sterling crisis had really upset his metabolism. He used to feel a pain in his chest, so he told me, whenever the official from the Bank of England came to announce another loss of gold. He could not understand why people sold sterling and bought dollars on such a big scale and what sort of people they were. They seemed to him to be a secret enemy. I had not realised what a terrible nervous strain he had been suffering. 'The seven months from mid-April to mid-November 1947' he wrote in *High Tide and After*, 'were the most unhappy of all my public life. . . . Very often during these months I lay awake at night doing mental arithmetic. . . . Sleeping pills could stop this mental arithmetic at some point in the night but when I woke next morning . . . there was no new hope in no. 11 Downing Street.' When we had arrived at Hinton on 25 August 1947 after the drive from the cheering crowds of Downing Street, I had noticed that Hugh was emotionally exhausted. After a few drinks he was holding my wife's hand and tears were running down his face. We feared a breakdown then and put him to bed early but he had recovered by lunchtime, for he was extraordinarily resilient. After lunch he seemed happy and relaxed and after a talk about the monetary crisis he suddenly said : 'Nicholas, would you like to go to the Lords ?' I replied that going to the Lords had no social attraction for me at all but if he wanted me to do any special job which required a Parliamentary status that was a different matter. He had nothing of that sort in mind at the moment, he said, but he would bring it up again in due course. I was spared the embarrassment, for very soon his own course ran out.

Both my wife and I felt that before long Hugh would crack. And so he did on 12 November when he was walking into the House of Commons for the presentation of his autumn budget. He met in the corridor leading to the central lobby Mr Carvel, the Lobby Correspondent, of *The Star* and briefly told him the main contents of his budget speech. Tired out, he was not aware of the risks of this encounter. He thought that Mr Carvel would enter the Chamber with him : he was too exhausted to imagine that the man would rush to the telephone and tell his paper the budget news for a 'stop press' edition which would actually be printed and on sale before he sat down. When I heard about the incident, I was greatly relieved that the breakdown had not involved Hugh in any serious indiscretion. It was a trivial matter, and Attlee need not have accepted his resignation, but Hugh insisted on going, because, apart from his highly developed sense of honour, he knew in his heart that he was no longer capable of carrying out his fearful responsibilities.

The next day Ruth Dalton telephoned to Olga to say that he could not sleep another night at no. 11. Could we put him up? We asked whether he would like to retreat to Hinton Manor where he always found peace and restoration. No, he could not leave London. At that time we had a small flat in Hertford Street and there was only a minute spare room, but we told Hugh to come along.

We dined that night in Soho, and John Wilmot joined us. Perhaps we had too much to drink to ease the strain of the moment. But by midnight we had seen Hugh to bed and I lay awake meditating on the sadness of his downfall. In the middle of the night I heard him go to the bathroom. Then I heard a thud and the sound of leaking water. Was it Hugh being incontinent? I rushed to the lobby and found him lying prostrate on the floor, muttering and groaning. In falling he had gripped the radiator and inadvertently had turned on the water. With difficulty I dragged the big man back to bed. I then fetched my wife. When she came he had just recovered consciousness and caught hold of her hands making her sit on his bed, and poured out all the feelings which had been suppressed during his crisis years at no. 11. The frustrations and anxieties of his office had been a slow torture and now that the tension had been broken and he felt released he cried his heart out. Somehow the hours passed and Hugh went to sleep. At eleven o'clock the next morning he had miraculously recovered and went to give an account of his indiscretion to the National Executive Committee. His collapse and faint were the first sign of the heart trouble which in the end carried him off.

I spoke to Ruth about the seriousness of the night attack in our Hertford Street flat, but she seemed incapable of looking after Hugh at their cottage, West Leaze, near Aldbourne. She was quite unable to make a home where Hugh could comfortably relax. She could not cook : she could hardly boil an egg. I always felt she was the wrong wife for Hugh – and he the wrong husband for her. She was an intellectual of distinction, with a fine knowledge of French literature and art, and needed a companion of the same tastes. She was excellent on committees and on the LCC, but she tended to bring out the schoolmaster in Hugh, which was the worst side of him. The marriage had nearly broken up during the war. They had a flat on the top of a building off Victoria Street. During the air-raids, Hugh used to sleep in the basement of the Millbank office of the Board of Trade when he was President. On one such occasion the bombs fell near Victoria Station and Ruth, a brave woman, thought her hour had come. After the explosions she heard the key turn in the front door of the flat. 'Ah!' she thought, 'Hugh has remembered me and has come home to see if I am safe.' 'Is that you Ruth?' he boomed. 'A terrible raid. I suddenly remembered that I had left my new suit in the flat. It would be a nuisance if that blew up.' Ruth determined there and then to leave him. And she did for the rest of the war, working, I believe, for the Free French. When 1945 came, and Hugh was made Chancellor of the Exchequer, John Wilmot persuaded her that it was her duty to be at his side in no. 11 Downing Street. She came back, and Hugh was relieved and pleased. They lived together, respecting one another but without intimacy, until he died in 1966.

After a lengthy convalescence, Hugh was fit enough to rejoin the Cabinet in July 1948. On a weekend visit to Hinton on 7 August 1948 he wrote in the house book : 'Recently appointed Chancellor of the Duchy of Lancaster with a large room in the

Privy Council Office. But as always there are Peace, Sense, Good
Food and Drink and Talk and Fun in this house'. And again in
May 1949 he came and wrote: 'This is a beautiful place of
renewal without fuss or effort'. We were happy to be able to
provide at Hinton relaxation and fun for Labour ministers under
stress. As they enjoyed good wine and food we christened them
the 'Fun Fabians' – as opposed to the Crippsian Puritan Millenarians. This tradition was kept up, on 26 September 1948,
when, according to the house book, Gavin Faringdon brought
over to Hinton for drinks, after a Fabian meeting at Buscot, Hugh
Dalton, Jim Callaghan, Dick Crossman, Maurice Edelman, Tony
Crosland, Kingsley Martin, Michael Young, Sidney Elliot and
Dick Acland. As Jim was then Under-Secretary at the Ministry of
Transport he was entrusted to the least drunk of those driving
home to Buscot Park.

The following two years Hugh was employed by Bevin on
occasional diplomatic missions over the formation of a Council of
Europe. He became deputy leader and finally leader of the
British delegation at the first and second meetings of the
Consultative Assembly at Strasbourg. The Council of Europe was
not taken too seriously by the British leader. I remember an
occasion when, after a debate in which Hugh spoke in excellent
French, he was explaining to a Norwegian delegate how English
ministers put their feet on the despatch box in the House of
Commons if their legs were long enough. He demonstrated by
projecting his feet onto a small table in the cocktail bar, sweeping
the bottles and glasses on the floor in a loud clatter to the alarm of
the assembly. The Alsatian wine always went a little to his head.

This occasion was in 1950. I had motored Dick Crossman and
his charming second wife Zita to Strasbourg to meet Hugh. He
was somewhat peeved because we were late for lunch, having
been listening on the car radio to Churchill's speech calling for a
European army, but the lunch was memorable for the quantities
of good Alsatian wine we had consumed. 'Now we are going to
walk this off', said Hugh, taking with him Jim Callaghan, Tony
Crosland and Dennis Healey on a trek up the mountain which he
describes in *High Tide and After*. 'We had a lovely sweat, an
ardent thirst, a magnificent view . . . after which we sat up talking
till a late hour.' Sweating obviously gave Hugh some sensual
pleasure, but his greatest pleasure came from the bright and

bawdy conversation of clever, handsome young men. The Crossmans and I had arranged to meet them for lunch on the next day but when we arrived at their hotel we were confronted with solemn faces on the part of the management. The English delegation had disturbed the whole hotel the previous night by singing bawdy songs until a late hour and they were now, they said, fast asleep. We decided to move on and I never referred again to the lost lunch which Hugh had clearly forgotten in the swoon of that companionable binge in the Vosges hotel.

After the General Election of February 1950, Hugh was appointed Minister of Town and Country Planning, keeping his seniority in the Cabinet by ranking five. This office was later enlarged into the Ministry of Local Government and Planning. Hugh's chief interest lay in the New Towns and the National Parks. He appointed me to the board of one of the most interesting of the New Towns – Basildon in Essex. 'I want you to go in and help to get a move on,' he wrote in a letter of 27 October 1950. 'It is vital that they should start to build new houses and new factories very soon. Only in this way can they meet the malicious propaganda of the Tory MP who is telling all the poor slum householders that for them the New Town means death and liquidation.' This appointment to Basildon was for me, as a practitioner in applied economics, a fascinating experience. I saw how vital cheap money was for social investment on this huge scale. We started with green fields and a few rural slums : we had to put in land drainage and a sewage works, make roads, build thousands of houses, even public houses, churches and recreation halls, not to mention schools and hospitals, and finally a town centre and shopping precinct. I saw what damage was done when the interest rate began to move up. It was three per cent when I arrived, and we were paying seven per cent to the Treasury when I left in 1952 during the Tory administration. I was chairman of the finance committee and had to revise the rents upwards giving a new stimulus to the wage claims in the Dagenham area. Dear money is always inflationary. Hugh wanted me, he said, eventually to become chairman of the Corporation, but that opportunity was denied. Hugh carried on happily in Local Government and Planning until the fall of the Labour Government in the 1951 election. But he was never the same man after his ordeal by torture at the Treasury.

As a postscript to Hugh's collapse over our monetary affairs I must add this charming story. When he lost office, he came to me and said : 'I wish, Nicholas, you would look after my money. I haven't got much.' He sent his portfolio and to my dismay and admiration he had put it all into 'Daltons'! I said to him : 'A painful operation is necessary. An impacted wisdom tooth must be pulled out. I am going to sell all your Daltons.' He seemed shocked, but I got him out at over 75 and, as we all know, the stock eventually went below 17. I re-invested the money in well-chosen equity shares and eventually trebled the value of his original portfolio. When he died in 1966 some people remarked that they never knew he had so much money. Nor did Hugh.

The Treasury also killed Dalton's successor, Stafford Cripps. The effort to try and make the trade unions see sense, and not join in the spiral game of wages chasing prices and prices chasing wages was too much for him. 'Our party !' – he cried in tones of despair and disgust at the Blackpool Conference when he refused to listen to the delegates or depart from one line of his prepared statement – 'our party has always insisted on the supremacy of moral values'. But they could not have cared less. They just wanted more cash down.

In July 1949 Stafford was forced to go to a clinic in Switzerland for two months rest and convalescence. This was the time when it had become evident that the sterling exchange rate of $4.03 could not be held against the ever worsening price-inflation. Stafford had set himself against devaluation, but he was finally won over by Hugh Gaitskell and Douglas Jay, his fellow Wykehamists at the Treasury. Many of us in the City used to tremble at the thought of Britain being run by three Wykehamists. Happily, Gaitskell and Jay were really moderating forces. They pressed for a devaluation to only $3.00. But Stafford by this time – 1949 – had become nervously and mentally exhausted. He outbid them in a fever and made it $2.80, which from the level of $4.03 involved a devaluation of no less than thirty per cent. The result was in the end a worse price inflation than ever before. Yet in 1949 he won a temporary victory over the trade unions. Wages in that year slightly declined in real terms – for the first time in the long struggle for the raising of the working man's standard of living. Stafford did not long survive his bitter moral victory. He was succeeded – much to Hugh Dalton's delight – by Hugh Gaitskell.

Every one in the Press had lauded Stafford's deflationary efforts at the Treasury, but I have found a letter from Hugh Dalton in my files which throws a different light on Cripps' budget:

DEAR NICHOLAS,

I am rather angry with both the *Statesman* and the *Economist* this week. The *Statesman*, in a good-bye to Stafford, suggests that I lack 'rigid moral courage' and 'concentrated power of decision,' and, though I will have my own tale to tell of all that time later on, I confess I found this characterisation rather irritating.

But little Piggy Crowther in this last *Economist* tells *statistical* lies and this makes me much angrier. You'll read on p. 639: 'in 1948 inflation was checked in the only way then possible. *The higher taxes of Sir Stafford's first budget* were the necessary method of securing a large Budget Surplus.'

Tony, in an anonymous defence of me in *Tribune* in Feb. 1949 pointed out that Stafford's big 'real' surplus for 1948–9, announced in April 1948, of £319 million (on the basis of existing taxation) was all due to my two budgets of 1947, both of which increased taxation. To this Stafford himself only added £11 million by the 'higher taxes' Crowther speaks about. I really would like someone to write to the *Economist* and expose this statistical lie, and, without even seeming faintly anti-Cripps, to put these simple facts. Crowther's personal animosity towards me is such that he can't even get his arithmetic correct when I'm about. Would you like to do it? Perhaps anonymously? Yours ever,

HUGH

I did what I could and Hugh was pleased.

The Treasury, having destroyed Dalton and Cripps, in the end broke Attlee's nerves. Because it resisted their inflationary wage claims, the Government had become unpopular with the trade unions. Rationing had gone on for too long and there were far too many Government restrictions in force – too much licensing for this and that – to suit the workers' tastes. When Attlee had to go

to the country in 1950 he lost over eighty seats and was returned
with a bare majority of eight.

Driving Hugh Dalton one day in 1951 up to Hinton for the
weekend, I pointed to a wooden hut in a farm worker's garden on
the edge of the village. 'Do you know, Hugh,' I said, 'that that
little hut could not have been erected legally without a licence
from the Minister of Town and Country Planning' – which he
then was! He looked amazed. At the end of the Levellers' reign it
seemed as if a new Cromwell had taken over and was subjecting
the countryside to the regimentation of another lot of Major-
Generals. I had had a taste of this Cromwellian regimentation
back in 1947 when my farm, which was being managed by a
young man from the north, was suddenly 'seized' and put under
supervision by the local Agricultural Committee under a clause of
the Agricultural Act of 1946, which related to 'bad' farming. The
manager had apparently over-stocked with a dairy herd and bull
and heifer calves which he could not adequately feed. The point
of outrage was that the Act made the local Agricultural Committee the accuser, the judge, the judge on appeal and the execu-
tioner. It was contrary to all our notions of equity and fair play. I
wrote a protest to Dalton but he could do nothing. Under this
and other Acts passed by the 'Leveller' government we all felt
that our native liberties had begun to shrink. We were moving
into an authoritarian state and we did not like it.

Naturally we all tried to get round the regulations by ingenious
deceptions. The most meritorious was a publishing venture by
George Weidenfeld and Nigel Nicolson. The paper shortage had
brought in a regulation that no new magazines could be
launched. So they started publishing *Contact Books* quarterly in a
stiff book-like cover. They contained lively criticism of the
contemporary scene and I was privileged to write for several
numbers of this 'book'.

The harsh anti-worker deflationary policies, which the
Treasury foisted upon Chancellor after Chancellor, eventually
split the Labour Party, as it did under Wilson eighteen years
later. Nye Bevan, Harold Wilson and John Freeman resigned
when Chancellor Gaitskell, trying bravely to finance rearmament
for the Korean war, as well as improved social welfare, proposed
to impose on the National Health Service the now familiar charge
for false teeth and spectacles. Attlee did not betray his colleagues

as Ramsay MacDonald had done, but he lost his nerve: he had had enough. So he threw in the sponge (which the old Protector would never have done) and went again to the country in 1951 to be heavily defeated. 'There are those who claim,' said George Wigg in his autobiography, 'that Attlee betrayed the social revolution. But he did not believe in social revolution'.

How shall we explain the failure of the second Puritan revolution? The Cabinet had the strongest mandate for revolutionary change ever given to a democratic government. Yet within a few years it had lost touch with its people and was void of any sense of direction. By 1950–1 it had wisely abandoned any thought of carrying its socialism forward to the completion of Clause 4 and the inauguration of the Socialist Commonwealth. Yet by its hatred of the profit-motive it had never allowed a mixed economy to flourish; it had never encouraged its business men to maximise profits and so raise the standard of living of their workers. It fell down on its socialism, yet never tried out the middle way. Years later it was said that Harold Wilson also had fallen down on his socialism, but he, too, had never tried the middle way, which was Gaitskellism.

One must not forget that the new Leveller leaders were a tired lot of Labour politicians, exhausted by their wartime offices, trying to carry out a revolutionary socialist programme, the economic and financial implications of which they had not carefully thought out before-hand – and the revolutionary implications of which they did not dare to think about. It must also be remembered that the revolutionary programme had been prepared by Marxist intellectuals who were no longer in power or in fashion. The Parliamentary leaders were *au fond* social reformers. Their kind of socialism was social reform. George Wigg – to quote his autobiography again – remarked that Prime Minister Attlee 'regarded the Labour manifesto of 1945 as a blueprint for what he himself called "an adventure of social justice".' That, indeed, was all there was to this jump in social 'revolution'. There was only one potential red revolutionary socialist in the Government – and that was Aneurin Bevan. His National Health Service stands out as the sole radical socialist measure of the 'Leveller' government. That and the New Towns, let me add.

I think the reason why the Government lost popular support was, first, because it failed to bring the workers into the social

G

'revolution'. This was entirely due to Herbert Morrison, whose concept of nationalisation was a bureaucratic managerial board on the lines of the London Transport Board with which he was familiar as a member of the LCC. The workers' social status remained unchanged. All that happened was a change of management. The top hats of the former owners were exchanged for the bowler hats of the new bureaucrats. There was no attempt to make the worker feel involved in the new State management. The great dynamism of the coal miners – the finest body of men in the Labour movement – was wasted and thrown away. The men were made to feel neglected; they were never consulted at any stage by the new Coal Board which began to be universally loathed. The same thing happened in the other nationalised industries; they were all bureaucratically, not democratically, managed. Morrison had created a vast new bureaucracy, which was unpopular both with the workers and the business men. Who really believes that the man in Whitehall knows best, as Douglas Jay once claimed? I remember once having a long private discussion alone with Herbert Morrison when he was Lord President of the Council and leaving amazed at his complete lack of understanding of the psychological aspects of his 'social revolution'.

Dick Crossman had this criticism to make, in an article which he wrote for the *New Statesman* of 19 April 1963 which I find a fair and correct summing up :

> In the history of the British left there can seldom have been an administration so conservative in its solicitude for the stuffier constitutional conventions, so instinctively suspicious of all suggestions for popular participation in decision-taking and workers control, and so determined to damp down the fiery demands for a new social order that had won them the election. . . . If in 1931 the MacDonald government was killed by the aristocratic embrace, in 1951 the Attlee Government quietly expired in the arms of the Whitehall establishment.

In the second place, the Labour Government left the rich richer, and the workers only slightly better off. The Nationalisation Acts, handing out Government stock to the former owners, restored liquidity to the capitalists and gave them the opportunity to increase their wealth by safer and more profitable investments. For example, I pointed out in several letters, to Hugh Dalton that the market valuation of the railway stocks before the election was about £846½ million, that it went down to about £836 million after the election and recovered – because of the rise in the gilt-edged market – to just over £850 million. As the owners of the marginal stocks, like L & NE preferred, expected to lose their dividend income in due course, there was no ground for compensating the railway owners on the basis of the wartime rental paid by the State. The market price was I said, fair enough. Yet the Government issued £1054 million of Treasury 3% stock 1978–88 in January 1948. I remember that the railway take-over became a bonanza for the Stock Exchange. Brokers did a roaring business in the marginal stocks on behalf of their speculative clients who 'cleaned up' on the Government's generous terms.

As for redistribution of wealth, the national pensions scheme, accepting the flat-rate contributions of the Beveridge Plan of 1943, actually took income away from the younger workers and passed it on to the pensioners. This was all the 'Levelling' of wealth the Government ever achieved. But they 'levelled up' the holders of the marginal railway nationalisation stocks.

By attacking, at the dictate of the Treasury, the wage rounds of the trade unions the Labour Government had made the working class feel bitter and more alienated than ever before from the governing clique. Certainly, the workers' standard of living had improved under the regime but it was painfully slow. There was a modest rise in average weekly earnings from £5 14s to £8 between 1946 and 1951. Allowing for the rise in prices wages in real terms managed to gain about 7% – a little over 1% a year. For a socialist government, pledged to level wealth and usher in the 'Socialist Commonwealth' it was surely a risible performance.

The second Puritan revolution, leaving the workers disgruntled, the rich richer, and the City still in control of the 'Commanding heights of the economy', must, in fact, be written off as an anti-climax in the march towards the 'Socialist Commonwealth.' Having suspected that this would happen I could not shed any tears.

The Labour Party is rarely generous to its leaders or friends. (I always felt that its bitchiness was so well reflected by the *New Statesman* under Kingsley Martin's editorship.) Certainly it has never recognised the debt it owed to Hugh Dalton for enriching, first, the intellectual life of his party and, secondly, the outdoor life of the middle-class who are potential Labour voters. The first contribution is, I think, the most valuable a politician can ever make to his country. By spotting or encouraging or bringing forward the bright young men of the left – Gaitskell, Callaghan, Jay, Crosland and Healey – he virtually transformed the intellectual force of the whole Labour movement. It would have been a dismal affair if the movement had been left to the dullards of the trade unions and the Co-operative party. These Dalton intellectuals gave it the chance to sheer away from the stultifying doctrines of bureaucratic Marxism and follow the course of an enlightened social democracy.

Secondly, by enlarging the national parks and forests, Dalton enriched the life of the middle-class who had then an extraordinary passion for hiking. I was always amazed to find the 'Fun-Fabians' who came to Hinton would immediately go out to range the Berkshire downs like a pack of beagles. It was a passion which was not shared by the working-class, who probably disliked Dalton enlarging the national parks and interfering with their poaching of rabbits and game. When he was Chancellor, Hugh created a National Land Fund for the purchase of land of recreational and scenic value. He was overjoyed when the Fund bought the estate covering Loch Lomond and thirteen miles of its banks and then the mountains of Merioneth and the beautiful Lake Bala. Hugh also added greatly to the forests of the Forestry Commission and was the first Chancellor to help the National Trust. I remember he made me become a life member of the Trust in the year when he undertook to double all their life subscriptions. There was no holiday he enjoyed better than visiting the national parks and forests and seeing the youth hostels crammed with ardent hikers, sweating over the mountains by day and under the sheets by night. For the enlargement of the national life in these ways Hugh should be remembered – not for his ineffectual attempt to control the Bank of England and the City.

My wife and I value a letter which Hugh wrote to me on 7 June 1948, from the Privy Council Office after his recovery from his first heart attack. I had written to condole with him and got this reply :

MY DEAR NICHOLAS,

I was very happy, on personal grounds, to get your letter. You and Olga were the most steadfast friends last November as you have so often shown yourselves to be at other times. I am less happy at the general look of things. Your apprehensions are, I know, shared by many. I am only just back so can't yet form any really firm opinions. And it is a great advantage to be free for the present of departmental detail. We shall love to come to Hinton. Love to Olga,

HUGH

On 1 December 1951, when the Daltons and the Crossmans were staying at Hinton for the weekend we tried to analyse the failure of the second Puritan revolution, but Hugh was really too tired to listen. In the house book he wrote: 'How beautiful is release from heavy responsibilities!' and Dick Crossman added: 'And how much sweeter not to have had them – yet!' The truth of that will emerge in Chapter 12.

11

The Tory Restoration

The Restoration of 1660 was re-enacted in 1951 when the Tories returned to power. As in 1606, so in 1951 everyone had had enough of 'Puritan socialism'. The workers were relieved that there was no longer a Leveller's moral conscience to make them feel guilty about their wage claims. They wanted to forget Stafford Cripps' cry that 'Our party has always insisted upon the supremacy of moral values.' They preferred the supremacy of money values – and much more fun.

The employers were also relieved because controls were being dismantled and they were now free, not only to make money for their shareholders, but also to get down to the more serious business of increasing their own private wealth. The rise in wages did not worry them. In an age of 'full employment', which had now become a built-in Government policy, they could easily pass higher wages on to the consumer in higher prices. There was no Prices and Incomes Board to stop them in 1951. What was important for the capitalist was the rise in the market value of his equity shares, which could at any time be cashed in for a tax free capital profit. Since companies were free once again to distribute share bonuses and to raise fresh capital by 'Rights' issues, the Stock Exchange was able to shake off its socialist freeze and show what a policy of economic growth meant in terms of rising capital values in the market.

When Hugh Dalton put a ten per cent tax on bonus issues I remember telling him that it would be laughed at and ignored. Companies would wait till he had gone and the tax removed, knowing full well that their assets would be growing silently and surely, if well managed, and would be reflected in market values. And so they were. The Stock Exchange began to boom in 1952.

There were in fact two major booms during the Tory 'Restoration' and how they enriched both capitalist and worker will shortly be told.

After the 'Restoration' I retired to Hinton to think things out and plan another book. I had resigned from the City partnership of Chase Henderson & Tennant during the second Puritan revolution. My known sympathy for the Levellers had made relations with my partners too unpleasant to tolerate. Some of them had objected to my serving on the National Investment Council under Dalton, and some had even opposed my appointment by Harold Wilson to the board of the National Film Finance Corporation. No one in the City, they said, should collaborate with dirty socialists. They were no doubt glad to see me go, and I was overjoyed to be free.

Some years later I was asked to write an economic commentary for a much larger firm of stockbrokers, L. Messel and Company, who were more broadminded, more adult and more alive to economics and sociology. What made it more pleasant was that the partners, while extremely efficient and hardworking, were the reverse of stuffy and seemed to be possessed of an infectious *joie de vivre*. At that time, the senior partner was Jock Hunter, a member of the Stock Exchange Council and one of the outstanding men in the City. His great integrity and decisive judgements – as positive and dogmatic as only a Wykehamist can make them – were famed far outside his firm. He was succeeded by Robbie Calvert, a quietly able, tall man of great charm whose wife was famous for her stud farm of Arab thoroughbreds. Of course I had to take a lot of leg-pulling from the younger bloods on account of my unorthodoxies but it was on the whole good humoured. My economic commentaries were circulated throughout their vast clientele and it was good to feel that they may have contributed to forward thinking in the City. Commendations came from as high up as the Governor of the Bank of England who was a friend of Jock Hunter.

I have to confess that the retreat to Hinton was also an aesthetic indulgence. I loved wandering round the garden, turning on the fountains or the cascade in the wood, watching the idle goldfish or the carp leaping in the moat, gazing at the splashing light of the little waterfall among the ferns, falling under the spell of the long yew walk with its statuary in the morning light, and in the evening watching the red glow of the setting sun slant horizontally, like a theatrical spot light, on to the great limbs of the three-hundred-year-old cedars of Lebanon, until they seemed to be on fire. There was not a part of this paradise which did not hold some magic for me, or reveal some new beauty each time I walked from one vista to another. And if it rained I used to shuffle through the rooms of the house, sometimes sitting in the bedrooms with their different period furniture – my own was panelled in stripped oak of 1700 with a Tudor four-poster, three seventeenth-century chests, a Cromwellian bible box and William and Mary chairs – sometimes looking at the Tudor portraits and finding some new features in the face of Henry vii or Edward vi, sometimes just standing entranced by the fine proportions and classical doorways of dining room or drawing room, with their cherub and lion carvings and period clocks. Even politicians without any aesthetic sense used to fall under the spell of the place.

At such times I liked to get myself 'tucked out' of the rush and bustle of the daily routine. I use the phrase 'tucked out' because I remember a letter which Lydia Keynes wrote to me in answer to my condolences after the first of Maynard's heart attacks. It ran – after thanking me – as follows :

4 June 1937

MY DEAR NICHOLAS,
You must remember that Poles are very jealous but Englishmen so different. They don't lock their wives but tie them invisibly. All the same in the end, only the pressure is subtle and more agreeable.

Maynard is better. For the first time he sat today on a chair for quite a few minutes, listened in to Toscanini on the sofa, read *Economica* and in lighter vein as well. By now he is tucked in. I always tuck myself out. I think Mr Baldwin is tucked in and so are you – the whole of the English nation. With love,

LYDIA

What a wonderful wife Lydia became for Maynard. After this heart attack she assumed the role of a dragon guarding the house against intruders upon Maynard's peace, keeping away stress and strain and insisting upon the rest and sleep the doctors had ordered. The last thing he wanted was for her to follow his economics. She gave him what he desired – love and understanding and the amusement of her quaint and often penetrating talk. My last vision of her was saying goodbye after a weekend I spent with them at their farmhouse at Firle in Sussex. The car had come to take me to the station after an early breakfast. Lydia called goodbye at the top of the staircase. She was in her black tights, doing her ballet exercises, using the bannisters as the bar.

The English nation, eight years after Lydia's letter, had gone through another Puritan revolution, and fourteen years on was embarking on a second Restoration. It was certainly not 'tucked in'. It might look like that to a rare and sensitive Russian ballet-dancer who had witnessed as a child the bloody Bolshevik upheaval, but England is always stirring underneath its crust. Its moral conscience is as plastic as the molten magma underneath the hard crust of the earth.

It seemed to me that the 'Restoration' of 1951 was as important a climacteric in our history as that of 1660. Consider what 'Restoration' meant in each case. In the Stuart Restoration, the new gentry, the surviving noble landowners, and the rich City merchants and lawyers, got together in common funk of the revolutionary radicalism which the Civil War had incited. They feared the socialism preached by the political Levellers and the soldier Agitators. Fortunately for them, they had some support from the common people who had had their fill of soldiers being billeted on their homes and of Puritan interference with their Sunday fun and games. Likewise in 1951 the gentry and the middle-class, the farmers and the business men, all got together in common funk of Marxist or Fabian socialism and, being supported by a considerable part of the working-class who were fed up with socialist interference with wage claims, they were able to regain power. What is more, a lot of working people instinctively felt that Labour politicians who had never had any money themselves were incapable of looking after the public finance and managing the national budget. There was some truth lurking behind that peasant-like suspicion.

The Restoration of 1660–89 saw the origin of the moneyed ruling-class, whose remnant was now being restored to power in 1951. After the accession of William III, this moneyed ruling-class split into two camps – Whigs and Tories – the Whigs representing the landed aristocrats and the newly rich merchants and lawyers, and the Tories the less wealthy, but more numerous country gentry like the Squire of Hinton, John Loder, who succeeded Henry Marten. Gradually a new capitalism emerged, first, out of the agrarian revolution of the eighteenth century, in which the squires of Hinton participated, and then out of the industrial revolution of the nineteenth century, which left the squires of Hinton in the cold. In the prosperous, mercantile era this new capitalism developed into finance-capitalism. Its stronghold was the Bank of England and its elite were the merchant bankers and financiers of the City. Its policy was to extend its investments overseas and its world banking, insurance and broking business. When the industrial demand for capital had become too great to be financed out of retained local profits, the industrialists in the provinces were forced to come to the capital market in the City. This gave finance-capitalism in the City a further opportunity to extend its money power at home. The curious feature of this finance-capitalism was that it was in the old Whig tradition. The poor Tory county squire was on the way out. With the cheap food imports of the new mercantilism he was no longer of any political significance. Power had passed to the financiers.

Naturally, the first action taken by the restoration of the old moneyed ruling clique was to restore freedom to the money market and the bond market. On the instructions of 'Rab' Butler, then Chancellor, the Bank of England removed the peg in the gilt-edged market, that is, it allowed the market to find its own level instead of instructing the Government broker to support it at the level of the agreed 3% yield. Before Gaitskell had left office in 1951 the long term rate of interest had already risen to $3\frac{3}{4}$%. With the Tory removal of the peg 'Daltons' immediately fell to a price which allowed a yield of $4\frac{1}{2}$%. Before the Tories left office in 1964 the rate of interest had jumped to over 6%.

In his memoirs *The Art of the Possible* Lord Butler glibly remarks that cheap money had proved to be the opposite of what the post-war situation demanded. He gave no reasons for this extraordinary statement. He just moved Bank rate up from 2% to $2\frac{1}{2}$% on taking office and up to 4% in March 1952. He did not seem to realise that dear money aggravates an inflation and that any attempt to control the economy by the use of interest rates was an outworn and discredited technique. (Alas! Edward Heath tried to bring it back in 1971 with fatal results) But 'Rab' had one sound idea which sadly he was dissuaded from trying out. This was to make the pound convertible for non-residents at a floating rate of exchange. But 'Rab', within his Treasury conventions, was an honest Chancellor and did not realise the wild extent of the rampage to get rich, which was bound to come out of the Tory restoration of freedom. He reduced Bank rate to three per cent in May 1954, and took 6d off the income tax in April 1955. Then sterling came under pressure and he had to put on a 'stop' in an autumn budget. It was the first of 'stop-go'. He relates in his memoirs that when driving home from a Yorkshire shoot he pulled up in a byway in the Lincolnshire fens and read all the 'stop' measures his advisers wanted. 'It was then in that lonely place that I first saw the necessity for an autumn budget which, as Nicholas Davenport wrote in the *Spectator* in October, was conceived in honesty.' So it was, but sometimes, commercial brains are more useful to the economy than a Chancellor's honesty.

At first there was some hesitancy in the equity share market after the fall in Government stocks which 'Rab' had induced by raising Bank rate but they soon recovered, and before long a breath-taking boom began to develop.

There were two outstanding 'bull' markets during this Tory regime. The first began in June 1952 and went on for three years to July 1955. Industrial equity shares won an advance of 118%. The next started in February 1958 – after a fall of 30% over 1955–6 – and lasted nearly two years till January 1960. In this the rise scored was 123%. The reason why an interval of two and a half years intervened between these two 'bull' markets was clear enough. To sustain a major 'bull' market you have to have a conjuncture of both favourable politics and favourable economics. From 1952–5 the conjuncture was divinely set for the 'bulls'. Then the political factor began to disintegrate. Prime Minister Eden went mad about Hitlerite Nasser and invaded Egypt with the French in 1956. The nation was humiliated; the Tory Party seemed doomed. But gradually Macmillan pulled it round, and Tory politics once more recovered with the economy. So a second 'bull' market developed and became a bonanza. The rise in industrial shares as I said, was 123%, but property shares outdid them all with a rise of nearly 200%. The land development charge had been lifted in 1953 and on 2 November 1954 Nigel Birch, Minister of Works, had announced in the House of Commons that building licences were to be dropped entirely, which caused an immediate spurt in building site values throughout the land. All this was tax free. And there was no capital gains tax on the market rise in shares. Oliver Marriott has written the story of it in his fascinating book *The Property Boom*. He listed over a hundred new millionaires: 'Army corporals and accountants, estate agents and furriers, all with one gift in common – the ability to use profitably the millions lent by banks and insurance companies.' He added: 'They built success on bricks and brains.' The most successful was Harry Hyams. He had made £27 million by the age of thirty-nine out of his office blocks, which usually remained empty, the annual appreciation in capital value not being taxable. But there were many others just as clever, if slightly less lucky. I am all for the capitalist who has a flair for creating wealth out of the skilful organisation of labour and materials – on him largely depends the growth of the economy and the export trade – but to allow over a hundred millionaires to grow untaxed out of the manipulation of development sites and life assurance money on long term was a nasty blot on the Tory 'Restoration'.

Between 1952 and 1964 the average capitalist, that is, the man who held the *Financial Times* index of thirty industrial shares, had enjoyed a capital gain – tax free – of 255%. In real terms it was 180%. Because there was no public unit trust into which the savings of the workers could be invested – as I had been advocating – the employee could not match the employer in capital gain but in income he followed suit. Between 1951 and 1964 the trade unions were able to push up their weekly wage rates by 76% and their weekly earnings by 119%. As retail prices rose by 54% in this period their gain in real terms was only 42%. It was not to be compared with that of the capitalist, but it enabled Harold Macmillan to tell the workers: 'You've never had it so good.' Strictly it was true, but it was a vulgar phrase which gave the British people a wrong image. Bernard Levin in his book *The Pendulum Years* remarked: 'The more assiduous students of Macmillans's style knew that beneath the fastidious exterior there lurked a vulgarian, and somehow his attempts to ape the idiom of the masses, as in his claim that "There aint gonna be no war" or "exporting is fun" seemed not patronising but genuine.' But those of us who had studied his career could not fail to notice that under Macmillan the nation took on an acquisitiveness which had not been seen since the days of Edward VII. Under those pontifical hooded eyes of the Prime Minister, everyone was on the make. Indeed, Macmillan encouraged the acquisitive instinct by introducing the Premium Prize Bonds. They were a great success. The more the value of the money depreciated, the more the public was willing to take a gamble on £1 of stock which could win a prize of £5000. Harold Wilson described the bonds as 'a squalid raffle,' but when he assumed power – and the cynicism which goes with it – he increased the top prize to £25,000. It is now £50,000.

Now, the Tories realised that a full employment policy with everyone on the make could lead to a wage-cost inflation, especially if skilled labour were in short supply. They were therefore determined to make full use of the monetary weapons they had brought back into play, although they had no sure knowledge of their economic effects. A monetary deflation, that is, dear money and tight money, if applied firmly enough on the right occasions, could teach the trade unions, they thought, a useful lesson by throwing men out of work, as in the twenties and thirties, if their wage demands became excessive. To prepare public opinion for this *dénouement* they set up a new Council on Prices, Productivity & Incomes and appointed as chairman a distinguished Cambridge economist, Sir Dennis Robertson, a contemporary of Keynes but not a Keynesian. Dennis had been a friend of mine – I had met him long ago at Cambridge when visiting my elder brother at Sidney Sussex College – and I had advised him on his family portfolio – an arduous job because he could never make up his mind. He was a great academic economist and a writer of mordant prose but he had no concept of the psychology of working people. Under his guidance the Council issued a series of reports calling attention to the danger of wages rising ahead of the increase in productivity although it insisted always on the need to keep prices stable. It seemed to me after reading them that the Tories were pursuing a class-war monetary policy which was bound to alienate the workers still more and produce a dangerously split society.

Happily, about this time (1953) I was asked by Walter

Taplin, an economist who was then editor of the *Spectator*, to write a weekly column on money and economics. This gave me a wonderful chance to criticise in length the Tory monetary policy which was giving me acute sociological pains. Here I must add that every subsequent editor of the *Spectat*or allowed me complete liberty of criticism and never attempted to change my words or influence my column. For me the *Spectator* has always been the most independent of the weeklies, and Iain MacLeod the most charming and considerate of editors. When he left he sent this brief note : 'My dear Nicholas, It's been delightful working with you at the *Spectator* and I can scratch your back in return. *I admire your work very much.* Happy New Year. Ever Iain.'

The staff loved Iain MacLeod. His courtesy was unfailing. He would telephone to say that he would arrive at, say, 11.30 and leave at 12.45 and he would not vary a minute. He was meticulous as well as brilliant. His most famous *Spectator* piece was his disclosure of how Macmillan 'fixed' his succession.

My criticism in the *Spectator* of the Council on Prices, Productivity and Incomes led to an unhappy split between myself and Dennis Robertson who, being the brains of the council, had drafted their reports. He believed that the root of all inflation was demand inflation and that it was caused by workers being paid too much in wages, and creating an excess demand for goods. The only way to counter it in his view was to damp down demand and increase unemployment. 'We believe', said the Council in its first Robertson report, 'that the decline in the intensity of demand will tend to moderate the insistence with which wage claims are pressed.' This might be true for a short period but it never lasted. Yet this theory of Dennis Robertson was the base of the Tory 'stop-go-stop' philosophy.

The theory behind the 'stop' – the sudden application of the deflationary brakes when the economy is said to be 'over-heated' or the balance of payments in deficit – is that it reduces imports, stimulates export and restores the balance of payments to surplus. But cutting down the home trade does not necessarily stimulate exports unless there is currently a boom in world trade, and British goods are just right in design and price. What it certainly does do is reduce output, raise industrial costs and so worsen our future competitive position abroad. By denying factories their long production runs, it pulls down the productivity of even the most efficient industries. It also lessens profitability – the home trade usually allowing a higher margin of profit – and creates a feeling of despondency throughout industry. It makes the business man feel less inclined to undertake new investment at home or to spend money on improving his sales organisation abroad. And it certainly does not stop the worker from asking for higher wages. Wages went on rising at much the same pace in each Tory period of 'stop'.

The second calculated 'stop' after 'Rab' was that of Thorney-croft who, under the encouragement of Professor (Lord) Robbins, became a 'hard money' fanatic. Thorneycroft decided that we must suffer deflation because the pound was in grave danger. So he raised Bank rate to 7% on 19 September 1957 in order to protect it. He calmly told the bankers at the Mansion House dinner: 'If one can regard the economy as an electric current, we are ensuring that if the current overloads it, the fuse will not be the pound sterling. The strain must be taken in other areas of policy.' This was bad imagery, because a growing economy has not, like an electric circuit, a fixed maximum capacity, but Thorneycroft apparently thought (quite wrongly) that the economy was overloaded and he desired to see the volume of employment (that is, the workers' livelihood) become the fuse which would blow if the overload went on. I remember going to the Tuesday Club dinner with 'Foxy' Falk at the time when the principal guest was Sir Leslie Rowan from the Treasury who had come to explain the Thorneycroft policy. Foxy demolished him by reading a short but devastating paper from which I quote the following:

Sound money as an aim overriding all others was rejected explicitly in the days of the Napoleonic wars and throughout world history it has been proved unattainable over and over again. In this new-fangled world, in which we have to struggle for survival against the advantages of great Continental economies, we shall be fatally handicapped if we listen to the Polonius-like maxims of a rentier-minded Government. Borrowing does not dull the edge of husbandry. On the contrary, it is the instrument of progress. At present it appears likely that after a short business recession we shall experience again the high rate of activity associated with rapid technical changes and other innovations. If a rising price level proves to be the inevitable and not unusual feature of this phase of history, we shall be wise to accept it as part of the cost. Better fifty years inflating than a cycle of decay.

Sir Leslie was so shocked that the meeting broke up abruptly. At that time this rebuke needed saying, but I doubt whether Foxy would have been so vehement if he had lived to see in 1973 the inflation rate go up to ten per cent.

Later on, when Thorneycroft informed the Cabinet that as guardian of the pound he must have the last word on Government expenditure, he was rebuffed by the Prime Minister and quickly forced to resign in January 1958. Macmillan, having seen the terrible effects of 'hard money' extremism in the twenties and thirties, was no doubt glad to see him go, together with his two Treasury ministers – Enoch Powell and Angus Maude. He called this drastic Treasury purge 'a little local difficulty'.

This 'hard money' fanatic was succeeded at the Treasury early in 1958 by a mild and genial business man, Heathcoat Amory, who reversed the controls from 'stop' to 'go' and allowed a hire purchase boom to develop. Under his régime Bank rate was reduced to four per cent. Of course, Amory overdid the 'go' as Thorneycroft had overdone the 'stop'. By April 1960, 'demand', he told the House of Commons, 'seemed to be in danger of out-running the capacity of the economy'. So in his April budget he had to reverse the controls from 'go' to 'stop'. Lord Kilmuir wrote in his memoirs: 'Many of us had been disappointed by his (Amory's) performance after 1959.... Whether it was merely that the sheer weight of departmental work overwhelmed him in his last months at the Treasury, I do not know, but it was evident that he had lost his grasp over economic matters.' This was evident, too, of his successor Selwyn Lloyd.

It was Selwyn Lloyd who applied the worst 'stop' of all. He literally froze wages and put on the brake of the so-called 'regulator' – the ten per cent addition to the purchase taxes and excise duties. Growth in the economy stopped; the steel industry was reduced to working at seventy-five per cent capacity; industrial investment came to a standstill. Advised by Frank Lee, the chief of his Treasury hierarchs, Selwyn Lloyd decided to have a showdown with the trade unions. There were thirty-five different wage claims pending in the spring of 1961 which could have added £500 million to the national wage bill, so he was determined to put an end once and for all to the wage-cost inflationary spiral. He had been driven to take this drastic decision, partly because he had been told that the increase in incomes in 1961 would be about fifty per cent greater than the increase in output, partly because of the sterling exchange crisis which followed on a large deficit in the 1960 balance of payments. In the first half of 1961 there was a flight of foreign money from London of around £700 million and the pound was saved only by borrowing heavily from the IMF. The IMF loan was, as usual, conditional on steps being taken to end the domestic inflation and the Chancellor at once decided upon a seven per cent Bank rate and a wages freeze. To enforce his pay pause he took the unprecedented step of refusing to implement not only the Burnham Committee's award to the teachers, but the other arbitration awards currently being made by the wage councils. At the same time the Chancellor took power to impose a ten per cent surcharge on all excise duties – and forthwith exercised it. He will go down in Labour history as the Chancellor who, having raised the standard of living of the surtax payer (not indeed before it was due) took steps to lower the standard of living of the working man.

Naturally these harsh deflationary measures were extremely unpopular and the Tory Government found itself in great trouble. Its Chancellors had committed many mistakes of judgment on economic affairs and had made the 'stop-go-stop' technique a national headache. They had carried the 1955 boom too far and reversed it too late. From 1956 they held stagnation too long – two and a half years – and in reversing it they then pushed consumer spending too far. Then, fifteen months afterwards, they had to reverse engines again. But that was not all. It was left to Selwyn Lloyd to throw the baby out with the bath water. So Macmillan decided to make Selwyn Lloyd the scapegoat for all his errors. And along with Selwyn Lloyd he sacked six other close friends from his Cabinet. He replaced Selwyn Lloyd with Reggie Maudling and instructed him to reverse engines – from 'stop' to 'go'. It was Reggie Maudling who left the famous deficit on the balance of payments of £800 million – later corrected to under £700 million – which Harold Wilson paraded before the nation

H

when he took office in 1964. It was said that Macmillan chose July for his 'night of the long knives' because Hitler had had his in June.

Dennis Robertson had retired from the Council on Prices, Productivity and Incomes in 1961. In the *Marshall Lectures* for 1960 he said :

> In the *Spectator* of 4 December 1959, Mr Davenport, one of the most sharp-tongued and contemptuous critics of the Thorneycroft policies and of the Cohen Council as originally composed, wrote these words : 'Mr Heathcoat Amory ... assumed office at the Treasury after the dangerous shock treatment had been given and the patient had come round. To everyone's surprise the mental condition of the TUC had been improved by the shock, and thereafter excessive wage claims were either not pushed or were successfully resisted, as in the case of the London busmen'. I could not help sending Mr Davenport a brief note, saying : 'Not to everyone's surprise; not to that of the much abused Cohen Council : see paras. 136–7 of their *First Report*. I neither asked for, nor received a reply to my note, nor did Mr Davenport, as far as I know, take any occasion to qualify that 'everyone'.

As a weekly columnist I really saw no reason why I should refer to the occasion again. The council never succeeded in getting any restraint in wage claims to last more than a few months. So I went on bombasting the Government for its stupid policy and I had a great ally in Robert Boothby who sent me this extract from a speech he made in the House of Lords on 27 July 1961 :

> Before I sit down, perhaps I may be allowed to detain your Lordships for a moment or two with a quotation from a very trenchant paragraph by a friend of mine, the outspoken, fearless and independent financial correspondent of the *Spectator*, Nicholas Davenport, because he succeeded last week in putting into one paragraph what I have been trying to say, and saying much less well, in the last twenty minutes. He wrote :
> 'If anyone should repent it, it is the Government itself. It should confess that it has been pursuing idiotic economic policies, refusing to plan and direct the two sides of industry, refusing to apply a building control and so allowing the build-

ing and contracting industry to over-reach itself and force up wages, relying on higher rates of interest and credit restrictions to do the impossible act of balancing the economy, encouraging the wrong domestic investment by indiscriminate investment allowances, refusing to control our overseas investment and allowing foreign exchange we have earned to stay abroad instead of coming home, trying to protect sterling with "hot money", that is, short-term foreign loans, expecting to boost exports by knocking the home trade in consumer durables, raising the price level at home by higher indirect taxes and dearer money and then complaining of the uncompetitive prices of British exports! This catalogue of ghastly mistakes is enough to make the nation rise up in anger and tell the Prime Minister that they have never had it so bad.'

That is powerful stuff, but I think that if you read it in Hansard tomorrow you will agree there is more than an element of truth in it.

In August 1962 the BBC did a programme on the 'Weeklies' and I took the opportunity when the *Spectator* turn came to hit again at the Treasury Knights. The BBC quoted dreary, repetitious speeches from the Tory Chancellors and I interjected:

This is the sixth financial crisis since the end of the war and you hear the same old speeches and get the same old remedies. The Treasury hierarchs can think of nothing better than damping down the whole economy. They are like a lot of old-fashioned doctors desperately applying leeches to a raving lunatic. We alas! are the lunatic driven mad by their stop-go policies.

Peter Black's review of this broadcast in the *Evening News* said: 'There was a mesmerising performance by the paper's financial pundit, Nicholas Davenport. With his big, sad, worldly face Davenport is the most promising personality I've seen on TV since the Orpington bye election'. How foolish, I thought, to go on writing painstakingly for a weekly paper when I might be exploiting 'a big, sad, worldly face' on television.

After Dennis Robertson's departure, the Council on Prices, Productivity and Incomes came round to the idea of a 'cost-push' inflation – against his 'demand-pull' – as our besetting national sin. But the sin really lay with the Tory Government which was applying the harsh monetary policy of the old moneyed ruling clique. It seemed incredible to me that the working-class should have to bear the brunt of the suffering whenever the ruling-class felt that they must deflate the economy in defence of the sterling exchange parity. Could managements never be expected to use their brains to offset a rise in wages by some more intelligent organisation of their business? The more I thought about it, the more I became convinced that this maladroit handling of monetary policy, this monetary attack on the living standard of the workers, would end in an explosion: the alienated working-class would make war on the society of privilege. This was exactly what happened under Macmillan's successor – Edward Heath – in 1971–3

In the Macmillan epoch the sour 'browned-off' behaviour of the workers, which followed on his cynical class-war monetary policy, became pathological. This was made evident by the number of frivolous strikes they indulged in. Railwaymen struck because they could no longer get their hair cut by railway employees in railway time and on railway premises. Shipyard workers struck because joiners and metal workers could not agree who should drill holes in metal sheets. Car workers even struck because managements dared to alter time arrangements for the tea break. Psychiatrists will recognise these frivolous strikes as the mood of the 'obstructive psychopath' – the man who will lie down on the job regardless of the public inconvenience he causes because he is discontented with, and sick of the society in which he lives.

I had long realised that economics without psychology was meaningless and that it was foolish to apply economic measures or pursue an economic policy without studying the behaviour of the human mind, particularly the mind of the workers. My wife is a voracious reader of Freud, Jung and the modern psychologists, and our lively discussions inspired me to psychoanalyse the split society. I do not claim to have the professional skill of a psychiatrist but it was easy to distinguish five psychological stages in the public mood over the past forty years – stress in the 1920s, depression in the 1930s, sublimation in the war years, frustration and disillusionment during the Labour régime of 1945–52 and finally pathological cynicism during the Tory régime of 1951–64. By the time the fifth stage was reached, our whole society had become neurotic. Aldous Huxley once defined a neurotic individual as a person 'who responds to the challenges of the present in terms of the obsessively remembered past'. Both sides of the split society were cases for the psychiatrist.

I had, in fact, consulted a practising psychiatrist about the extraordinary insensitive approach to the wages problem made by Selwyn Lloyd when he introduced the pay 'stop'. The psychiatrist agreed that he had probably been motivated by a sado-masochistic impulse to bring suffering on himself and others in order to expiate a sense of guilt. In Selwyn's view the working-class had been sacrificing the national economy for the sake of their pay-packets and they would have to be taught a lesson by suffering. In a Freudian analysis this sadistic instinct would be an extroversion of his primary masochism and I am sure that his great hour came when he received an unexpected letter from his Prime Minister to say that he had been sacked.

The social folly and the economic risk of conducting a class-ridden financial policy, which had the reverse effect of its intentions, enraged me so much that I asked Iain Hamilton, then editor of the *Spectator,* if he would take four lengthy extracts from the book I had begun writing on the split society. He agreed with a warming readiness, and in November 1963 they appeared with a clever cartoon of a split head on the cover. They created quite a stir and roused a lot of controversy. Bob Boothby, always my staunch supporter – I rejoice he is now happily married to a charming Mediterranean girl who guards him as Lydia guarded Maynard Keynes – wrote to the editor :

> Congratulations to you for publishing the four best articles on economic policy since Maynard Keynes died. Together they constitute a classic document which should be made compulsory reading for professors, politicians, tycoons and the managerial society including all trade union leaders. I hope he will now develop his themes and turn them into the book they ought to be.

I did my best and added to the book a full statistical support for the main theme, analysing both the external and the internal problems of the economy. The book was published by Victor Gollancz in the summer of 1964. I received two letters which I cherish. One was from Michael Foot who said 'I think it is one of the most important books written about not merely economics but the politics of this country over the past thirty years.' But he could not review it in the *Evening Standard* because its publication date did not coincide with his weekly reviewing date. I wondered whether he had funked admitting that my diagnosis of the split society, and not his, had been right. The second was from Roy Harrod who wrote :

CHRISTCHURCH
OXFORD

MY DEAR NICHOLAS,

I have been most fascinated by your book. It is certainly a notable and memorable work. With its general drift I am, as you know, cordially in agreement – notably with your attitude to economic expansion and about the interest rate.

But, unlike most books, yours says a great many things on every page – things of interest and importance and it is almost inevitable that I should often find myself in disagreement, even violent disagreement, with many statements. . . .

I violently object to the Establishment, but don't associate it as closely with the old school tie as you appear to. The trouble with the Establishment is that they don't think for themselves, but take on views that are simply the fashion. This is allied to the appalling amateurism of this country at present. . . .

I think you are the sole living writer I know who has consistently written regardless of fashion, party or prevailing ideology. Yours ever,

ROY

This, coming from the biographer of Keynes and the most original thinker of the Oxbridge economic schools, made me more than delighted.

The reviews were encouraging and I was particularly pleased with that of the *Economist* which, as usual with that paper, penetrated beneath the surface of things. I give it in full as it contains a synopsis of the book :

Without Mr Davenport, a City radical, the world would be a duller place. He is the solace of the conscientious layman who struggles to digest the regular offerings of the economic pundits, and his column in the *Spectator* is among the lightest and liveliest of the week. Financial journalist and company director, investment advisor and Berkshire squire, he is also the most articulate of that rare and curious breed, the City radical. From a position slightly but firmly left of centre, he has recently turned his attention to the impact of mass psychology upon the British economy. The result is an immensely readable, often illuminating and very individual tract for the times.

According to Mr Davenport, ours is a 'split society exploited by two opposing interests each motivated solely by the acquisitive instinct'. Though 'tolerant, liberal and decent by comparison with many others', it is therefore 'a neurotic society', incapable of securing for its members the good life which the smooth working of a mixed economy could provide. The responsibility for this lamentable state of affairs rests squarely upon 'the Establishment'. Over the past forty years the short-sighted selfishness of its 'financial and economic mismanagement' under the influence of the City has led to 'the complete estrangement of the working class'. All too often, the worker's attitude is now that of 'the obstructive psychopath', 'indifferent to the interests of the nation as a whole'. Unless this disastrous interaction is brought to an end, we shall remain 'a society doomed to decline'.

Since the war, however, the continued domination of the City has driven both parties to put the balance of payments above the modernisation of industry, the prestige of the pound before the welfare of the people. It is now a matter of urgency to 'put men before money' by adopting 'a humane financial policy' which is clearly seen to be equitable in its operation. But an onslaught on capital gains and the imposition of corporation tax cannot ensure acceptance of an incomes policy. The worker must also be given 'a stake in the country' by way of state-sponsored unit trusts. Involved in growth and fired by the prospect of a better life, he will soon lose his 'sense of alienation'.

The *Economist* reviewer missed the sociological importance of the State Unit Trust as I will explain in the next chapter.

Throughout this excursion into sociology, [the *Economist* went on] Mr Davenport concentrates upon the devil he knows. By comparison with the bankers, Treasury Knights and simple-minded politicians, both sides of Industry appear to have been guiltless as babes unborn or neglected Keynesians. But can the cleavage in contemporary Britain really be dated from the return to the gold standard in 1925? And is the average worker in fact more likely to be alienated by the spectacle of property millionaires or killings on the Stock Exchange than by the daily stupidity and caprice of management from his chargehand upwards? Full of good stuff and rich in its denunciation of 'finance-capitalism', this remains a view from the Barbican. Still, it begins to look as though Mr Callaghan might benefit from a few more tutorials with Mr Davenport.

This he was never allowed to do. As I will tell in the next chapter he became, like his predecessors at no. 11, the slave of that closed monastic order, the Treasury Establishment.

12

The Socialist Miscarriage
1964-70

Shortly before the General Election of 1964 – and just before
The Split Society was published – I went to see Harold Wilson in
his room at the House of Commons. I told him about the book
and asked whether I might give him a brief synopsis. He lit his
pipe and courteously prepared to listen.

I said that economics was meaningless without an understanding of psychology. The Tory Party did not seem to realise
that you could not subject the working-class to a loss of jobs in
order to maintain the exchange value of the pound without
making them feel resentful and rebellious and in time alienated
from the rest of society. He puffed and agreed. What is more, I
went on, the monetary techniques employed – the 'stop-go-stops'
– must seem to them to emanate from a moneyed ruling clique
who did not have to suffer the same distress from deflation but
were, on the contrary, always enriched by the rise in the market
value of their investments when inflation came round again on
the Stock Exchange. I thought this was a very dangerous situation
and was bound eventually to lead to a confrontation between
rulers and ruled and perhaps to the explosion of class war. I
concluded by saying that I could see no Prime Minister capable
of healing the sore in our society – the widening split – except
himself. He smiled and assured me that he had no intention of
repeating the 'stop-go-stop' of the Tories. But, that, of course, was
exactly what he did.

Seeing my chance to advance some of the pet ideas of my *Split
Society* I went on to stress the importance of psychology in the
application of an economic policy. If any psychiatrist had to deal

with a sullen, resentful and unco-operative patient he would try to win his confidence by making him feel that he was on his side and able to help. In the same way a future Labour Prime Minister should try to make the working-class feel that they could share in the fruits of economic expansion in a capital way, like the rich, as well as in an income way through higher wages. This could be done, I said, by setting up a public unit trust and letting the workers buy equity units at the Post Office as they would Saving Bonds. They would quickly see the units appreciate in market value. Such an idea was entirely logical because Labour was allowed by the *New Statement of Aims* of 1960 to work a mixed economy. It would have the added attraction that in times of inflation the workers could have a small percentage of their pay deducted for 'Forced Savings' in the public unit trust. Incidentally, I added, we could at long last have a funded National Pensions Scheme if the Pensions Minister were authorised to invest his surpluses in units of the public unit trusts.

He ignored the last point but I could see he was interested. So I went on to explain how unit trusts operated and what management charges they exacted. A State unit trust would have a much lower management charge and would undoubtedly attract the small saver who was suspicious of the City and yet disliked seeing his Post Office Savings depreciate in real value through inflation. I told him that I had proposed a State unit trust as long ago as May 1958 in my column in the *Spectator* but it had not been taken up by anyone in his party until Douglas Jay appropriated the idea without acknowledgement in articles he had written in 1962 and 1963. The name I had given to it in my book was SPUT – State Participation Unit Trust – which, I suggested, would buy carefully selected equity shares of well managed enterprise companies quoted on the Stock Exchange, as well as shares offered by trustees of deceased estates in payment of death duties. It was essential, I added, to keep the management of SPUT in expert hands, independent of the Treasury and Government, so that it could have the status of a public board like the BBC. It would soon accumulate holdings larger in size than those of the private life and pension funds and unit trusts and would become a major factor in directing the public savings into worthwhile investment required for the growth of the economy. At the moment there was no government control over or any direction of the public savings which were in the hands of the managers of private life and pension funds and unit trusts who were at liberty, if they wished, to invest the whole lot abroad.

I recalled that I had written a letter to him in July 1963 referring to an article of mine in the *Spectator* on 'The Price of Money', which had contained this sentence :

A new Labour Government may, therefore, decide to take powers first to direct the life assurance companies as the main holders of the accumulated savings of the people to hold a certain proportion of their assets in Government bonds; secondly, to set up a State unit trust which might receive the deposits of savers who preferred equity shares to bonds.

I felt that I had made an impression on Harold's thought. Perhaps he could see socialism being introduced by the back door if the State acquired an increasing stake in private enterprise through a public unit trust. Perhaps he thought that this would be a step towards the ultimate collectivisation of capital. This was not, of course, my objective; my aim was simply to make the working-class feel involved in the business of wealth creation, by sharing in the capital profits as well as the dividends. It was surely the only way to remove their discontent and their growing sense of alienation from a capitalist society. It was also the only way to make a mixed economy work in harmony. He seemed to agree.

In a subsequent meeting with Jim Callaghan I also thought that I had won over the future Chancellor to my idea of a unit trust. I did not, of course, expect professional politicians to act on the spur of a rational argument. They had their political position to consider and it was awkward enough. The Labour Party, being a coalition, had its unreconcilable left and right and as the left was always more loud-mouthed than the right, the leaders of the party would inevitably have to play to the left. They could not, therefore, suddenly propose a public unit trust which might smack of capitalist practice. They could not admit that the appreciation in the market value of the units of this public unit trust would depend mainly upon the rise in company profits. They had to adopt an equivocal attitude towards company profits to please their left wing whose ultimate aim was still to destroy capitalism. It was, in fact, two years after taking up office before Callaghan allowed himself to say that he was not against profits.

When Wilson expressed agreement with that sentiment he was always careful to qualify it, if he was speaking to the 'comrades', with the proviso that profits must be made fairly and honestly, not by financial manipulation or by the exploitation of a monopolistic position. So neither Wilson nor Callaghan in office ever considered the setting-up of a public unit trust which might have healed the split society. Alas! I never had a favourable opportunity to bring up the subject with them again.

I always felt when talking with Jim Callaghan that it was like playing with a big Alsatian dog. All would be well and then suddenly you would get a nasty bite. With Wilson it was like being friendly with a cat. It would purr along and take delight at being stroked but suddenly it would arch its back and walk off in another direction. But it is futile to expect politicians to behave in a logical or straightforward manner. They are always too concerned about their own personal or party line. In the Labour ministry of talents of 1964 I knew personally at least half a dozen intellectuals of distinction in the Cabinet and often wondered why they so miserably failed to divert the Prime Minister one inch from his fatal course. What I found unpleasant about this Labour administration was that you only had to meet one Cabinet minister to hear some abuse or criticism of another. They seemed to have neither the loyalties of the working-class nor the manners of the upper.

There was only one politician I found really loveable and in tune with my ideas about a public unit trust. Not long after *The Split Society* was published, the telephone rang and a voice from St Moritz said that he had read it with excited interest and could he meet me? It was Harold Lever, the Labour Member for the Cheetham division of Manchester. He said he believed strongly in a mixed economy, in the creation of wealth and in the sharing of it, as I had proposed, through a public unit trust. He was at that time a member of the Wider Share Ownership Society which Maurice Macmillan was pushing. We arranged to meet at his London flat and I found him at the first encounter a fascinating talker, a serious thinker and a wit with a droll sense of humour.

Harold Lever was a rich man, having had a genius for making money out of money, which the prejudiced socialist always condemned. Before he was out of his teens he had made money by buying and selling houses on borrowed money as he had seen his family lawyer firm do. Then he found it easy to exploit the bond market, as Keynes had done, for he had an instinctive flair for the money market. A firm of Manchester stockbrokers called him in to advise on new issues. So his wealth grew out of his money management and expertise. Finally he became a barrister specialising in financial and tax cases. But he was not at first regarded as a serious politician. He headed the list for non-attendance at the House, perhaps because he found party politics frivolous, and bridge-playing and backgammon intellectually more satisfying. He introduced me to the charming Rixi Markus who was, and still is, the world's greatest woman bridge player. Any one who could partner her must be very gifted. But Harold was *au fond* a serious sociologist. He saw the social and economic dangers of the split society as I saw them and we used to have constant talks over morning coffee in his flat on how to manage a mixed economy and expand its wealth.

Olga and I were delighted when Harold married Diane Bashi, the ex-wife of Selim Silkha of Mothercare fame. (Harold always maintains that since he took Diane away, Selim, now many times a millionaire, has never looked back.) Diane came from the rich Iraqi banking family of Bashi. She had great beauty, charm, taste, determination and a quiet wit. She decorated their flat in Eaton Square with genuine panelling and furniture of the Louis XV period with exquisite *objets d'art* and pictures. 'What will the comrades say?' I asked Harold, as I watched a French artist painting the bathroom in *trompe l'oeil* style. 'I don't care', he replied, putting on a strong Manchester accent. 'My wife has been used to luxury all her life and I don't see why she should be deprived of it because she marries a poor Labour member from Manchester'. How right he was! When she went to his constituency, as beautifully dressed as she always is, the wives were fascinated by her clothes and jewellery; they were not envious of wealth, knowing that their rich member was doing his best to right wrongs and stand up for social justice.

Diane Lever made Harold take politics more seriously. He had always been recognised as a useful and witty party speaker. He once talked out a Tory films Bill by speaking non-stop for four hours – with the house often convulsed with laughter. His imitation of his brother Leslie, who had been made a Papal Count by the Pope for his gifts to Catholic schools in his Manchester

constituency, will long be remembered as the finest Parliamentary
burlesque. Yet for the first year of Wilson's administration he
remained a backbench Member and it was only his devastating
criticism of Jim Callaghan's first April Finance Bill which made
Wilson give him ministerial office. He began in the humble position of a junior minister at George Brown's new Ministry of
Economic Affairs.

As soon as Harold Wilson was installed at no. 10, complete
with Marcia Williams as personal secretary, George Wigg as
'security' adviser and Tommy Balogh as economic adviser – a
very formidable under-the-counter team – I sent him a warm
letter of congratulations and advice and received this kind, but
non-committal reply :

10, Downing St.

MY DEAR NICHOLAS,
Many thanks for your letter of the 21st and your very kind
encouragement. I will do my best to keep in touch with you
through the *Spectator* and I am glad you are keeping contact
with Jim. You will see that we are making an economic statement next week but I won't try to anticipate your comments on
the following Friday. All best wishes again – and warm regards
to Olga. Yours,

HAROLD

I sent him my book, suitably inscribed, as I heard he had been
quoting figures from it in his election speeches. In his reply of
thanks he said : 'We certainly intend to press on with solving the
problems you describe'. I had marked the passage where I said
that he was tailored for the job of uniting the split society – a
grammar-school boy, scholar and then Fellow of an Oxford
college, civil servant during the war, familiar with management
problems as well as labour resentments, tuned to the technological
revolution. There had never been a Prime Minister so fitted to
unite the nation. Hitherto, nice ineffectual men from the right
family and public school had risen to the top of Tory ministries.
No one could say that Harold Wilson was either nice or ineffectual. And he seemed to have destiny behind him, as we were
constantly reminded by that photograph of him as a little boy,
standing on the threshold of no. 10.

The time was indeed ripe for uniting the two halves of the

nation. As Frank Cousins had been declaring *ad nauseam*, in the Selwyn Lloyd period, that he would never agree to an incomes policy under a Conservative government but that if Labour were returned he would accept some restraint of wages provided other incomes – profits, dividends and rents – were also subject to restraint, I thought that the grand opportunity had arrived – that Prime Minister Wilson could close the ranks. All he had to do was first to convince the TUC that social justice would be done through a reform of the taxation system, removing the tax advantages accruing to the possessors of capital. Secondly he should persuade the CBI that companies in the private sector would be encouraged to make sufficient profits to enlarge their investment and improve their productivity, provided they took their workers into a kind of partnership, involving them in the lay-out of their work. On the basis of an expanding economy – with the balance of power held firmly between workers and management – a voluntary incomes policy could, I thought, become practical politics. This was also the view of Harold Lever with whom I discussed endlessly the working of a mixed economy.

I assumed that as Harold Wilson had practised economics at Oxford he would know enough to be able to steer the economy safely through the rough currency weather blowing up from the balance of payments deficit. But alas! the sterling crisis of 1964 seemed to be beyond his comprehension. When foreign bankers began selling sterling he thought it was a wicked fascist conspiracy to wreck socialism in England. He rushed to the defence of the pound and applied – guess what – the conventional monetary policies of finance-capitalism! He told the City at his first Lord Mayor's banquet : 'I want to take this opportunity tonight, in the heart of this financial centre, to proclaim not only our faith but our determination to keep sterling strong and to see it riding high.' His only break with City tradition on that occasion was to wear a black tie and dinner jacket instead of the customary white tie and tails, and decorations. Eventually – who would have believed it of a 'socialist' government? – the deflationary policies he applied during his term of office for the protection of the old exchange rate of sterling were progressively so harsh that the economy began to stagnate and unemployment to rise. He had outdone even the 'stop-go-stop' policies of Tory finance-capitalism!

It was clear to most economists in 1964 that an exchange rate of $2.80 was becoming a difficult position to maintain. The official economic adviser to the Treasury at that time was Robert Neild, whom I had recruited to the Board of the National Mutual Life office when I was Deputy Chairman. I knew Robert to be a devaluationist and I am sure he expected to preside over the devaluation of the pound on taking up his job at the Treasury. His shock on finding that politics came before economics with the Prime Minister caused him to resign his post in 1966, after Wilson had been returned to power with an increased majority and still did nothing about devaluation.

Robert Neild had been a colleague of Nicky Kaldor at Cambridge – the second of the Hungarian-born economists called in by Wilson to the consternation of the Central European bankers – and Nicky too was a convinced devaluationist. But Nicky had been posted to the Inland Revenue Department – to put the fear of God into the hearts of the rich – and was out of reach of Wilson's ear, which Tommy Balogh had. So Wilson took George Brown and Jim Callaghan into the Cabinet room one day – the door being shut without any economist or civil servant being present to advise – and told them firmly that they had to stand by the pound. The Labour Party, he said, could not survive if it were said that every time it took office there was a flight from the pound – as in 1931 and 1949. So it was a political, not an economic, decision.

There had been a great tussle between Wilson and Lord Cromer, the Governor of the Bank, over the raising of Bank rate from five to seven per cent before the first international loan was negotiated in defence of sterling. Cromer had wanted to have it raised earlier, and to have it accompanied with a statement that wages would be frozen and Government expenditure cut, which Wilson properly refused to make. I remember that Olga and I went to dine with Dick Crossman at his house Prescote Manor, near Banbury, on the Sunday before Bank rate was raised which was 23 November 1964. Dick apologised for cutting the dinner short because he had a train to catch. 'The PM', he said, 'has called a Cabinet meeting early on Monday. God knows what for'. I said I could tell him; the pound was in grave danger. 'Really?' he replied. 'No one has told me.' The astonishing thing was that Wilson had kept the first sterling crisis away from the Cabinet until the last moment. He knew that a decision to stand by the pound and adopt the Tory deflationary finance policies would be likely to arouse a lot of opposition in his party. So he conspired only with the two ministers on the financial front – George Brown, who was not too willing, and Jim Callaghan who (according to George Wigg's memoirs) was in a state of jitters. It is curious that Ramsay MacDonald, when he decided to stand by the pound in 1931, conspired also with two senior ministers only – Snowden and Thomas. In socialist betrayals, Judas perhaps, assumes a trinity like the Godhead.

'Don't mention the name of "Roley Cromer" to me again', snapped George Brown when I called on him one evening at the DEA after this first sterling crisis. We were alone in his palatial office and he pulled out the bottom drawer of his desk to disclose a bottle of whisky to moisten our talk. After he had blown up, I reminded him that the Governor had really saved his Government's life. 'Roley Cromer' had called up his Central Bank friends on the telephone on 26 November 1964 and had persuaded them to support sterling to the tune of $3000 million in spite of the terrible things Wilson had been saying about the financial mess left by Maudling. Wilson had actually sent two senior ministers – the Foreign Secretary Gordon Walker and the President of the Board of Trade, Douglas Jay – to a meeting of the Ministerial Council of EFTA to justify our breach of faith in imposing a fifteen per cent surcharge on imports. Tell them, he said, that we had no time to consult them because we were 'sunk'.

Douglas Jay told me afterwards that he had never favoured this breach of faith : he had proposed import quotas which would have been permissible under IMF rules. But ministers in those days never thought of resigning on points of principle : they obeyed the Wilson rules of expediency. It was Wilson's tactic to discredit his Tory opponents by telling the world that they had left Britain in a financial mess. But what business man would have thought of trying to raise an overdraft from his bank by confessing to the manager that he was 'in a financial mess' ?

Incidentally, the trumpeted '£800 million deficit' turned out to be a gross exaggeration. The Central Statistical Office published new tables in August 1970 which revealed that the total deficit in 1964 was £695 million, of which £395 million was on the current trading account and £300 million on capital account. The trading deficit was swollen up by stocking-up at a time when the terms of trade were worsening. The capital account, which is only in debit when more assets are acquired abroad by British residents than are acquired in Britain by foreign residents, was unfortunately heavy that year. But any British government which commanded respect abroad, as Harold Lever always insisted, could have financed a £395 million trading deficit. Edward Heath did not panic when his deficit went over £1000 million but he was protected of course by a floating pound.

After the first attack on sterling, I asked the private office at no. 10 to arrange an interview for me as financial correspondent of the *Spectator*. In January 1965 Harold Wilson received me in the Cabinet Room. The first impression I got of the Cabinet Room was its vulgarity : too much gold leaf and green brocade. But it seemed to suit the ebullient Prime Minister. He was in great form and exceeding good humour. He was sitting in his armchair in the middle of the huge oval Cabinet table smoking his pipe as usual. I noticed that he was much better dressed than he used to be and was wearing new brown suede shoes. He sat back in his chair, put his feet neatly on the Cabinet table and began puffing his pipe. 'You know, Nicholas,' he said, 'I had to take control of this little affair with the Governor. [One gathers from Wigg's memoirs that Jim Callaghan had collapsed.] I sent for the Governor and we had a proper confrontation in this room. I heard what he had to say. You know the stuff about freezing wages and cutting government expenditures. So I said : "Mr Governor, I would like to ask you one question. Who is governing Britain? The Governor of the Bank or the Prime Minister?" [Puff! Puff!] He didn't like it [Puff! Puff!] No banker likes being deflated. They like to impose deflation on others'.

There were in all four sterling crises – November to December 1964, June to September 1965, June to September 1966 (when a wages and prices freeze was imposed) and May to November 1967. Wilson might be forgiven for his refusal to devalue on the first occasion, when he was new to the game and had a majority of only six in the House, but not on the second or the third. On each occasion he borrowed heavily from the IMF and the Central bankers until he had finally to submit like an undischarged bankrupt to the annual supervision of the IMF and write them 'letters of good intent'. On each occasion he handed out the harsh doses of deflation which he had promised the workers he would never do when unemployment was high. On each occasion he adopted the 'stop-go-stop' techniques of the Tories which he had railed against when he was in opposition. The only difference was that his 'stops' became more severe as they went on until he ended up with the worst kind of economic crisis we had ever seen. It was called 'stagflation' because it embraced simultaneously an economic stagnation and a raging wage-cost inflation.

In *The Labour Government's Economic Record 1964–70* Wilfred Beckerman, who had been economic adviser at the Board of Trade, declared that Wilson's biggest mistake was not to devalue in 1966 immediately after the general election had given him a majority of ninety-seven. I do not agree. It seems obvious to me that a modest devaluation should have been put through early in 1965 when it would not have provoked a wild rush into the shops, or a sharp rise in prices and wages. Wilson should have gone to Washington as soon as the first crisis had blown over and should have told American and IMF officials that it would take five years to 'restructure British industry' (his favourite phrase) and that in the meantime the export trade would have to have the stimulus of a ten per cent devaluation. If they refused he should have threatened to float the pound. But they would not have refused. Sterling had an immense nuisance value. The Americans were scared that if the pound collapsed the dollar would follow. The IMF were scared that if sterling and the dollar collapsed, the whole international monetary system would fall apart. Our nuisance value at that time was so great that we could almost have dictated the terms of support for a modestly devalued pound. Of course, we would have to have agreed to a partial dismantling of the sterling area, which was in any case overdue. We would have had to tie up the sterling balances as we did in the Basle agreement of 1968, which Harold Lever helped to negotiate when he was Financial Secretary of the Treasury, but if we could pull off a Basle agreement in 1968 we could have done the same in 1965 when the sterling situation was far less critical. But 1965 went by without a move on the part of the Prime Minister to avert the coming tragedy or to employ the financial expertise of Harold Lever who was the only minister who could talk to bankers overseas in their own language.

Actually Wilson was very nearly driven into devaluation in 1966. In July of that year M. Pompidou had arrived for a courtesy visit and, to Wilson's annoyance, had recommended devaluation. The Cabinet at that time was split over devaluation and tempers were frayed. Wilson denounced the Press talk of devaluation and spoke contemptuously of 'the moaning minnies, the wet editorials'. The ministers who favoured devaluation were George Brown, Roy Jenkins and Tony Crosland on the right and Dick Crossman, Barbara Castle and Tony Greenwood on the left. On the night before the great Cabinet row, which was on 19 July, I dined with Dick Crossman in the House of Commons. He asked me, as one practising in applied economics, whether devaluation was practicable here and now. I replied: 'Of course it is – provided you take powers, being a socialist government, to control the subsequent movement in prices and wages'. Partly because the six were not prepared to resign *en bloc* if their advice was rejected, partly because Wilson, supported by the vacillating Callaghan, was able to carry the rest of the Cabinet with him, devaluation was again rejected. It was about this time that a story went the rounds of Whitehall that Wilson had complained to a friend about the uselessness of so many of his Cabinet colleagues. 'Why, then, don't you sack them?' asked the friend. 'Are you mad?' came the reply, 'they are the only ones whose votes I can rely on'.

I had first hand evidence of the reasonable French attitude to sterling devaluation in 1965 and 1966 because shortly after the visit of Pompidou I flew to Paris to have lunch with M. Wormser, whose sister was a friend of my wife. M. Wormser was then an economic adviser to De Gaulle, and was subsequently ambassador in Moscow. He is now chairman of the Bank of France. After lunch in his small and charming flat he gave me a dissertation on the French view of the English sickness and told me that they had always been prepared to support a devaluation of the pound of the order of ten to fifteen per cent. I went to see Callaghan on my return to report this frank and helpful conversation and was curtly told that I had been talking to the enemy!

Wilson's misadventure over the pound was matched by Callaghan's misadventure over his budget, but I must bear witness to Jim's good intentions. He did genuinely try to heal the split society, by carrying through the taxation reforms which the unions had demanded, not merely as an act of social justice, but as a prerequisite for their co-operation with the Government on any incomes policy. As every one knew, the possessors of capital had enjoyed many tax advantages, and companies trading abroad had been able to get away with revenue murder by offsetting British tax against tax paid overseas. Jim's mistake was to do too much too quickly – the opposite of Wilson's mistake over sterling. He frightened the business world by giving notice in November 1964 that he would introduce a capital gains tax as well as a new corporation tax in his 1965 Budget. When April came round there was consternation in the City. It was worse than they had expected. It was an affront to private enterprise. There were clauses in his revolutionary Finance Bill which laid such heavy restrictions and penalties on 'close' companies that some of the merchant banks in the City would have had to close their doors. Nicky Kaldor had apparently convinced Jim that all private companies – the fount of all our private enterprise – were mere dodges to evade or mitigate taxation!

The hundreds of amendments to the Bill which were tabled were signs not only of the City's dismay but of the bad draughtmanship of a complicated Bill which caused despair to settle on the offices of the Inland Revenue for the rest of Jim's tenure of office at no. 11. Harold Lever won his Parliamentary spurs by speaking against the most noxious clauses in the Committee stages of the Bill. It was probably this brave act of opposition to his party which drove Wilson to offer him ministerial office.

Jim's budget speech, everyone agreed, was a remarkable *tour de force* and I wrote on 8 April 1965 to congratulate him on it. I said : 'I was personally gratified because your taxation reforms carried out the recommendations of the last part of my book *The Split Society* except that I prefer a steady taxation of capital *increment* to a capital gains tax. I do not know what Macleod is saying but I am giving it full praise in my part of the *Spectator* although, as I say, I think you have overdone the deflation'. Although he delivered a fine peroration in the speech about uniting a divided nation, I fear that Jim made the split worse; he antagonised the business world and lost their support for good and all. And he did not add to this reputation when he said in a speech in June : 'As a result of the Budget we have now reached a stage when not even the most doubting Thomas believes that the pound is likely to be devalued.' I felt sorry for Jim, for he was aware of the causes of the social split and was never thanked by the trade unions for trying to remove the social injustices of the tax system. He had studied *The Split Society,* as I was made painfully aware when he insulted me at a dinner party in Harold Lever's flat, accusing me of running down my friends when they were dead (this must have referred to my criticism of Hugh Dalton which I had felt bound to make in the interests of economic truth). I remember sitting in my City office one after-noon, worrying over the fact that Jim had gone too far in his April Budget – two revolutions in one Finance Bill ! – when the telephone rang and a gravelly voice said : 'This is Jim speaking. I thought I would let you know that your book had really inspired my budget.' It was a nice gesture. It showed that he had honestly tried to heal the split society. But it gave me a sinking feeling, for I realised that he had no idea of what made one half of the split society tick.

I tried to explain to Jim the misgivings of the private sector when he and his charming wife Audrey came to stay a weekend with us at Hinton on 5 March 1966. But it was of no avail. Jim wrote his name in red ink in the house book : 'Red ink until the BOP (balance of payments) is in the black.' In spite of his brave words in public he was still desperately worried about the pound. Yet because he had to be looking over his shoulder all the time at his left wing he was not prepared to go all out for company profits. Only a highly profitable private sector and a cheaper pound could have brought a surplus to the balance of payments.

My depression deepened when Jim introduced his 1966 Budget. He brought in a new tax which again upset the business world – the Selective Employment Tax. This administratively complicated tax, involving payments out, and re-credits in hundreds of millions, imposed a pay-roll tax on essential service industries, including the building trades, and handed out a pay-roll bonus to all manufacturers, including the manufacturers of candy-floss and luxuries. I remember going to Great George Street at about six o'clock on Budget day to collect the Treasury papers for the *Spectator* article I had to write when I ran into Nicky Kaldor, the inventor of the tax, in Whitehall. 'Nicky' I cried, 'what have you done ! Putting a pay-roll tax on builders in a housing shortage and giving a bonus to the manufacturers of one-arm-bandits in the pubs!' He roared with laughter – he was always a congenial man to meet – and as I went down the steps to the Underground I could hear his laughter echoing in the street. 'Poor Jim!' I thought. 'He is now in the hands of quite the cleverest of the academic lunatics of the left.'

I wrote a letter of protest and concern to Jim after his July 1966 deflationary measures, and received this letter in return :

DEAR NICHOLAS,

Many thanks for your letter of 8th September. I hope that you will point out, in any article you write, all the differences between the measures of July, 1961 and those of July, 1966! I mention some of them below.

The total effect of all our measures is of course greater than that of those taken five years ago; that is because the size of the deficits, and the pressures on the economy, are much greater. But there is all the difference in the way the restraints have been applied.

Though we have cut back on public investment, we have excluded housing, schools, hospitals and Government financed factories built in development areas. The contrast with 1961 is clear; on that occasion cuts were made in educational programmes, the house purchase scheme was suspended, and the growth of expenditure on the health services was curtailed.

I believe that the new investment grants will discriminate more effectively than the old system in favour of the poorer regions; and that, with the greater selectivity of the grants system, there will be a decided advantage for investment in manufacturing industry.

While there should be some easing in the pressure of demand, and hence some rise in unemployment, our regional policies are designed to ensure a more even spread over the country.

Our measures to improve the balance of payments have partly taken the form of curbing home demand, but we have also done a great deal, before 20th July, to control investment overseas. In this we have gone a great deal further than Selwyn Lloyd in 1961; thus we were able to deflate by less than would otherwise have been necessary.

I do not see how anyone can deny that the prices and

incomes standstill is a different, and much better, prospect than the Pay Pause. The standstill is extremely stringent and wide ranging; it can, if necessary, be enforced, so that justice can be seen to be done; and it covers commitments outstanding from the date of operation. In all these respects, the standstill is substantially different from the Pay Pause. Moreover it was introduced after a series of measures, such as capital gains tax and a surcharge on surtax, designed to secure a fairer distribution of income; not, as in 1961, only a matter of weeks after big concessions to surtax payers. Yours sincerely,

JIM CALLAGHAN

I continued to fight against these Treasury measures in my column, in the *Spectator* and received once again – bless him! – encouragement from Bob Boothby. Here is another letter:

HOUSE OF LORDS

DEAR NICHOLAS,

What good articles these last two. You continue to surpass yourself.

I don't know whether you saw the enclosed (Hansard). It's all coming true. The maddest thing of all is this clamping down on private investment in productive industries overseas.

Is it Balogh? Is it Kaldor? Or is it just the dear old old Treasury, who have fucked this country up for forty years? Yours ever,

BOB

Bob followed up this explosion with another, in a letter to Jim Callaghan dated 2 December 1966 which began: 'Dear Jim. A Christmas thought from Boothby. Put it on your mantelpiece, when the time for reflation comes, Keynes' greatest single sentence: "Investment is governed by the expectation of Profit". Yours ever, Bob.'

But how can you really expect a Labour Chancellor to run a mixed economy when, as a professed socialist, he does not believe in profit and despises the profit-motive?

It is to Jim's credit that he could not stomach the savage deflationary package of 1966 and left it to Harold Wilson to take control over the economy. Jim's end followed quickly on the sterling crisis of 1967. After a 'no change' budget came the Six Day War in the Middle East, the closing of the Suez Canal, a huge balance of payments deficit and a climacteric flight from the pound. In November he had to announce that the pound would be cut from $2.80 to $2.40. With devaluation he had also to announce his resignation. Wilson moved him to the Home Office where his undoubted political talents were far better employed.

One of the tragedies of 1967 was the sacking of Douglas Jay from the Board of Trade. I could not feel great sympathy for Douglas. He had long been a fanatical anti-European, in spite of the fact that Wilson was urging the nation to join the European Common Market. When Wilson had said : 'The Common Market is of such transcendent importance to Britain that the whole Cabinet must be involved and that's the way I am playing it.' I asked Douglas to lunch at the Athenaeum to tell him, as an old friend, that he was in danger of losing all public respect if he did not make his position clear – that he would resign if the party accepted the terms and was only staying on in the Cabinet while the issue remained undecided. He grumbled and said he would think it over before his next speech in the country. The speech duly came and the *Daily Mail* gave this headline : 'Douglas Jay toes the line' !

On 25 August Jay's eldest son Peter, and his beautiful wife Margaret (the daughter of Jim and Audrey Callaghan) were staying the weekend with us at Hinton. Some evil tension must have been in the air, for their lovely child Tamsin, aged two, fell into the fountain while we were noisily talking politics on the terrace. Fortunately my wife suddenly asked : 'Where's Tamsin?' Peter leapt to his feet, rushed to the fountain and discovered Tamsin floating face downwards in the water. He revived her and all was well. But while the shock seemed to hang over the dinner table that night, the telephone rang from Cornwall and a sepulchral voice said : 'It's Douglas. Can I speak to Peter?' He then told Peter that Harold Wilson, journeying back from the Scilly Isles, had asked to meet him on Plymouth railway station. Walking up and down on the draughty platform, Wilson had given him the sack. Peter was livid, and after dinner he went into the drawing room alone and in a white rage wrote a leader for the 'Business News' in *The Times* which contained the most vitriolic criticism of Wilson and his economic policy that had yet appeared in that 'neutral' paper. There was never any love lost between the Jays and the Wilsons.

Jim was succeeded at the Treasury by Roy Jenkins who brought to the office an intellectual distinction it badly needed. It is always unfair to criticise a minister for mistakes made in the first six months of a change. The British habit of switching ministers constantly from office to office at the Prime Minister's whim is a ridiculous and dangerous one, which presupposes a mental agility few of them possess. There could have been no minister of greater intellectual capacity than Dick Crossman. Yet he told me that it took him nearly two years for him to master the comparatively simple Ministry of Housing, and at that point he was suddenly moved by Wilson to become Lord President of the Council and Leader of the House. I therefore criticise the civil servants, not Roy Jenkins, for allowing the public to indulge in a buying spree from the day of devaluation in November 1967 until the budget of 1968 which imposed the heavy taxation designed to stop the spending mania. Everyone knew that prices were going to rise as a result of devaluation and the rush into the shops created the dangerous inflationary fever that swept the country. The extra taxation should have been imposed at once to prevent the fever rising. It was 1968 before the Prices and Incomes Act was passed.

It grieved me to find that when Harold Lever became Financial Secretary of the Treasury a close working partnership between Financial Secretary and Chancellor did not develop. Harold had the banking-financial expertise which the academic Roy did not possess. It was Harold who prevented Henry Fowler, the Secretary of the American Treasury, from making a fool of himself in 1968 when the Americans were hell-bent on demonetising gold. The civil servants, who found Roy the eminently orthodox, if not Gladstonian, Chancellor, used to regard Harold as a maverick. Thus frustration developed and Harold had to go to bed with an ulcer, which is often the sign of emotional stress, as I know from my own experience. Recovering from his illness Harold made a speech to a Press Association about the way he would settle the short term debts abroad. The speech had not been cleared with Roy and the rift widened. Harold felt bound to leave the Treasury, which he did when Wilson offered him a higher post at the Ministry of Trade and Industry. It was sad for me and bad for the nation, for a close-working Jenkins-Lever partnership at the Treasury would have solved many monetary problems and would have made the mixed economy not only work but expand. Left to himself and his conventional advisers in 1970, Roy failed to introduce the stimulating expansionary budget Harold desired, which might have won them the election.

The break-up of the Wilson Government came after its abject surrender to the trade unions over Barbara Castle's Industrial Relations Bill. Her White Paper, called *In Place of Strife* was aptly renamed by Harold Lever 'In Chase of Strife'. I always felt that it was a mistake to leave these critical negotiations to a strident Amazon. Barbara really upset the old trade union boys who hate nagging women always trying to get their way. I hasten to add that Barbara is far from a nagging wife. Her home life with her husband Ted is sweet and loving. But her frenetic public image, her pertinacity, her vehemence, her aggressiveness had a terrifying effect upon the old-fashioned trade union negotiators. Her White Paper was like a bomb thrown by a Womens-Lib fanatic into a quiet front parlour while Dad was having his high tea. Barbara's frenzied drive for her Industrial Relations Bill certainly caused a furore in the trade union Establishment. The union leaders had never liked the wages and prices freeze in 1966, nor the 1968 Prices and Incomes Act which gave the Government the power to order delays in implementing wage agreements. When Roy gave notice in his budget speech of 1969 that legislation would be coming forward to implement the more important provisions of *In Place of Strife*, war was virtually declared between Smith Square and Downing Street. When it was found that the bill went further than the Donovan Committee – and contained penal clauses under which a trade union could be fined if it disobeyed orders for the resumption of work – hell broke loose. What really upset Transport House was the idea that the Parliamentary Labour Party, which had been financed by the trade unions, and elected for the ultimate purpose of destroying capitalism, as its old constitution proclaimed, should have presumed to act as a national government and put the trade unions in their place in a mixed economy. They had never accepted a mixed economy. Clause 4 was still in the constitution and their goal was a socialised economy with a workers' government in Whitehall, dominated by the TUC. So when the Bill was brought forward in the House, Douglas Houghton, chairman of the Labour Party, had to tell Wilson that he would not get it through. 'It can only be done with us', he said. 'It can't be done without us'. There were at least fifty members of the Labour Party who were convinced Marxist socialists and would never accept Wilson's idea of a national government running a consensus-mixed economy. So Wilson had to eat his words. He had told the party on 12 April that 'the passage of the Bill is essential to the Government's continuance in office.' But he had spoken out of turn, without consulting his masters! One must have great sympathy with him in trying to run a government in the broad national interest when the fanatical anti-capitalist interests in his party held the balance of power.

Wilson's line of retreat was to pretend that the TUC had agreed to alter their rules. They didn't. They only entered into a 'solemn and binding obligation to take energetic steps to obtain an immediate resumption of work within the rules', that is, when the TUC deemed strikers to be at fault! Tell that to Jimmy Reid on the Upper Clyde, or Bernie Steer in the docks and hear the ribald laughter it would arouse. This abject surrender of Wilson and Barbara Castle let loose the flood of pent-up wage demands, sent the wage-price spiral spinning and cost the Labour Party its defeat in the 1970 Election. In his rush to the polls, Wilson scrapped no less than twenty-two bills which were before Parliament, including the much publicised National Pensions Bill – the residue of the great social reforms with which he was claiming to bring a fairer socialistic society to the people.

There is no doubt in my mind the split society might have been unified if George Brown had been Prime Minister instead of Wilson. When I sent him my book to read in the Autumn of 1964, I got this witty reply:

FIRST SECRETARY OF STATE
DEPARTMENT OF ECONOMIC AFFAIRS
12 November 1964

DEAR NICHOLAS DAVENPORT,
Thank you for your letter of the 6'th November sending me a copy of your book *The Split Society* – bless you! I will now read it and find out what I am doing! With best wishes, yours sincerely,

GEORGE BROWN

In spite of his outrageous behaviour on occasions – I recall that Aubrey said of Henry Marten : 'His company was incomparable but he would be drunk too soon' – George was able to get at the heart of things and galvanise both managements and trade unions into co-operative action. Both sides trusted him : neither at that time trusted Wilson. The fact that George got the CBI and the TUC to sign the Tripartite Declaration of Intent on 13 December 1964 – it constituted a voluntary prices and incomes policy – was a tremendous achievement. So was the National Plan of September 1965 – again agreed to by both sides – which aimed at a twenty-five per cent growth of the economy between 1964 and 1970. But all this fine drive to organise a partnership between the Government, employers and workers in the working of an expanding mixed economy was frustrated by Harold Wilson when he adopted the 'stop-go-stop' policies of the old moneyed ruling clique and clung on to an over-valued rate for sterling. It was all the more pathetic because George Brown's new Ministry of Economic Affairs was conceived to prevent such a thing happening. But the Treasury came out on top again because it was left with the responsibility of short-term 'demand management'. This was the Treasury Knight's trick, a trump card which they did not hesitate to play.

I came to know George fairly well when my wife and I stayed with Harold and Diane Lever at a villa they had rented near Cap d'Antibes in the summer of 1965. George and Sophie, his wife, were there when we arrived : they had been invited for a long weekend and stayed for a long three weeks. On the first night of heated argument George wanted me to join him at the Ministry of Economic Affairs. Nine o'clock in the morning face to face with George was not an alluring prospect. But I was greatly impressed by his understanding of how a mixed economy should be run in a genuine partnership between Government, employers and trade unions.

George's vitality was remarkable. He would burst into song at any moment. His favourite song was one I particularly detested – *Hello Dolly* – which he could never fully remember in words or tune. So my wife went out to buy him a record of the music of the film. This was fatal, for we had in future the full accompaniment from George at the top of his voice. But I could see that he was on edge. He would call up to his Ministry frequently, and one day he had his two top civil servants – Sir Eric Roll and Sir Douglas Allen – fly down for an afternoon's discussion on some 'vital' matter. I was introduced to them in the swimming pool. I shall always remember their look of consternation when the First Secretary of State ended their talk with a burst of *Hello Dolly*. I suspected that what was making George on edge was the fact that the telephone had never rung from the Scilly Isles where the Prime Minister was relaxing in his bungalow. Was influence and power slipping away from the Deputy Prime Minister? I feared it was. It must have been galling to George to know that the man at the top who had made a mockery of his National Plan, who allowed the Treasury to undermine all his fine efforts to expand the economy, had not even bothered to give him a call on the telephone. The tension eventually became unbearable. George finally resigned from the Ministry of Economic Affairs, after it had been murdered by Wilson's July 1966 deflationary poison package. He was given the Foreign Office. I went to see him in the vast room of the Secretary of State and found him more on edge than ever because he had to sit under a huge portrait of George III. I was told later that he had it exchanged for a portrait of Ernie Bevin. Then in 1968 he resigned from the Government altogether and I can well understand his feelings as he ran shouting down the corridors at the House: 'I can't stand this bloody little man any longer'.

I used to travel frequently down to Cardiff to see the remarkable Julian Hodge, the quiet and humble accountant who built a prosperous financial centre out of nothing in the commercial capital of Wales. Brinley Thomas, the economist, and I drew up the portfolio of the Welsh Dragon, the first unit trust that Julian created. The BBC heard of this, and in December 1968 I was interviewed in Cardiff by David Bevan for the Welsh television programme of the BBC. He held up a copy of my book *The Split Society* and asked: 'Do you remember what you wrote on page 185?' He read it out:

> If Harold Wilson leads a government which wins the confidence of both managements and men, which understands the technical application of science not only to industry but to industrial relations, which knows how to pursue a policy of

economic growth without looking over its shoulder at the state of the gold reserves, he will have a good chance of making a success of it, that is, of healing the split society.

I had to confess that my hero had made a hash of it and I explained why. Instead of making a stand on *The New Statement of Aims* of 1960 he never attempted to define a mixed economy and explain how he proposed to run it. He never clearly defined the public sector and its role in the mixed economy. He talked about re-structuring British industry but left everyone in doubt as to how he would bring it under public control. He played first to one side and then to the other side. He prevaricated continually. He was devious in the extreme. Instead of bringing the two sides of industry together he widened the split. If only he had declared that he wanted to see wages rise on sound productivity agreements, and profits rise on sound investment, if only he had brought the shop-stewards into factory floor management and held out for a partnership in industry between government, the CBI, and trade unions, as George Brown intended, and as Edward Heath has tried, he could have made the British mixed economy an exemplary economic success. But he got himself befogged by prices and incomes policies in a vain attempt to defend the wrong exchange rate of sterling.

At this point Bevan asked me an odd question. Did I think it wrong for a Prime Minister to have assumed the overlordship of the economy in 1966? Yes. I thought it was inviting divine displeasure. In classical time 'hubris' always preceded 'nemesis'. In Greek tragedy the gods took a special delight in humbling the cocky, self-assured man. They would lay before the mortal hero the chance to make a fatal mistake, and if he fell for it, they would drive him on to his own ruin and destruction. This they did to Wilson in the battle for sterling. In February 1965, after the first sterling crisis, he had told a Parliamentary Party meeting: 'The economic crisis is now virtually over. The future is bright with promise.' In October 1965 he boasted: 'The economy is strong. Sterling is strong. Employment is strong.' The cheers of his supporters were strong. He repeated the boast in January 1966 when he claimed that he was going to build 500,000 houses. (The highest he ever got was 380,000 in 1968.) He was going to deal with the 'speculators and the sell-Britain-short brigade' from a position of strength. In April 1966 he did attain Parliamentary strength, having won a majority of ninety-seven in the General Election. So in July 1966 he denounced 'the defeatist cries, the moaning minnies, and wet editorials'. But then he had to clap on his prices and wages freeze. Early in 1967 his cockiness returned. He promised a surplus of £200 millions on the balance of payments! But another flight from the pound blew up and the £200 million surplus became a deficit of no less than £670 million! The gods finally humiliated him when he was forced into devaluation in November 1967. When he came to make his devaluation speech – with its gaffe about the 'pound in your pocket' – it was said that he was so emotionally upset that he had to have sedation. It was not surprising. To me, watching the television, he certainly looked a broken man. Remembering the ebullient figure who received me in the Cabinet room in January 1965, I thought of *Oedipus at Colonnus*.

In the train going home after this television interview, which David Bevan said had been viewed 'with tremendous interest', I began to think of the Greek tragedies and was struck by the similarity between the tragedy of Harold Wilson and the Sophoclean tragedy of Oedipus. It was a conventional theme of Greek tragedy that misfortune would fall upon an eminent man not because he was basically wicked but because there was some flaw or misdeed or accident which the gods had to punish. Sophocles did not attribute to Oedipus any personal fault beyond a sharp temper and a certain stubbornness; in fact, he gave him extraordinary powers to meet his terrible fate. The same powers of resilience and resistance, as well as a sharp temper and stubbornness, were given to Wilson. He was able to sleep peacefully every night in spite of failure after failure in his economic management. Like Oedipus the King, Wilson was an undoubted king in the world of politics. Like Oedipus he was a man of outstanding abilities far above the common lot. His mental powers, his tenacity, his political cunning were unique. And like the egocentric Oedipus, Wilson's weakness lay in his ignorance of certain frightening facts which were bound to bring disaster upon him. Wilson was so ego-centred that he was completely unaware not only of the frightening facts but of what people outside Britain thought of him and his fine words. He could solemnly give a lecture at the White House to the President of the USA and be quite ignorant of the fact that they were all laughing at him behind his back.

In the Sophoclean drama, calamity was bound to come because Oedipus did not know that the man he killed in the brawl at the crossroads was his own father. Wilson did not know – or shut his eyes and refused to see – that in the financial brawl at the sterling cross-roads he too had killed his own father – Clause 4 socialism.

It must not be forgotten that when Hugh Gaitskell proposed in 1960 the removal from the Labour Party constitution of the Marxist Clause 4 – the socialisation of all the means of production, distribution and exchange – it was Harold Wilson who allowed himself to be put at the head of the opposition. The honest Gaitskell, who was essentially a social democrat reformer, had felt quite rightly that the nation would not stand any further enlargement of Fabian socialism. He was the first leader of the party to see that any extension of it would land the economy into the strait-jacket of a centrally-controlled state, in which our traditional liberties would have to be abandoned. But he had run into stiff opposition, and a majority of the party had refused to abandon its socialist-commonwealth dreams. Harold Wilson had allowed himself to be identified with that opposition. A compromise had been reached – it was called a new *Statement of Aims* – which recognised the intervening state of a mixed economy, but it was clear at the time that the party had no stomach for it. So when Gaitskell died in 1963 Harold Wilson was elected leader – and not George Brown – because he was regarded as the fit guardian of this sacred Marxist cow. Clause 4 had, in fact, fathered him and now unintentionally he proceeded to kill it. It is curious that all historians except Paul Foot and the Marxists have so far overlooked this tragic patricide, which the gods were bound to punish.

To complete the Sophoclean tragedy, Oedipus did not know when he assumed the kingship of Thebes and went to bed with Queen Jocasta that he was sleeping with his mother. Wilson did not appear to realise that when he assumed his economic over-lordship and adopted the deflationary monetary techniques of the Tories he was going to bed with finance-capitalism. Oh, you may object, but that was not his mother! Curiously enough it was – in an historical sense. Harold Wilson was *au fond* a social democrat, like his leaders in the Attlee administration, and historically social democracy derived from liberalism. Wilson started under-graduate life at Oxford as a Liberal and he may well have studied the evolution of Liberalism from the post-Restoration Whigs. Now the modern version of the mercantile capitalism of the post-Restoration Whigs is finance-capitalism. That Wilson should go to bed with finance-capitalism was not surprising for a politician who was by nature and education an anti-Marxist social democrat, who was also trying to prove that a social democrat Labour government could govern Britain and maintain the pound sterling as firmly as the old moneyed ruling clique.

Wilson was, of course, right to choose the freedoms of social democracy instead of the tyrannies of a centralised communist State into which the Clause 4 fanatics would drive us. But as he was elected to bring in Clause 4 socialism, so he was doomed to be the victim of an Oedipus tragedy.

Consider what the Marxists expected of the son whom Clause 4 had fathered. It was made crystal clear in the compromise state-ment of 1960 which contained these words: 'It [the Party] is convinced that these social and economic objectives can be achieved only through an expansion of common ownership substantial enough to give the community power over the com-manding heights of the economy.' It was in the City where these 'commanding heights of the economy' lay. To get control of them meant – for the Marxists – taking over the life assurance companies, the mutual life societies, the private pension funds, the building societies, the hire-purchase finance companies, the joint stock banks – indeed, the whole financial apparatus. (The merchant banks were untouchable because they could easily emigrate and set themselves up in Switzerland.) But not a step in that direction was ever made by Harold Wilson. It was not, of course, possible for him to make such a Marxist move while he had a tiny majority of five or six, but when he had a majority of ninety-seven after the 1966 Election, it was expected by his Marxist supporters that he would do something to show that he believed in the advance of Marxist socialism. But he never expressed his faith in Marxist socialism. Certainly he kept talking about 're-structuring' British industry, but not of socialising the whole of it – only the parts of it which had got into financial trouble. For example, he set up the Industrial Reorganisation Corporation which was to take British industry, he said, 'by the scruff of its neck and drag it kicking and screaming into the twentieth century'. But he appointed not a Marxist socialist, but an able merchant banker, Ronald Grierson, late of Warburgs, to be its head. The left had expected an active Marxist politician. Incidentally, the IRC aims were so ambiguous, that while industrialists feared that it might be back-door socialism, the Marxists regarded it as front-door State capitalism. Again the Industrial Expansion Bill was supposed to give the Government powers to acquire shares in private industry, as the Marxists desired, but the Act, as passed, merely enabled the State to hold risk capital when it came to the rescue of a company or trade. Of course, Wilson carried out his mandate to re-nationalise steel but he appointed a liberal-minded peer, Lord Melchett, to run it as a commercial enterprise, not a full-blooded Marxist socialist to run it as a State benevolence for the workers. There was a provision in the Steel Act for putting workers on boards but it never came to anything meaningful in a socialist sense. The men were never consulted. Here I must pay tribute to Julian Melchett, who died after a heart attack brought on by his over-work in the national cause. He had fought too hard to secure from the Treasury sufficient money to finance the vast costly programme for the modernisation of the British steel industry.

Now I always insisted with Dalton that taking over 'the commanding heights of the economy' as the Marxists desired was really quite unnecessary provided he secured from the life and pension funds a promise to place an agreed proportion of their investments in public and local authority agencies and the gilt-edge market. I got very near to securing such an agreement when Jim Callaghan was Chancellor of the Exchequer. By special appointment I brought some influential 'Life' friends to see Jim at the Treasury in May 1966. They were Haynes, then chairman and managing-director of the Royal London Mutual, Crabbe, general manager of the Provident Life Association and then chairman of the Life Offices pension committee, and Cahill, general manager of the Legal and General and deputy chairman of the British Insurance Association. They were prepared, I knew, to co-operate with, and support financially a Public Works Loan Agency if Jim was prepared to launch such a body. We were received by Jim and his Treasury Knights and an amicable discussion followed, except that Crabbe was worried by the rate of inflation and the rate of interest allowed by the Treasury. I wrote to Jim as follows:

Hinton Manor
19 May 1966

DEAR JIM,

It was very good of you to receive us yesterday but dear Crabbe must 'crab' everything. He was trying to maintain a relationship between inflation and the rate of interest which no Chancellor could possibly accept. However, they are all quite prepared to subscribe to a 'tap' issue of the Public Works Loan Agency or the National Loans Agency (whatever you like to call it) on market terms identical with, say, the L.C.C. issues, and I am sure that you could rely upon an annual subscription of around £150 – £200 million out of their new money without disturbing their present holdings of gilt-edged. Of course, if you were to allow the life companies to transfer their existing tax credits within their portfolio from stock to stock you would galvanize the gilt-edged market into great activity and would have no difficulty in getting all the money you want for the agency.

My 'Life' friends greatly appreciated the opportunity to talk to you. In the past they have always had to go to the Bank of England and have had no direct contact with the Treasury.
Yours ever,

NICHOLAS

I regret to say that nothing came of this meeting. I suppose that pre-occupation with sterling prevented Jim from considering any long-term reform of the financial system. The financial institutions – the commanding heights of the economy – naturally went on increasing their power and influence. The direction of the vast flow of private savings – now approaching £2000 million a year – remains completely in the hands of directors to do as they please with them.

The power of these financial institutions was made apparent when Dick Crossman, once the leader of the 'keep left' movement, was told to introduce a National Superannuation Bill as a partnership between State and private enterprise and to allow partial contracting-out of the State scheme for workers who were in private occupational pension schemes. Every Clause 4 Marxist expected, of course, a socialist government to take over the life companies and their private pension schemes, especially as some were run by mutual societies without a trace of equity capital, and the great private companies – Prudential, Equity and Law, and Legal and General – had already confined their equity shareholders to a mere ten per cent of their net surplus. But this was not to be. Apparently the Labour 'Shadow Cabinet' had decided in 1956 – so Dick told me after he had lost office – to abandon the idea of nationalising life assurance companies and to concentrate on national superannuation. Dick had therefore to bow before the great private 'Life' interests, and I was happy to introduce him to Crabbe, who was chairman of their pensions committee. We had several lunches together at the Athenaeum Club and Crabbe was as helpful as he could be. Dick Crossman would, of course, have jumped at the opportunity of nationalising these 'commanding heights of the economy', the financial institutions. It would have given him the chance of funding his National Pensions Scheme. Apart from the private funds taken over he could then have invested his surpluses in units of a State unit trust if that institution had been set up as I had advised. It could then have become the richest pension fund in the world and could have provided the highest pensions in the world. The compromise bill, which happily never reached the statute book, compelled the rich wage-earners to hand over more of their wages in the form of higher contributions to the state scheme in order to provide for the elderly. The contribution of a worker earning thirty-three pounds a week was due to go up under Dick's scheme from 25s 5d to 44s 7d a week – nearly one pound extra. Wealth-distributive it certainly was, but not in the socialist sense desired by the Marxists.

Another point which angered the Marxists was that under the Wilson administration the workers were never consulted about anything. There was no 'worker participation'. They were never brought into management, as German workers are, who elect their own representatives on supervisory boards of directors; they were left as second-class citizens without a voice in the running of their working life. They were certainly given a statutory right to redundancy pay on dismissal but this is the hall-mark of a liberal Welfare State, not a socialist one. A Marxist State would have nationalised any large company – like the newly merged GEC – AEI – which was likely to embark on wholesale sackings.

As the years went by Wilson took on the character of a new National Establishment figure. In the 1966 currency crisis he complained as much about the restrictive practices of labour as about the inefficient practices of management. At the TUC Blackpool conference of 5 September 1966, he was bold enough to say : 'The restrictive practices that are still too prevalent today amount simply to a means of laying claim to a full day's pay for less than a full day's work'. At times he seemed to be anti-labour. There was a rumour that he had disparaged the working-class in a speech to the Economic Club in New York in February 1966. I have a letter from a friend who was a bank adviser, John Smith of 64, Wall Street, dated 28 February 1966 saying : 'Prime Minister Wilson placed a perceptive finger on the root of the British recent performance in affairs economic, which he aptly termed as "the sheer damned laziness of the British workman".' I wrote to Mr Smith for chapter and verse and on 14 March 1966 he corrected it by replying : 'According to Sydney Gampell's *Economic X-Ray* Mr Wilson's condemnation covered the nation at large rather than being confined, as I interpreted it from my previous source of information, to be the British working man'. But the rumour stuck, and when Wilson added 'One man's wage rise is another man's price rise', the workers regarded it as a conventional remark for a Tory Prime Minister, but not one that should fall from the lips of a socialist premier who was supposed to be one of their own.

When Wilson finally adopted, in 1967, the full deflationary policies of finance – capitalism in defence of the pound, which meant a continuing high level of unemployment, the workers had had enough of his Establishment image. The devaluation of 1967 was the last straw. Wilson's closest confidant, Professor Balogh, let the cat out of the bag in a letter to *The Times* in which he said that devaluation was simply a means of depreciating the real value of their wages. He was merely repeating what Jim Callaghan had said in the House of Commons on 24 July 1967 when he was resisting devaluation : 'The logical purpose of devaluation is a reduction in the standard of life and home'. The enraged workers, the frustrated Marxist socialists, wrote off the Wilson team as another bunch of power politicians clinging to office for the pay and rewards. It was significant that Peter Shore, the Minister of Economic Affairs, said on BBC television on 28 March 1968 : 'We have not the slightest intention of quitting or resigning or being hounded out. We shall cling on to office'. And so they did – until every Clause 4 Marxist hated and despised them for it.

Looking back on the Oedipus tragedy staged in 1964–70, I cannot help feeling how cruelly the gods treated Harold Wilson. He had extraordinary talents. His mental powers, his physical endurance were fantastic. He must have realised that his policies were bound to kill his Clause 4 father, but he did his best to keep him alive by various subtle 'socialist' acts of Parliament. As for sleeping with his mother, finance-capitalism, he must have assured himself that a little incest would not hurt, provided it was not allowed to produce offspring. One is glad that Harold never contemplated Oedipus' fate : he never thought of retiring, which would have meant putting out his political eyes. As I write he has actually recovered his power and is again leading his party. It is a pleasant change to have a Greek tragedy with a happy ending.

Epilogue
The Revolution Game

In this memoir I have been telling the story of social conflict as I have seen it in England in the 1640s – through the eyes of Henry Marten, the regicide – and in the 1920s to 70s through the eyes of a radical in the City who happened to be a friend of a few ministers in the post-war Labour governments. I have not attempted to give a history of 'the revolutions of our time'. This had been done brilliantly enough by John Vaizey, now Professor of Economics at Brunel University, in his *Social Democracy* (Weidenfeld and Nicolson, 1971). I have simply set down how and why the well-meaning social reformers I knew came to grief because they failed in a capitalist State to understand money and the money-makers and to adapt their 'socialism' to a mixed economy with a private sector dependent on profit.

As I cling to the idea that the purpose of life is the lifting of the human consciousness into a higher plane of understanding and happiness, I have always taken my stand, as any sane student of history would, on evolution as opposed to revolution in our economic affairs. The Russian Revolution came out of terrible suffering and violence and world war and it is small wonder that in a society unused to democracy the so-called dictatorship of the proletariat, which Marx imagined would be temporary, turned into the worst form of political tyranny the world has seen since the Middle Ages.

The original Marxist concept of a class war between the bourgeoisie, the beneficiaries of capitalism, and the proletariat, the victims of capitalism, now seems plainly ridiculous when, thanks to the Keynesian full-employment White Paper of 1944, the proletariat hold the trump cards at the bargaining table and the workers of the strong-arm unions are able to dictate to their puppets at Westminster. The notion that the capitalist mode of production – in the rapidly changing forms of capitalism today – deprives man of his 'authentic' humanity is as silly as the idea that the communist mode of production – in the authoritarian Eastern half of Europe and the vast fortress of Russia – gives man an enlarged humanity. What the romantic type of student revolutionary believes today is that man can only enlarge his capacities and enrich his nature when he is freed altogether from the production process, whether it be capitalist or communist. One has some sympathy for that point of view but, of course, it would bring disaster to a country dependent for nearly half its food on foreign supplies. One cannot go about smashing up what remains of the evolving capitalist system with the Marxist hammer if the result is starvation – or a beggar-like dependence on Russian charity.

Dialetical materialism was an ingenious theory of its time but the later development of quantum physics proved it to be non-sensical. A *coup de grace* was given to the theory by Professor Jacques Monod, the eminent molecular biologist, in his book *Chance and Necessity*. He made it clear that the inversion by which Marx substituted dialetical materialism for the idealist dialectic of Hegel was nothing but animism. Hegel's postulate was that as the Absolute Whole is Mind, which thinks dialectically in terms of thesis, antithesis and synthesis, so the laws governing the movement of the natural universe must be of a dialectical order.

The late J. B. S. Haldane, a Marxist as well as a brilliant scientist, wrote: 'In dialectics they (Marx and Engels) saw the science of the general laws of change, not only in society and in human thought, but in the external world which is mirrored by human thought.' Professor Monod, quoting this passage, described it as sheer animist projection. Dialectical materialism would have us return to the animism of primitive man who saw devils in the lightning and the thunderstorm. The Marxist sees devils in the development of capitalism; we Keynesians see in its liberal and technological evolution the emancipation of economic man.

Two Oxford Marxist economists – Andrew Glyn and Bob Sutcliffe – have lately written a book *British Capitalism, Workers and the Profits Squeeze*, in which they claim that the basic contradictions of capitalism are still at work, as the prophet said, and that the militant trade unions, by exacting higher and higher wages, are eating into company profit margins, so that our capitalists are cutting back on investment, slowing down growth and preparing for death. There is some truth in what they say. It is notable that since we joined the European Common Market there has been no rush on the part of foreign capitalists to build factories in Britain. However, Wilfrid Beckerman, now an economics professor at London University, replied angrily to the authors in the *New Statesman*, accusing them of betraying the working class. To quote Beckerman : 'It is important that the recent academic attempt to provide a sophisticated justification for excessive union militancy be exposed at the outset for what it is, namely, a distortion of the facts combined with a nonsensical theory in order to justify predictions that are without any scientific basis whatsoever.' He pointed out that their theory of capitalist collapse, in stark contrast to Marx's, was not based on the increasing impoverishment of the workers but on the increasing enrichment of the members of the militant trade unions. It is they who now hold the political reins.

Now it is true that capitalism has not yet been overturned by the Marxist tactics of the militant trade unionists but in Britain it has had a narrow shave and has had to have the injection of a powerful pick-me-up-drug. To get British industry to invest, Edward Heath, when he assumed power, had to pump £3000 million into the economy by way of taxation relief and hand out another £3000 million in subsidies to lame ducks in the regions. Certainly he got the economy to grow for a time at the rate of over 5% a year – and company profits, when labour co-operated, bounded upwards with wages – but by the end of 1973 the militancy of the non-co-operating miners had forced the Government to impose a three-day working week.

Today the miners dictate not only terms of economic growth but the terms of political power. They have even assumed political power. I quote from an article by John Grigg in *The Observer Review* of 31 March 1974:

On the morning of 28 November 1973 Michael McGahey, Vice-President of the National Union of Mineworkers, told the then British Prime Minister, Edward Heath, that it was his intention to smash the Government's pay policy and to remove Mr Heath from office. He was speaking across the Cabinet table at 10 Downing Street. Witnesses differ as to the exact words but agree that was the gist.

It was not an idle threat because within little more than three months Edward Heath was thrown out of office and his pay policy was truly smashed. It is a pity that he did not have a tape machine under the Cabinet table. Mr McGahey's rough language might have shocked the British people as much as President Nixon's did the American people when the Watergate tapes were transcribed.

This was perhaps the first time that trade union brute force had been deliberately used to smash the Parliamentary process of law-making. But worse was to come. Mr Hugh Scanlon on behalf of the Amalgamated Union of Engineering Workers refused even to acknowledge the existence of the Industrial Relations Act which had been duly passed by Parliament and was accepted, although detested, by the Labour Party as the law of the land. He refused to appear before its court; he refused to pay the fines which had been levied on his union for malfeasance. As Sir John Donaldson, President of the Industrial Relations Court, remarked, the union had adopted a policy which had not been seen in this country for centuries. To quote his words:

> Making great play of the claim that its executive is bound by the democratic decision of its members it has denied the democratic rights of the rest of the community to make laws which bind us all. If it can veto laws which do not appeal to it, why should not others do the same? This way lies tyranny and anarchy.

Clearly Mr McGahey and Mr Scanlon have proved that it is now possible for strong-arm trade unions to smash not only our capitalism but our democratic and Parliamentary way of life. They have not yet done so, partly because they know that public opinion is not on their side, partly because they must first have a reliably subservient Labour government at Westminster to effect the legal processes they have flouted and give them control of the army and the police. Even Hitler did not attempt revolution until he had won constitutional control.

And how could they expect to win public support? What

worker could believe that he would be better off under a Mc-Gahey-Scanlon dictatorship? Compared with the communist half of the world the rise in the standard of living in the capitalist democracies has been fantastic. I have seen in my own lifetime in my own village, the workers' style of living transformed from the near-neolithic to the luxury of the electrical age. With the national average earnings now over £40 a week, which means that the skilled élite will be earning £100 and more a week, the higher paid workers can take their holidays abroad and eat and drink like a lord (assuming the lord likes fish and chips). All this has been achieved in one generation through the Keynesian 'full employment' policies of the 'de-humanising' capitalist system. And the workers retain their freedom, changing jobs as they please, which they would never be able to do in the authoritarian communist countries where strikes and militancy of any kind are taboo. The only trouble has been the depreciation in the purchasing power of their money wages – a secular trend which can be disguised in the communist countries but not in the democracies. Wars and natural calamities like droughts are the main causes of the big jumps in the price level but in recent times price inflation has spurted because British workers are not really interested in offsetting cost increases by productivity increases. Some of our present inflation has, of course, been imported from abroad but most of it is generated at home because the powerful unions stupidly insist that their wages must always go ahead faster than prices, thus speeding up the wage-price spiral. As employers turn higher wages into higher consumer prices, the unreasonable wage claim of a strong-arm trade union is simply twisting the arm of fellow-workers who are less powerful. Occasionally governments add to a wage-cost inflation with a demand – inflation by mismanaging government spending, stepping it up too far or too fast. Indeed the gross financial bungling of both Labour and Tory Governments – from the nuclear-power muddle to bad macro-economic planning – must share the responsibility for our present disaster. But the excessive annual wage claims by militant unions have now become the ritual of our decline and fall.

In spite of the evolution of capitalism towards a fairer and more efficient system for the creation of wealth, the dangerous sense of alienation from the governing Establishment which the workers began to feel under the Tory administrations still persists under Labour. Arthur Koestler wrote in *Encounter* (October 1973): 'The same lovable bloke who risked his life on D-Day to keep the country free would not lift a finger at Dagenham to put the country back on its feet'. That is because he still does not feel part of the nation. Why? I think it is partly because he has not been brought into any share of the management and the capital profits arising from it, partly because he has lost faith in Parliament and despises politicans and partly because he has been 'got at', being a complacent and easygoing bloke, by a few intellectual power-ambitious revolutionaries who really do want to smash up our existing free and democratic society.

The technique of these revolutionaries has changed since the days of the great depression. In the 1920s the only effective weapon at hand was the general strike. It failed in 1926 because the Establishment was then more efficient and less soft. It did not hesitate to call out the troops and to send Marxist propagandists to gaol. Today the revolutionaries are more subtle. First of all, they work on trade union officials, who stupidly react to the old cries about exploitation, make them press inflationary wage claims and provoke strike action in order to hit at company profits and investment, hoping that this will undermine the capitalist system. Secondly, they organise strong-arm gangs in the unions to intimidate the mass of workers into strike action by mass picketing. I have myself seen, from my office window in the City, a force of bully-boys march into a building site and 'persuade', by the threat of physical violence, reluctant workers to down tools and follow meekly behind a column of men shouting 'Out, Out, Out'. This form of picketing is, of course, illegal, and the Courts have now more clearly defined it and imposed some exemplary sentences on those convicted of it. Their third tactic is the sit-in. This worked well on the Clyde, not only because the leader was an exceptionally able communist, Jimmy Reid, but because all the physical equipment for finishing the job – completing the ships in the yards – was on site and did not have to be hired or financed. Recently the management has actually tried to help a sit-in at a motor cycle works by arranging for the finance of the job. There is no reason why workers should not hire managers if they can secure finance. Finally there are the 'squatters' who take possession of empty buildings. On the whole these long-haired do-

gooders excite public sympathy as they are providing shelter for
the homeless. It is the pleasant side of the British that we have
such a decent fair-minded bourgeoisie as to allow good points,
when they have them, even to the revolutionaries who are seeking
to destroy their easy way of life.

The tactic of the general strike remains, of course, the ultimate
revolutionary weapon but the revolutionaries who would use it
are not a unified force. They are, in fact, hopelessly split on points
of tactics and ideology. The Communist Party has about thirty
thousand members and most of the militant shop stewards belong
to it. While they are now infiltrating the unions they are still
making no headway in the constituencies as a Parliamentary
party. The groups to the left of the communists are three – the
International Socialists with perhaps five thousand members who
publish a weekly *Socialist Worker*, the Socialist Labour League,
now the Workers Revolutionary Party, with perhaps five
thousand members who print the *Workers Press*, and the International Marxist Group with less than five thousand members
who publish the *Red Weekly*. There are also a number of smaller
Trotskyist and Maoist groups which attract ardent young
teachers, social workers, community organisers and bearded
idealists. The contacts between all these Marxist groups are
spasmodic and chancy. They join up mostly in street demonstrations where a jolly rowdy time is had by all. But our saving grace
is that the weapon of the general strike cannot be used without
the full co-operation of the TUC, which is by no means to be
taken for granted. Some unions are communist-led, but the
majority are still anti-communist and will certainly not allow
their union affairs to be run by crackpot revolutionaries.
Although the Labour socialist is, like the communist, pledged to
destroy capitalism, he is still more inclined to do it by persuasion
than by force.

A fascinating exchange of letters came recently in *The Times*.
A Labour MP, Norman Atkinson, claimed that although the
Labour Party was a Marxist party by virtue of its constitution
(Clause 4 and all) it was essentially a democratic party and
would never let go of Parliament. Marxism, he said, stood for
democracy. That this remark was plain silly was exposed by Mr
T. A. Pickard two days later in a letter of 28 September 1973
which pointed out that Marxism stood for *revolutionary*

socialism, meaning a change of society by force, not by Parliamentary vote. In contradistinction, he said, German revisionists, British Fabians and the British Labour Party believe that Parliamentary processes *can* produce socialism, that a sufficient number of bourgeois *will* gradually and gracefully share power with the proleteriat, that any material affluence which capitalism brings will mean a blurring, not a sharpening, of class differences, and that a common interest can be found in promoting a liberal egalitarian society. In short, he said, revolution is an irrelevance. One can agree almost wholeheartedly with him, provided he does not over-emphasise the egalitarianism. Inequalities of income and wealth will never be eradicated in any society, capitalist or communist. The most we can do in a free democratic society is to check the growth of inequality and eliminate its gross extravagances by direct-taxation of a selective kind.

There was a fine trenchant article in the *New Statesman* of 3 September 1971 by a social democrat Member of Parliament, Brian Walden, on 'The Myth of Revolution'. He was complaining of the well-known Marxist cries – 'Parliamentary democracy is a fraud' – 'The Labour Party is a sham' – 'Capitalism is in crisis' – 'The workers are in a state of militancy and will shortly be converted to the need for revolution' and so on. Brian Walden replied : 'Most people do not want a revolution. Why should they? Revolutions are unpleasant happenings and the rewards, if any, are never conferred on the revolutionary generation. Men have to be driven to desperation before they will risk everything for a dream. No such situation presently exists in Britain.'

I cannot believe there is any deep-laid revolutionary plot on hand in Britain to smash the British way of life, but it could be done by mere accident. Certainly the continual erosion of the purchasing power of money through wage-cost inflation could disrupt society. Did not Lenin say that if you want to destroy capitalism, debauch the currency? Did not Stafford Cripps once say during his communist flirtation : 'We (the Labour Party) must create chaos because it is only out of chaos that communism can arise'? But the facts suggest that our present chaotic wage-cost inflation is not deliberately set in motion by a Machiavellian plot but by the action of honest but pig-headed and misguided trade unionists who are too stupid to see that time is on their side.

I often discussed the socialist miscarriage of 1964–70 with the wisest of the elder Labour statesmen, (now Lord) Douglas Houghton. Douglas had been appointed by Wilson to be the co-ordinator of social welfare policies with a seat in the Cabinet. He was abruptly dismissed in 1966 and became chairman of the party. After one of our discussions he wrote this revealing letter. It was dated 13 May 1967 :

DEAR NICHOLAS,
The British trade unionist has an inbred fear of being exploited : he is taught his history of exploitation; so-called 'trade union principles' are about exploitation and the solidarity necessary to check them.

The weakness of our industrial system is the failure of the trade unions to get interested in efficiency and profitability. Attempts to get worker participation have failed because the unions are suspicious of it. The worker representatives on productivity councils are usually kept apart from union activity and are regarded coolly by their union officers.

I once gave some lectures to the United Steel Company's productivity conference where this point came up. I stressed that in the public service the scope (and constitution) of the joint machinery for negotiation of wages and conditions included worker participation in methods and management problems. We never separated the two. In industry they generally do. Worker members of management boards and production committees will be classed as bosses' men unless they come from and retain their place in the union.

Will Ron Smith at £15,000 a year on the Steel Board be regarded as a worker-representative?

The TUC have always been too little interested in this because the unions have never wanted their men to have a foot in both camps. For one thing they fear that drinks and cigars in the board-room will be their undoing. And to understand the problems of management would undermine their confidence in union affairs and would bring the voice of management into union meetings. That of course would be most unpopular. So long as this attitude continues we shall not get the best out of the endeavours we are making to succeed in the middle way.

Trade union philosophy is for the destruction of capitalism :

it created the Labour Party to do it. And now, when public ownership has lost its attraction and capitalism is not so bad after all, the trade unions don't know what to believe. Their reflexes, however, continue to work as they did in 1911. Yours ever,

DOUGLAS

Douglas was right. A strong Labour Prime Minister who had the economic truth at heart could have told the trade unions what they *must* believe in. Gaitskell could have done it. He was the only Labour leader I knew who really understood money and the monetary system and the working of a mixed economy in which rising profits in the private sector would support rising wages, rising investment and economic growth. And if he had lived to back a public unit trust he would have seen to it that the workers take their share of a rising capital profit. He would have made them all realise that this was the only alternative to a centralised authoritarian communist economy in which their traditional liberties would be lost, their right to strike prohibited and their standard of living reduced. The left may sneer at Gaitskell but Gaitskellism was never alas! tried.

The question today is whether the militant unions are prepared to co-operate with any Labour government which prefers democracy and evolution to dictatorship and revolution. The Marxist revolutionaries are trying hard to turn the trade unions against the parliamentary system which they regard as a load of crap. It was significant that when the TUC organised their massive demonstration against the Industrial Relations Bill in Trafalgar Square in February 1971 they told the Parliamentary Labour Party that there was no room for them on the rostrum; they did not want distrusted politicians to upset the harmony and solidarity of the workers. It was in effect a demonstration against the Labour leadership as much as against the Tory Government.

For the moment the revolutionary militants seem to have the initiative. But I doubt if they will succeed in the end. Happily, our outstanding left-wing political leader, Michael Foot, is one of our greatest Parliamentarians. He would never sacrifice the House of Commons to a rabble in the streets. I am not so sure about Tony Benn. According to Leo Abse he has an Oedipus complex and as his father, Lord Stansgate, was the most devoted adherent of

Parliamentary democracy I have ever known – I first met this charming man on a Parliamentary delegation in Rome – I hope the Oedipus complex will not carry his ambitious son into a Marxist revolutionary escapade.

The ridiculous feature of the militants' programme for more and more nationalisation is that if implemented it would intensify the sense of alienation from the ruling Establishment which the mass of workers now feel. On 2 October 1972 there appeared in *The Times* a fascinating article by Ota Sik, a Czechoslovakian who was Deputy Prime Minister under Dubchek. I quote from it a passage which illuminates my argument: 'The nationalisation of the means of production by communist states has in no way overcome the alienation of the workers from the factories but has even deepened it because of the extraordinary bureaucratisation of management.' This would surely be repeated in Britain if an authoritarian, anti-democratic communist regime were ever to take us over. It was a dramatic and a moving occasion to hear the old Jugoslav Marxist Djilas say recently on BBC television that he would sooner go back to prison than accept a communist regime, denying, as it always must, freedom to the individual.

Let us hope that radicalism will yet have a comeback within our Parliamentary system. It could still be made to appear more attractive than revolution. As Brian Walden said in the article I have quoted: 'Social democracy is not the barren mule of politics that its critics pretend. There is no reason to suppose that it cannot bring about further changes in ownership, education, social welfare and amenity'. But it needs an imaginative leader. Can Roy Jenkins grasp the leadership to which his great ability, his intellectual *gravitas* and his genuine feeling for European social democracy entitle him? Can Tony Crosland step into the front seat? What a tragedy it was that the strongest leader the Labour Party has ever had, who was capable of steering a social democratic movement to victory, died so mysteriously in 1963 when he was on the eve of success!

In one sense the story I have been telling is the story of political failure. The Levellers of the 1640s were broken by Cromwell; the Levellers of 1945–51 and 1964–70 were beaten by the Tories. The Heath idea of Tory revolution was smashed by the miners. But in another sense it is a story of achievement, for one can see in these levelling movements a microcosm of the advance of the human consciousness towards a higher understanding and happiness. Out of the Leveller movements of the 1640s came the first principles of democratic government which we in America and Britain now enjoy. Out of the Leveller governments of 1945–51 and 1964–70 came changes in the form and practice of capitalism which have immensely improved the lot of the working masses. Even a Tory Prime Minister feels upset today when he thinks he sees 'an unacceptable face of capitalism'. We have certainly travelled far from the twenties and thirties when the capitalism practised by the then moneyed ruling clique was an inefficient system – and with an odious face.

My great regret is that I did not succeed in getting my specialised financial ideas taken up by the Levellers who came to Hinton as my friends. I thought they were good, healing ideas. Curiously enough, the same thing happened to my predecessor at Hinton Manor, Henry Marten. It is a strange quirk of English history that a former owner of the house should have been caught up in the Puritan revolution of the 1640s while I was caught up in the Puritan revolution of the 1940s. Henry, of course, had a leading role to play on the politican stage while mine was always behind the political scenes or in the prompting box or writing scripts for some of the players. But we both failed in our advisory roles which were – to put it baldly – attempts to put some economic commonsense, and feasibility into the muddled policies and programmes of the Levelling politicians. However, we might both claim to have helped a little in the advance of the English social conscience. At least that is my hope. But sometimes I hear in the old haunted house at night the sound of an ironic laugh echoing faintly down the stairs. I am sure – I know – it is Henry Marten, the wit of the Long Parliament, laughing at the idea of history repeating itself in the Levellers' revolution game. Who would sense better than the regicide that any attempt at revolution which the Levellers may make today is sure to be smashed by another Cromwell?

Appendix

For the negative business of preventing the misuse of the machinery for making public issues of Stock Exchange 'introductions' a National Investment Board should be set up to act as a supervisory body to receive and adjudicate on all applications for permission to make a public issue of capital or Stock Exchange 'introduction'. The members of the National Investment Board would be appointed by the Government and would be attached to the Ministry of Finance. They would have a status similar to that of the Tariff Advisory Council. The National Investment Board would receive applications from all the issuing houses, banks, finance companies, stockbrokers and so on, who are now in the habit of making the public issues of capital. Foreign borrowers would have to apply through their agents and would appear on the same footing as domestic borrowers – the only difference from existing practice being that their application would be made openly to the National Investment Board instead of secretly to the Governor of the Bank.

In deciding to approve or reject applications the National Investment Board would receive instructions from the Ministry of Finance as to broad principles. For example it would be informed that the estimates of the Ministry of Finance of the balance on international account for the year allowed for a surplus of so many millions, or a deficit. With this knowledge the National Investment Board would decide whether it could permit any foreign issue or not. If it could, it would then use its own judgment as to whether it considered the loan to be a productive one and likely to benefit the British export trades. As regards domestic issues the Board would receive from the Ministry of Finance statistics showing estimated national income and the estimated output and productivity of the various industries. It would be particularly advised if certain industries showed signs of being over-equipped with plant. With this knowledge the Board would decide whether the particular domestic issue was desirable for the industry concerned.

The Board would not attempt to reject any application merely because the prospectus showed an over-optimistic estimate of profits but it would send back for emendation any prospectus which did not give the investing public a fair deal. The approval of the Board would not be construed as a recommendation to the public to subscribe because so many issues would be passed in normal times that the Board's machinery would be recognised for what it was, namely the licensing authority which allows company promoters to use the efficient machinery of the capital market. The enterprising and honest promoters would still be able to make a speculative issue if the Board considered a sufficient supply of the national savings was available, and of course the Board would not interfere with the raising of money for private enterprise without recourse to the capital market.

It would be futile for the National Investment Board to prohibit a public issue and then to find that the promoters had placed the issue privately and arranged for the stock or shares to be introduced on the Stock Exchange through the help of stock-jobbers and stock-brokers. This menace would be removed by requiring the Stock Exchange Committee not to grant 'leave to deal' unless the proposition had received the imprimatur of the National Investment Board. I believe the Stock Exchange Committee would be glad to be relieved of part of the odious responsibility of granting or refusing 'leave to deal'.

It will be seen that the functions of the Investment Board are purely advisory. It would have no power to issue stock or to initiate public issues of capital. To a large extent it would be negative in its advisory work, discouraging private enterprise which it considered to be against the public interest and preventing further investment in highly prosperous industries in periods of Stock Exchange activity. But it will also be constructive. By the mere fact of its co-ordinating influence it would enable all domestic issues to make a businesslike and intelligent entry upon the capital market. Moreover it would facilitate constructive borrowing if it had subsidiary Investment Boards for special spheres of enterprise such as municipal works, the development of Crown Colonies, the improvement of docks etc.... To what extent the industries of the country can borrow centrally through Finance Boards is a question discussed in Mr Quigley's memorandum.

INDUSTRIAL FINANCE CORPORATION

For the more constructive work of initiating finance for basic or new industries new machinery should be set up. I suggest that an Industrial Finance Corporation under state control should take over and enlarge upon the Bankers Industrial Development Company. This Corporation would do more for industry than what the Agricultural Mortgage Corporation does for agriculture, as it would initiate financing schemes. The first step is for the Government to set up a commission to enquire into the industrial loans of the joint stock banks. Industries would have to be considered as a whole. In cases where new development could take place if the frozen loans of the joint stock banks were thawed, the joint stock banks would be required to take shares in the Industrial Finance Corporation at a valuation in exchange for their loans. In cases where the company was hopelessly insolvent the banks would be required to write off their frozen loans.

The Industrial Finance Corporation would have a share capital owned partly by the joint stock banks as considerations for loans or mortgages released, and partly by the Bank of England on behalf of the Government. The Government would have the controlling voice on the board of directors, by appointment of the Chairman. Both the stock banks and the Bank of England would subscribe fresh capital so that the Industrial Finance Corporation would become a finance house and would promote industrial issues.

The Industrial Finance Corporation would be the State controlled machinery for directing the flow of savings into industrial enterprises which the Government considered desirable to promote. The issue made by the Industrial Finance Corporation would be without Government guarantee. They would be made on their merits, just as the issues made by the Central Electricity Board.

The question whether the State should not assume control or supervision of the basic industries through Central Boards is one which is outside my province, but which has been dealt with in Mr Quigley's paper.

NICHOLAS DAVENPORT

January 1932.

Index